Reputation and
International Politics

This book is a volume in the series

CORNELL STUDIES IN SECURITY AFFAIRS

edited by Robert J. Art, Robert Jervis, *and* Stephen M. Walt

A complete listing appears at the end of the book.

Reputation and International Politics

Jonathan Mercer

Cornell University Press

Ithaca and London

First published 1996 by Cornell University Press.

First printing, Cornell Paperbacks, 2010
Printed in the United States of America

☉ The paper in this book meets the minimum requirements
of the American National Standard for Information Sciences—
Permanence of Paper for Printed Library Materials, ANSI Z39.48–1984.

Library of Congress Cataloging-in-Publication Data

Mercer, Jonathan (Jonathan Loveridge), 1959–
Reputation and international politics / Jonathan Mercer.
p. cm.—(Cornell studies in security affairs)
Includes bibliographical references and index.
ISBN 978-0-8014-7489-7
1. International relations. 2. Security, International. 3. Reputation (Law)
4. United States—Foreign relations—1993– I. Title. II. Series.
JX1391.M437 1995
327.1'01—dc20   95-35449

To my parents, Elspeth and Benjamin

Contents

Acknowledgments

Many friends, colleagues, and teachers helped me while I was writing this book. Robert Jervis and Jack Snyder influenced my ideas more than they know—the book could not have been written without their support, criticism, and scholarship. Susan Peterson was the first to notice problems and the last to be satisfied with my solutions; I could not have asked for a better friend or reader. Lynn Eden, Ted Hopf, Chaim Kaufmann, Alan Rousso, and Scott Sagan each read most or all of the manuscript with an insight and an attention to detail that would astonish only those who do not know them. Robert Art, Richard Ned Lebow, Janice Stein, and an anonymous reader offered valuable and detailed suggestions for revising the manuscript. Thomas Christensen and Randall Schweller were extremely helpful because they were never satisfied. Rose McDermott and Lee Ross were excellent critics and helped me to improve my use of psychology. I also thank Bruce Clark, Eileen Crum, Barry O'Neill, and Robert Powell for sharpening my discussion of game theory.

For comments and suggestions on individual chapters, I am no less indebted to Mark Barnett, Victor Cha, David Dessler, Robert Keohane, Deborah Larson, Peter Liberman, John Owen, Paul Pierson, and William Wohlforth. Roger Haydon and Kay Scheuer at Cornell University Press were careful editors and insightful critics; Lisa Turner, the copy editor, did splendid work on the manuscript. For their friendship and support I thank Louise Melling, Rebecca and Mark Brown, and Amy and Gary Johnson; for his teaching I thank Oberlin College professor Harlan Wilson; and for her remarkable talents as an administrator I thank Marguerite Freund of Columbia University. I also thank

Lesley Kao of Stanford University for her assistance in preparing the manuscript for publication.

The support I received from a variety of individuals and institutions made this book possible. The Institute for the Study of World Politics supported the project when it was only a proposal. Samuel Huntington and Stephen Rosen invited me to spend two rewarding years at the John M. Olin Institute for Strategic Studies at Harvard. I was also fortunate to spend a year at Richard Rosecrance's Center for International Relations at UCLA. And David Holloway and Michael May brought me to the collegial and stimulating Center for International Security and Arms Control at Stanford. It has been my good fortune to learn from these scholars and to spend time in their institutions.

My greatest debt is to Elizabeth Kier. Beth critiqued innumerable drafts of each chapter, helped me to escape from a variety of problems, and forced me to rethink many of my beliefs about theory and international politics. Beth's intellectual contribution to this book was enormous; her personal contribution is greater. Finally, I dedicate this book to my parents: Elspeth and Benjamin—they have *always* been there.

J. M.

Reputation and
International Politics

Introduction

I see how peoples are set against one another, and in silence, un-
knowingly, foolishly, obediently, innocently slay one another. I see
that the keenest brains of the world invent weapons and words to
make it yet more refined and enduring.
— Erich Maria Remarque, *All Quiet on the Western Front*

This book is more about words than about weapons. It is about how
the keenest minds in the world made formal an argument to support
conflict today in order to avoid conflict tomorrow. Since Thucydides,
leaders have worried that both friend and foe sit in judgment over their
every act. Any sign of irresolution will, they fear, cause allies to defect
and adversaries to challenge. Deterrence theorists transformed these
fears of decision-makers into strategic theory. The crucial importance of
reputation is now common sense. It is also wrong.

It is wrong to believe that a state's reputation for resolve is worth
fighting for. This belief in the importance of reputation is premised
on a mistaken view of how people tend to explain behavior and on an
empirically unsupported belief that people expect a state to behave in
the future just as it behaved in the past. Before another politician de-
clares that America's reputation requires us to spend lives and money
today to ensure peace tomorrow, we need to think carefully about the
logic and evidence behind the argument. This book critiques the conventional view of the importance of reputation, offers an alternative
explanation of how reputations form, and then tests both views
against evidence from three major crises. In contrast to deterrence
theorists, I contend that we should never go to war because of our
reputation.

If we abandon a commitment, or if we stand firm and fight, how will
others interpret our behavior? Deterrence theory holds that a reputation
for resolve—the extent to which a state will risk war to achieve its ob-

[1]

jectives—is critical to credibility. A reputation for resolve means that others will be more likely to believe one's threats and therefore less likely to challenge one's interests. Woe to the state that has a reputation for irresolution, for it will suffer the indignity of repeated challenges, and its threats and promises will pass unheeded by friend and foe. A reputation for resolve, said the influential deterrence theorist Thomas Schelling, "is one of the few things worth fighting over."[1]

American presidents agree that a reputation for resolve is worth fighting for. President Truman thought that failure to defeat the aggressors in Korea "would be an open invitation to new acts of aggression elsewhere." President Nixon believed that if the United States abandoned Vietnam, "the cause of peace might not survive the damage that would be done to other nations' confidence in our reliability." President Reagan argued that if the United States could not win in Central America, "our credibility would collapse and our alliances would crumble." And President Bush said that a failure to respond to Iraqi aggression "would be a signal to actual and potential despots around the world."[2]

It is usually argued that the loss of life in peripheral conflicts is regrettable but unavoidable. In order to deter future aggressors and ensure future peace, we must be willing to absorb short-term costs. To earn a reputation for resoluteness, or to avoid one of irresoluteness, we must signal our firmness to allies and adversaries by fighting today. As Herman Kahn bluntly put it, sometimes U.S. security depends on "a willingness to incur casualties in limited wars just to improve our bargaining position moderately."[3]

We cannot sensibly assess the grim trade-off between lives lost and reputation gained until we understand how and when a reputation for resolve forms. In spite of the wars fought, lives lost, and billions spent for the sake of reputation, we know very little about how reputations are gained and lost. Robert Jervis observed that despite the importance of credibility to deterrence theory, "scholars know remarkably little"

[1] Thomas Schelling, *Arms and Influence* (New Haven: Yale University Press, 1966), p. 124.
[2] Truman quoted in John Lewis Gaddis, *Strategies of Containment: A Critical Appraisal of Postwar American National Security Policy* (New York: Oxford University Press, 1982), p. 110; Nixon quoted in Seymour Hersh, *The Price of Power: Kissinger in the Nixon White House* (New York: Summit Books, 1983), p. 119; "Speech to a Joint Session of Congress on Central America," *New York Times*, April 28, 1983, p. A12; "Text of President's Address to Joint Session of Congress," *New York Times*, September 12, 1990, p. A20.
[3] Herman Kahn, *On Thermonuclear War* (Princeton: Princeton University Press, 1960), p. 566.

about how people determine whether something is credible. Jervis argued that while states can get reputations for being bold, reckless, or resolute, "it is not clear how these reputations are established and maintained or how important they are compared to the other influences on credibility. We cannot predict with great assurance how a given behavior (e.g., refusing to change one's position on an issue) will influence others' expectations of how the state will act in the future. . . . On these points we have neither theoretically grounded expectations nor solid evidence."[4]

Little has changed since Jervis made this observation in the early 1980s.[5] Our theoretical understanding of reputation remains shallow. Although there has been an explosion of interest in reputation among game theorists and economists (as I discuss in the next chapter), these scholars are uninterested in how reputations form. Instead, they assume the conditions that must obtain for a reputation to form and then use the concept (as an independent variable) to solve problems. Not surprisingly, weak theory and an absence of supporting evidence go together. After canvassing the literature on deterrence theory, one recent study found the evidence for reputation's effect on credibility "virtually nonexistent."[6]

Yet the absence of theory and evidence have not slowed the use of reputation to solve difficult problems. Deterrence theorists and security experts continue to assume the value of building a good reputation.[7] Scholars extend the concept to cover other areas as well. Reputation is flexible enough that it can be used to deter terrorists, to enforce international banking agreements, to facilitate mutually advantageous international agreements, to explain disinflation in the European Monetary

[4] Robert Jervis, "Deterrence and Perception," *International Security* 7 (Winter 1982/3): 9.

[5] For example, Jonathan Shimshoni writes that "in the future a major area of study must be the creation and decay of reputations." Shimshoni, *Israel and Conventional Deterrence: Border Warfare from 1953 to 1970* (Ithaca: Cornell University Press, 1988), p. 215.

[6] The same study found "relatively little work" that examines how managers in businesses assess the behavior of their rivals. See Bruce Clark, "Deterrence, Reputations and Competitive Cognitions" (Ph.D. diss., Stanford University, 1993), pp. 16, 2.

[7] James Alt, Randall Calvert, Brian Humes, "Reputation and Hegemonic Stability: A Game-Theoretic Analysis," *American Political Science Review* 82 (June 1988): 445–466; Steven J. Brams, *Superpower Games: Applying Game Theory to Superpower Conflict* (New Haven: Yale University Press, 1985); Paul Huth, *Extended Deterrence and the Prevention of War* (New Haven: Yale University Press, 1988); John D. Orme, *Deterrence, Reputation, and Cold-War Cycles* (London: Macmillan, 1992); Barry Nalebuff, "Rational Deterrence in an Imperfect World," *World Politics* 43 (April 1991): 313–335; R. Harrison Wagner, "Rationality and Misperception in Deterrence Theory," *Journal of Theoretical Politics* 4/2 (1992): 115–141.

[3]

System, to interpret a monopolist's pricing strategies, or to keep host governments from exploiting multinationals.[8]

Political scientists and economists use reputation to solve problems. It is rare, however, that we see reputation itself treated as a problem. The simplest questions have not been addressed. What is a reputation? When does it form? Does it form easily or rarely? Do reputations form differently between allies and adversaries or between threats and promises? We cannot advise decision-makers how *they* should behave until we know how *others* explain their behavior. Do observers always, sometimes, or never infer from our behavior character traits that they believe will predict our behavior? The answer to this last question determines when reputations form. If others infer an irresolute character from a state's abandonment of a commitment, and as a result expect that state to be irresolute in the future, then President Johnson was right when he said that "surrender anywhere threatens defeat everywhere."[9]

The belief that reputation is central to a state's security is not an artifact of the Cold War. Thucydides discussed how the Melians and Athenians tried to manipulate reputation to make credible threats, and how some actors worried about their reputations with adversaries. After the Sicilians heard rumors that the Athenians were going to attack them, the Sicilian Hermocrates chastised his countrymen: "They [the Athenians] are attacking us on the assumption that we are not going to defend ourselves, and they have a right to hold such a poor view of us, because we failed to help the Spartans to destroy them."[10]

President Clinton expressed similar concerns. With pressure building on him to withdraw American troops from a humanitarian mission in Somalia after twenty-five U.S. soldiers were killed, the president asked rhetorically: What would happen if we abandoned Somalia? "Our own

---

[8] John L. Scott, "Deterring Terrorism through Reputation Building," in *Defense Spending and Economic Growth*, ed. James E. Payne and Anandi P. Sahu (Boulder: Westview, 1993), pp. 257–268; Charles Lipson, "Banker's Dilemmas: Private Cooperation in Rescheduling Sovereign Debts," in *Cooperation under Anarchy*, ed. Kenneth Oye (Princeton: Princeton University Press, 1986), pp. 200–225; Robert Keohane, *After Hegemony: Cooperation and Discord in the World Political Economy* (Princeton: Princeton University Press, 1984); Axel Weber, "The Role of Reputation in the EMS Disinflations," *European Economic Review* 36 (October 1992): 1473–1492; Kannan Srinivasan, "Multiple Market Entry, Cost Signalling, and Entry Deterrence," *Management Science* 37/12 (1991): 1539–1555; Reinhilde Veugelers, "Reputation as a Mechanism Alleviating Opportunistic Host Government Behavior against MNEs," *Journal of Industrial Economics* 41 (March 1993): 1–17.

[9] Quoted in Gaddis, *Strategies of Containment*, p. 211.

[10] Thucydides, *History of the Peloponnesian War*, trans. Rex Warner (New York: Penguin, 1979), p. 433. Also see the Melian Dialogue, pp. 400–408.

credibility with friends and allies would be severely damaged. Our leadership in world affairs would be undermined at the very time when people are looking to America to help promote peace and freedom in the post-cold-war world. And all around the world, aggressors, thugs and terrorists will conclude that the best way to get us to change our policies is to kill our people. It would be open season on Americans."[11] We can know if President Clinton is right only if we have some way of determining how friends, allies, aggressors, thugs, and terrorists are likely to explain U.S. behavior. How they explain U.S. behavior determines whether the president needs to worry about national reputation.

Like the Sicilians, President Clinton may have had no need to worry. The Athenians did not think the Sicilians were irresolute because of their past behavior. They viewed Sicily as a great power that would resist invasion by Athens. The Athenian Nicias warned his countrymen against the coming battle with Sicily: "So we must leave Athens with a force that is not only a match for their forces . . . but actually much superior to them in every direction; and even so we shall find it hard enough to conquer the enemy and come off safely ourselves."[12] Although Sicily's failure to help Sparta destroy Athens led some Sicilians to worry about their reputation, it does not seem to have influenced the Athenians.

When do we need to worry about our reputation? Deterrence theorists and decision-makers argue that a reputation for resolve is central to a state's security. As Thomas Schelling wrote: "We lost thirty thousand dead in Korea to save face for the United States and the United Nations, not to save South Korea for the South Koreans, and it was undoubtedly worth it."[13] But in fact it *is* doubtable. I offer an alternative explanation for how and when reputations form and conclude that enormous human and material sacrifice made in the name of reputation is probably a waste of precious resources.

Whatever one thinks about the importance of reputation should be based on sound theory, method, and evidence. I hope that by presenting competing theories of how reputations form, and by testing them against historical cases, I can help readers to break free from "common sense" and draw their own conclusions about reputation and international politics.

[11] "Clinton's Words on Somalia: 'The Responsibilities of American Leadership,' " *New York Times*, October 8, 1993, p. A15.

[12] Thucydides, *History of the Peloponnesian War*, p. 424.

[13] Schelling, *Arms and Influence*, pp. 124–125.

What Is a Reputation and When Does It Form?

How much should we worry about our reputations? We can address this question once we know what we are looking for. Two conditions are necessary for a reputation to form. First, we need to know when decision-makers are most likely to explain an ally's or an adversary's behavior in dispositional (or character) terms. Second, we need to know when they will use these explanations to predict or explain similar behavior in the future. The heart of the problem with the deterrence argument concerns when these two conditions obtain.

A reputation is a judgment of someone's character (or disposition) that is then used to predict or explain future behavior. A reputation forms when two things happen. First, an observer uses what are called dispositional or character-based attributions to explain another's behavior. A dispositional explanation is one where the nature or character of an individual determines an action. Consider, for example, the sentence "Mary kept her promise because she is a reliable person." Mary's disposition or character trait of "reliability" explains her behavior. We expect Mary to keep her promise unless she finds herself in a situation that compels her to break her promise. For example, "Mary broke her promise because there was a gun to her head." Mary's situation, not her disposition, explains her behavior. A situational attribution means that most people in the same situation would behave similarly. Situational attributions do not have cross-situational validity. In a different situation, where there was no gun to her head, she might keep her promise.

Whereas dispositional attributions are valid and constant in most situations, situational attributions are explanations based on the transient features of a particular context. Because a reputation is a judgment about another's character, only dispositional attributions can generate a reputation. A dispositional attribution is necessary but not sufficient for a reputation to form.

The second point to examine is the use of past behavior to predict future behavior. A reputation forms only when people perceive commitments as interdependent or coupled: "Because Mary was reliable in the past, she will be reliable in the future." However, if we believe she kept her promise only because of the situation—she had a gun to her head—then we cannot know how she will behave in a different situation. Because a situational attribution does not have cross-situational validity, it cannot be used to predict behavior in a different situation and so cannot generate a reputation.

[6]

In short, a dispositional attribution is necessary but not sufficient for a reputation to form. A reputation forms if two conditions are met. First, observers must explain an actor's behavior in dispositional—not situational—terms (e.g., French decision-makers were resolute). Second, observers must use the past to predict similar behavior in the future (e.g., French decision-makers will be resolute). A reputation forms when both conditions are met (e.g., French decision-makers have a reputation for being resolute).

My reputation is not something I can keep in my pocket; it is what someone else thinks about me. I do not own my reputation. Because different people can think differently about me, I can have different, even competing, reputations. Some people may think I am generous, some may think I am stingy. Recognizing that reputation is not a property that I own and control has two important consequences. First, because people can differ in how they explain my behavior, they can give me different reputations based on the same behavior. Second, because people can give me different reputations, I cannot sensibly talk about my reputation; instead, I should speak of my reputations.

This is not the way most people, including deterrence theorists, think of reputation. For example, in an incident that occurred several months before American troops occupied Haiti, a small number of armed Haitian demonstrators directed by Haitian security forces blocked U.S. troops on a United Nations mission from landing at Port-au-Prince. Although only selected members of the international force were equipped with sidearms, and although there were no provisions for American troops to fight their way to shore, an American policy-maker remarked: "This embarrassment has dealt a blow to American credibility, one of our most precious assets."[14] Implicit in this statement are the three assumptions commonly made by deterrence theorists and economists about reputation.[15]

First, everyone will think our behavior should be attributed to our character. It signaled that we lacked resolve or backbone. Had we landed the troops, our behavior would have demonstrated our resolve. Second, everyone will view our behavior similarly. If we back down in

[14] Former Secretary of State James Baker, quoted in Thomas Friedman, "A Broken Truce: Clinton vs. Bush in Global Policy," *New York Times*, October 17, 1993, pp. A1, 12. For details, see Howard French, "Protesters Force a Retreat by Diplomats," *New York Times*, October 12, 1993, p. A1.

[15] For stylistic reasons, I refer to "deterrence theory" or to "the deterrence hypothesis." There is no one deterrence "theory" and so no one deterrence hypothesis on reputation.

[7]

a crisis, both friend and foe will interpret our action as indicating our irresolution. By failing to land troops in Haiti, we have caused everyone to think we lacked resolve. If everyone interprets our behavior similarly, it makes sense to speak of a reputation rather than reputations. We can get a reputation for resolution by standing firm. Third, everyone believes that however we behaved in the past, we will behave similarly in the future. Why has American credibility been damaged by our failure to land troops in Haiti? Because everyone thinks that our retreat revealed our irresolute character. Friends will be less likely to trust us, enemies more likely to challenge us.

These three assumptions mean we should worry about our reputation. If every time we back down in a crisis friend and foe will think we demonstrated irresolution and will therefore expect us to be irresolute in the future, then we had better stand firm in the present. Thus, every act generates one reputation. These three assumptions address only how reputations form, not how others will assess credibility more generally. Although other factors, such as interests and capability, also figure in one's credibility, we can determine the importance of a reputation for resolve only by distinguishing it from these other factors.

Unlike the deterrence argument, which finds its theoretical support in game theory, my argument is rooted in social psychology. Because a reputation is a judgment of someone's character that in turn is used to predict or explain future behavior, how we explain behavior determines whether or not a reputation can form. For deterrence theorists, how people explain behavior is unproblematic: every act generates a corresponding dispositional attribution. For social psychologists, in contrast, how people explain one another's behavior is a central concern of their discipline. Although I develop the argument in Chapter 2, let me foreshadow it by stressing how my assumptions about reputation differ from those of deterrence theory.

First, whereas deterrence theory assumes we explain another's behavior only in dispositional terms, we know that people often explain others' behavior in situational terms. If this is the case, rather than think the United States backed down in Haiti because it lacked resolve, an observer might explain away this behavior as a result of a transient feature of the particular context. For example, an observer may believe U.S. interests were best served by withdrawing its limited forces in order to return later with overwhelming force. In a different situation the Americans might stand and fight. When observers explain an outcome as a function of the transient nature of the situation, then they are not making a judgment of the actor's character. Because a reputation is a judgment of someone's character, whenever observers use transient sitauation (rather than enduring character) to explain an outcome, no reputation forms.

Second, whereas deterrence assumes we all explain the same behavior similarly, we know that people often explain the same behavior differently. For example, some observers may think we demonstrated irresolution by not landing troops in Haiti, whereas others may think we demonstrated wisdom, self-restraint, or maturity. Still others may think we had no choice: given the situation, the only sensible course was to back down. Because different people can explain the same behavior differently, our behavior can generate different, even competing, reputations.

Third, whereas deterrence assumes past behavior will be used to predict similar behavior in the future, it appears that commitments are more independent than interdependent. People may think that because we backed down in Haiti we will back down in the future. Equally logical observers may assume that because we backed down in Haiti we will be even more resolute in the future—this is the "Never Again!" phenomenon. Or, people may see no connection between our behavior in Haiti and our future behavior.

While these three points distinguish my approach from that of deterrence, they say nothing about how I think reputations form. To understand how reputations form, we must conduct two tests. The first is to determine when people are most likely to make dispositional explanations for another's behavior. When do we attribute behavior more to a person's character, and when do we explain another's behavior as a function of the transient situation? My approach uses social psychological research, which predicts the following: people interpret behavior in either situational or dispositional terms depending upon the desirability of that behavior. More specifically, observers use dispositional attributions to explain an out-group's undesirable behavior, and situational attributions to explain an out-group's desirable behavior. I use the term "out-group" to refer to either allies or adversaries.

Second, we must test for the interdependence of commitments. In this case, interdependence means using past behavior to predict or explain future behavior. The deterrence hypothesis assumes people use past behavior to predict the same behavior in the future; it assumes that commitments are more interdependent than independent. I assume the opposite in part because when people use transient situation to explain behavior, this explanation cannot be used to predict behavior in a different situation. If we think Mary kept her promise because she had a gun to her head, this belief tells us nothing about how Mary will behave when she does not have a gun to her head. I also expect commitments to be more independent than interdependent because the desirability of another's behavior—not the other's past behavior—determines whether we explain that behavior in dispositional or situational terms. In other words, it is the desirability of the target's immediate behavior rather than its past behavior that determines our type of explanation.

My hypothesis yields four propositions on when reputations for resolve are likely to form between states. I argue that while adversaries can get reputations for having resolve, they rarely get reputations for lacking resolve; and while allies can get reputations for lacking resolve, they rarely get reputations for having resolve. These propositions are intuitive. The danger of war usually encourages decision-makers to be cautious in their assessments of both friend and foe. They are more likely to think their adversary is resolute than to assume it is irresolute. Similarly, they are more likely to wonder whether their ally will be loyal in a conflict than to assume that it will be loyal. These four propositions fit Realist assumptions that anarchy and self-help characterize international politics.[16]

PLAN OF THE BOOK

I develop these arguments in the first two chapters and test them in the remaining three. Chapter 1 examines reputation's importance to deterrence theory and shows that states worry a great deal about their reputation. Of course, showing that policy-makers worry about their reputation does not show that they *need* to worry. After reviewing a few empirical studies of reputation, I critique the way deterrence theorists and game theorists use reputation. I then use this literature to develop a hypothesis on when reputations for resolve form that will compete against my own argument developed from social psychology.

Chapter 2 presents the theoretical basis for my argument. After introducing some basic concepts and theory in social psychology, I discuss how in-group/out-group and confirmatory attribution biases explain how we interpret our adversaries' behavior. The main task is to deduce

[16] See Kenneth Waltz, *Theory of International Politics* (New York: Random House, 1979).

a hypothesis that captures the behavior of both adversary and ally. The next section addresses this issue and explains the relationship between desires, allies, and adversaries. Having presented the logic behind my argument, I discuss my hypothesis and its four propositions on when reputations form. The last section discusses the use of psychology to examine international politics.

The next three chapters examine how decision-makers in England, France, Russia, Germany, and Austria explained the behavior of their allies and adversaries in three crises from 1905 to 1911. Although the competing hypotheses could be tested in any period, there are two important requirements. First, my research design requires access to the genuine beliefs of decision-makers. The more recent the case, the more severe are the practical data limitations. Probably more has been written about the origins of the First World War than about any other period in history. The enormous amount of source material makes it possible to determine how key actors explained one another's behavior.

The second requirement is a succession of crises involving the same states. The series of crises that I examine—beginning with the first Moroccan Crisis, followed two years later by the Bosnia-Herzegovina Crisis, and continuing two years later with a second Moroccan Crisis—involves the same states and many of the same policy-makers, often fighting over the same issues. This should be an easy case for deterrence theory. Not only did decision-makers at the time think their reputations important, but historians and political scientists today argue that Russia's reputation for irresolution was a cause of World War I.[17]

Some readers may doubt that we can learn much from historical cases. After all, the decision-makers I examine had never experienced a world war, let alone contemplated a nuclear war. It may be that today people think differently, and presumably more clearly, than people did a century ago. If people think differently today than yesterday, however, my arguments should fail when tested against historical evidence. I base my arguments on contemporary social psychological theories and these theories are designed to explain how people explain behavior

---

[17] Paul Huth argues that 1914 was one of the few times when reputation was important. See Huth, *Extended Deterrence*, pp. 149–198. See also Glenn Snyder and Paul Diesing, *Conflict among Nations: Bargaining, Decision-making, and System Structure in International Crises* (Princeton: Princeton University Press, 1977), p. 541; Imanuel Geiss, *German Foreign Policy, 1871–1914* (London: Routledge and Kegan Paul, 1976), p. 117; James Joll, *The Origins of the First World War* (New York: Longman, 1984), p. 10.

today. But if they are valid for people living in a different time and a different culture, we should have greater confidence that they are relevant today.

Not only do people process information today as they did in other eras, but their beliefs about the importance of reputation have not changed. Consider the following examples.

- According to Thucydides, the Athenians explained that they had to conquer the Melians to prevent their allies from viewing them as cowards, which would threaten the integrity of their empire: "So that by conquering you we shall increase not only the size but the security of our empire."[18]
- As the architect of Germany's Moroccan policy in 1905, Baron Friedrich von Holstein focused on Germany's reputation: "Not only for material reasons, but even more to preserve her prestige, Germany must oppose the intended annexation of Morocco by France. . . . But if we now allow our feet to be stepped on in Morocco without a protest we simply encourage others to do the same somewhere else."[19]
- A top Pentagon strategist during the Vietnam War advised in a secret memorandum in January 1966: "The reasons why we *went into* Vietnam to the present depth are varied; but they are now largely academic. Why we have *not withdrawn* from Vietnam is, by all odds, *one* reason: (1) to preserve our reputation as a guarantor, and thus to preserve our effectiveness in the rest of the world."[20]
- Before the Gulf War former president Richard Nixon advised: "If we succeed in getting Mr. Hussein out of Kuwait . . . we will have the credibility to deter aggression elsewhere without sending American forces." If we fail, Nixon warned that "other aggressors will be encouraged to wage war against their neighbors and peace will be in jeopardy everywhere in the world."[21]

---

[18] Thucydides, *History of the Peloponnesian War*, p. 403.

[19] Holstein memo (June 3, 1904), quoted in Norman Rich, *Friedrich von Holstein: Politics and Diplomacy in the Era of Bismarck and Wilhelm II*, vol. 2 (Cambridge: Cambridge University Press, 1965), p. 684.

[20] John T. McNaughton, "Further McNaughton Memo on Factors in Bombing Decision," *The Pentagon Papers* (New York: Bantam Books, 1971), pp. 491–492.

[21] Richard Nixon, "Why," *New York Times*, January 6, 1991, p. E19. For a similar view, see Zbigniew Brzezinski, "Three R's for the Middle East," *New York Times*, April 21, 1991, p. A17.

- More recently, a dozen State Department officials argued that a failure by the United States to take military action against the Serbs "would teach would-be conquerors and ethnic bigots throughout the world that their crimes will go unpunished."[22]

Whether it is right or wrong, the belief that our reputation is worth fighting for is as commonly held now as it was in Holstein's day.

Are these beliefs genuine? Sometimes actors use reputation arguments to bolster a policy they want for other reasons. One advantage of using historical cases is that it allows us to examine what decision-makers were saying in confidence to one another. Public statements are unreliable because they are usually meant to signal a particular disposition to friend and foe or to bolster an argument. The empirical chapters make clear that turn-of-the-century beliefs about the importance of reputation often governed policy decisions. Though the evidence is harder to gather, the same appears to be true today.

The three empirical chapters should make us think more carefully about the centrality of reputations for resolve to our security. Skeptics can rightly note that this is a limited study based on European men's explanations in a pre-nuclear era. Others may note different cases—such as Hitler's view of his adversaries after the Munich crisis or Saddam Hussein's view of the United States before the Gulf War—in which they expect results contrary to my argument. I address these issues in Chapter 6.

[22] Quoted in Michael Gordon, "12 in State Dept. Ask Military Move against the Serbs," *New York Times*, April 23, 1993, p. A12.

[1]

Reputation and Deterrence Theory

"I think we have an interest in standing up against the principle of ethnic cleansing," declared President Clinton. "If you look at the turmoil all through the Balkans, if you look at the other places where this could play itself out in other parts of the world, this is not just about Bosnia."[1] If this belief is right, then the costs of intervention may be more than offset by keeping other potential bullies in their place. If it is wrong, then we should stop using arguments about deterring tomorrow's aggressors to justify intervention today.

This chapter addresses the issue by examining reputation's importance to deterrence theory. While we know that decision-makers worry a great deal about their reputations, what little evidence we have suggests that they probably have nothing to worry about. After discussing the empirical support for the assumption that actors use past behavior to predict future behavior, I critique the deterrence theory literature on reputation. This scholarship has two strands. One is the traditional deterrence literature, the other is the more recent work that uses an explicitly rational-choice approach. A review of these approaches to reputation in deterrence theory allows me to show that the deterrence hypothesis I test in subsequent chapters is cogently deduced from this literature.

THE CENTRALITY OF REPUTATION TO DETERRENCE THEORY

Deterrence is a theory of influence. Actors use threats and promises to encourage the target state to behave however the actors think the target

[1] Quoted in Michael R. Gordon, "Clinton Considers a Tougher Policy to Halt the Serbs," *New York Times*, April 17, 1993, pp. A1, 4.

should behave. The objective of deterrent threats is to convince a would-be challenger that the costs and risks of a challenge outweigh its benefits. The defender needs to convince would-be challengers that it may defend its interests. We need to convince our adversaries and allies that we probably mean what we say. How do we get them to believe us?

The central problem in deterrence theory is making threats and promises credible. Credibility consists of resolve, capability, and interests. A threat may be incredible because observers think a state lacks either the capability or the interest to carry it out. A threat may be incredible because observers think the state lacks the resolve to make good on its threat. These distinctions often blur. Observers may expect us to be resolute because we have vital interests at stake, or they may believe that we view our reputation for resolve itself as a vital interest. Similarly, observers may believe a state's failure to build up its military shows it to be either incapable of defending itself, or unwilling to do so.

This book focuses on resolve. Resolve is the extent to which a state will risk war to keep its promises and uphold its threats.[2] I also examine the flip side of a reputation for resolve: a reputation for loyalty among allies.[3] As Clausewitz observed, it is generally easier to assess capability than resolve: "The extent of the means at his disposal is a matter—though not exclusively—of figures, and should be measurable. But the strength of his will is much less easy to determine and can only be gauged approximately by the strength of the motive animating it."[4] How do we assess another's resolve? When do we explain another's behavior as being driven more by "strength of will" or more by some other factor, such as interests or capability? Distinguishing resolve from other factors is the first step to understanding the important role a reputation for resolve plays in deterrence theory.

When decision-makers use capability to explain an outcome, they are using a situational attribution. In a different situation, one in which the target had greater (or lesser) capability, the outcome might be different. A situational attribution cannot sensibly be used to predict behavior in a different situation. When policy-makers use disposition (or character) to explain an outcome, this attribution can be used to explain behavior

---

[2] I base this definition on the one given by Robert Powell. See Powell, *Nuclear Deterrence Theory: The Search for Credibility* (New York: Cambridge University Press, 1990), p. 42.

[3] Glenn Snyder and Paul Diesing, *Conflict among Nations: Bargaining, Decision-Making, and System Structure in International Crises* (Princeton: Princeton University Press, 1977), p. 432.

[4] Carl von Clausewitz, *On War*, ed. and trans. Michael Howard and Peter Paret (Princeton: Princeton University Press, 1976), p. 77.

in a different situation. A reputation is a belief that someone has an enduring characteristic. More precisely, a reputation is a dispositional attribution that is then used to predict or explain future behavior.

Thomas Schelling illustrates nicely this distinction between resolve and capability. A child who wears glasses and cannot see without them cannot be expected to fight. This handicap provides an excuse for the child who wants to avoid a fight, but does not want to appear afraid to fight. "If one's motive for declining is manifestly not lack of nerve," observed Schelling, "there are no enduring costs in refusing to compete."[5] In this case, glasses provide the needed situational explanation to avoid the enduring dispositional explanation of cowardice. In a different situation, perhaps one where the fight were to take place in the darkness of night, the child might fight. When a state yields to a threat, and observers explain this retreat as a result of the distribution of capability, then no character judgment is made and no reputation for resolve can form.

The same distinction can be made between resolve and interests. If observers explain a target's behavior as a result of its interests, then a reputation for resolve cannot form. In this case, resolve becomes a function of interest. When interests are high, so is resolve; when interests are low, so is resolve. Like capability, interest-based explanations should be categorized as situational attributions: predicting the target's behavior depends upon how it views its interests in that situation. In contrast, if observers believe resolve drives a target's behavior, then a reputation for resolve can form. For example, a state that stands firm when its interests are thought minor, or a state that yields when its interests are considered vital, can get a reputation for either having or lacking resolve.

The credibility of a commitment depends upon some mix of situation (does the state have the interest and the capability to keep its commitment?) and disposition (does the state have the necessary resolve?). If resolve is a function of capability and interests, then we need to worry about maintaining our capability and establishing our interests. It also means that reputations for resolve cannot form. Because our capability and interests vary from situation to situation, then our resolve would also vary according to situation. *A reputation cannot form for something that varies according to situation.* In other words, situationally induced behavior cannot generate a reputation. For example, someone who is

---

[5] Thomas Schelling, *Arms and Influence* (New Haven: Yale University Press, 1966), p. 120.

repeatedly serious at funerals should not get a reputation for being a serious person based on this behavior. Most people are serious at such somber events. But someone who was repeatedly funny at funerals might get a reputation for being funny. Because funerals generally do not encourage hilarity, we are likely to use dispositional attributions to account for this behavior.

A situational attribution has only within-situation validity; it cannot be used to predict or explain behavior in a different situation. In contrast, a dispositional attribution can have cross-situational validity; it can be used to predict or explain behavior in a different situation. Later I discuss how a dispositional attribution can also be used to predict or explain behavior in the same situation (such as being funny only at funerals). Because situations in international politics are always somewhat different, and for the sake of clarity and simplicity, I will refer to dispositional attributions as having cross-situational validity. I will return to this issue when I discuss the differences between specific and general reputations for resolve.

In short, while there are different ways to define resolve, a *reputation* for resolve should be understood as a judgment of another's character that is then used to predict or explain future behavior. Behavior that observers attribute to a particular situation—being serious at funerals, fleeing a burning building, yielding to overwhelming force, or fighting to defend vital interests—cannot generate a reputation. By untangling resolve from interests and capability, we can assess how important a reputation for resolve is to our credibility.

Deterrence theorists and decision-makers worry about how to make credible commitments. How can seemingly incredible threats be made credible? One important strategy is to manipulate reputation.[6] But a reputation cannot be manipulated unless people think it exists, and it cannot exist unless commitments are interdependent. Reputation must first exist as a "fact" before it can be used as a "tool."

Deterrence theorists contend—and decision-makers believe—that threats and promises are interdependent whether we like it or not.[7] This

[6] See for example, Schelling, "The Art of Commitment," in *Arms and Influence*, pp. 35–91.

[7] Neither all deterrence theorists nor all decision-makers believe the world is tightly interdependent. However, since nearly everyone believes that reputations for resolve are important to a state's security, nearly everyone believes that commitments are somewhat interdependent. While I distinguish between these two views later, for stylistic reasons I refer to "deterrence theorists."

[17]

belief will sometimes result in bloody fights not for the immediate stake, but for saving and building a reputation. "The main reason why we are committed in many of these places," wrote Schelling, "is that our threats are interdependent. Essentially we tell the Soviets that we have to react here because, if we did not, they would not believe us when we say we will react there."[8] Most disputes are not about the issue at hand, but about expectations of future behavior: if we are timid now, they think we will be timid in the future, so we must be tough. Because interdependence is generally considered a "fact," decision-makers are obligated to play by its logic. This reasoning is similar to that found in the game of Chicken.

In the game of Chicken, the only thing more dangerous than acquiring a reputation as a chicken is attempting to fix that reputation. If I swerved off the road last time, how can I convince my adversary that this time I really am serious? Such an image, wrote Jervis, "can be a handicap almost impossible to overcome."[9] An effort to get rid of a chicken image can result in a head-on collision, killing both parties. It is argued that a good reputation is not only desirable, but essential to a state's security. Dean Rusk captures this view: "The integrity of the U.S. commitment is the principal pillar of peace throughout the world. If that commitment becomes unreliable, the communist world would draw conclusions that would lead to our ruin and almost certainly to a catastrophic war."[10] Because reputation is so important it can, like any other vital security interest, be manipulated to further diplomatic objectives. Reputation is thus believed to be not only a "fact," but also a "tool."

Decision-makers use reputation to help make their threats and promises credible. As Schelling put it: "A potent means of commitment, and sometimes the only means, is the pledge of one's reputation."[11] A common way to show resolve in bargaining is to stake one's reputation on the outcome.[12] Another way to increase one's commitment is by es-

---

[8] Schelling, *Arms and Influence*, p. 55. See also William W. Kaufmann, *The Requirements of Deterrence* (Princeton: Center for International Studies, 1954), p. 7.

[9] Robert Jervis, *The Logic of Images in International Relations* (Princeton: Princeton University Press, 1970), p. 6.

[10] Quoted in John Lewis Gaddis, *Strategies of Containment: A Critical Appraisal of Postwar American National Security Policy* (New York: Oxford University Press, 1982), p. 240.

[11] Thomas Schelling, *The Strategy of Conflict* (Cambridge: Harvard University Press, 1960), p. 29.

[12] Snyder and Diesing, *Conflict among Nations*, pp. 203–247; Robert Jervis, *The Meaning of the Nuclear Revolution: Statecraft and the Prospect of Armageddon* (Ithaca: Cornell University Press, 1989), pp. 39–40; Alexander George and Richard Smoke, *Deterrence in American Foreign Policy: Theory and Practice* (New York: Columbia University Press, 1974), p. 559.

tablishing a reputation at lower levels of conflict for keeping one's commitments. In this case, a state will want to show resolve either by provoking a crisis or by fighting a costly war over a minor issue in the "expectation of getting a 'free ride' on its resulting reputation."[13]

Deterrence means preventing certain events from happening; it is about the future. Interdependent commitments are ideal for deterrence theory because they allow one to use present behavior to suggest future behavior. At the same time, they allow one to justify present behavior because one is creating expectations of future behavior. Without the "fact" of interdependence, the "tool" of reputation is denied and with it an important means of imparting credibility to threats which may otherwise seem incredible.

Do States Worry about Their Reputations?

Reputation has played an important role among American decision-makers both in the design of nuclear strategy and as a reason for intervening—or not intervening—in foreign conflicts.[14] There are many cases where the United States apparently acted primarily out of concern for its reputation. For example, concern for reputation led the United States to create a government in Korea below the 38th parallel, then to deploy U.S. forces in Korea in 1950, and finally to move from containment of communism to liberation of Korea.[15] Reputational concerns appear to have been equally important in the Taiwan Straits Crises, the 1958 Lebanon intervention, and Vietnam.[16] President Bush used reputation as an important reason to fight Iraq in the Gulf War and President Clinton invoked reputation to support intervention in Bosnia, Somalia, and Haiti. American decision-makers apparently decided not to intervene in China in the late 1940s primarily because of the potential repu-

[13] Jervis, *Logic of Images*, p. 46.

[14] See Robert McMahon, "Credibility and World Power: Exploring the Psychological Dimension in Postwar American Diplomacy," *Diplomatic History* 15/4 (1991): 455–471; Fred Kaplan, *The Wizards of Armageddon* (New York: Simon and Schuster, 1983); Gaddis, *Strategies of Containment.*

[15] See William Whitney Stueck, Jr., *The Road to Confrontation: American Policy Toward China and Korea, 1947–1950* (Chapel Hill: University of North Carolina Press, 1981), pp. 7–8, 75, 152, 174, 186, 231; Richard Whelan, *Drawing the Line: The Korean War, 1950–1953* (Boston: Little, Brown, 1990), p. 52; Gaddis, *Strategies of Containment*, p. 111.

[16] McMahon, "Credibility and World Power," pp. 461–466; George and Smoke, *Deterrence in American Foreign Policy*, pp. 353, 385; Richard Ned Lebow and Janice Stein, "Deterrence: The Elusive Dependent Variable," *World Politics* 42 (April 1990): 354.

tational costs of failure.[17] Reputation was advanced as a reason not to intervene in defense of Quemoy and Matsu and as a reason for not deploying more ground troops in Vietnam.[18] Concern for America's reputation may have been a reason why President Bush decided against marching to Baghdad in the Gulf War and it might be a check on U.S. intervention against Serbia in the former Yugoslavia.[19]

While everyone agrees that U.S. decision-makers care a great deal about America's reputation, several scholars suggest that decision-makers in other countries are less influenced by reputational concerns.[20] Patrick Morgan puzzles over why American decision-makers are so concerned about reputation. This concern springs from self-doubt, he argues, not from a belief in interdependence as either a fact or a tool: "This converts a concern for reputation from a rational extension of the art of commitment into a pretense used to hide a pervasive insecurity over what to do if one's most important commitments are challenged."[21] Why are Americans plagued by such self-doubt? Morgan believes the answer may be found in American culture and decision-making patterns.[22]

If American decision-makers have an unusual concern about their reputation, it could more plausibly be attributed to the problem of extended deterrence than to deep-seated insecurities. The United States had many more allies that were non-contiguous with the United States than did the Soviet Union. To the extent that the United States had more of a problem with extended deterrence than did the Soviet Union, it would not be surprising if Americans more than Soviets sought to create and use a reputation for keeping commitments to make deterrent threats credible. The more difficult it is to make your threats credible, and the more important it is they be credible, the more likely you will use whatever is available to convince friend and foe that you are not bluffing.

---

[17] Stueck, *Road to Confrontation*, pp. 7, 94.

[18] See McMahon, "Credibility and World Power," p. 462; *The Pentagon Papers* (New York: Bantam Books, 1971), pp. 141–142.

[19] See Gerald F. Seib, "How Miscalculations Spawned U.S. Policy toward Postwar Iraq," *Wall Street Journal*, May 3, 1991, pp. A1, 4; Eric Schmitt, "U.S. Is Shying from Bosnian Conflict," *New York Times*, July 19, 1992, p. A10.

[20] Patrick Morgan, "Saving Face for the Sake of Deterrence," in *Psychology and Deterrence*, ed. Robert Jervis, Richard Ned Lebow, and Janice Stein (Baltimore: Johns Hopkins University Press, 1985), p. 142. See also Richard Ned Lebow, "Conclusions," in *Psychology and Deterrence*, p. 220; Snyder and Diesing, *Conflict among Nations*, p. 457.

[21] Morgan, "Saving Face," p. 134.

[22] Ibid., pp. 135–136.

Do other states worry less about their own reputation than Americans worry about the United States' reputation? Morgan argues that Britain and France are not that concerned about their reputation: "Neither they nor most other U.S. allies were ever fully in sympathy with the predominant U.S. rationale for involvement in Vietnam. There was no grave concern in Europe that U.S. credibility was at stake in the 1973 Middle East war or in a variety of earlier East-West crises. The same was true about Iran and Afghanistan during the Carter Administration."[23] Morgan is right that U.S. allies did not worry about U.S. reputation in these crises. But a concern for one's own reputation is different from a concern for someone else's. It was America's—not Britain's or France's—reputation at stake in Vietnam, the Middle East, Iran, and Afghanistan. The British and French worry about their reputation when it is directly engaged. For example, British concern for its reputation was evident in the Falklands War. A senior British defense official observed: "If we can't get the Argentineans out of the Falklands, how long do you think it will be before the Spaniards take a crack at Gibraltar?"[24]

Similarly, Morgan suggests that the Russians worry less about their reputation than do Americans. He notes that Soviet literature on deterrence paid little attention to the importance of reputation and, correspondingly, the Soviets have "often accepted the necessity for a retreat without apparently fearing that a disastrous erosion of its credibility would follow."[25] The Russians may care less about their reputation than do the Americans, but this cannot be inferred from Soviet defeats any more than from American defeats. Neither the Soviet retreat in the Cuban Missile Crisis, nor the American retreat in Vietnam, provides evidence that either state believed its reputation unimportant.

While some states may worry about reputation more than others, all states worry about their reputation for resolve to some degree. My three case studies provide ample evidence that Russian, British, French, German, and Austrian decision-makers were concerned with their reputations for resolve. Yet concern for one's reputation does not mean one needs to be concerned.

---

[23] Ibid., p. 142.

[24] Quoted in Richard Ned Lebow, "Miscalculation in the South Atlantic: The Origin of the Falklands War," *Psychology and Deterrence*, p. 117. See also William Borders, " 'Iron Lady' Displays Grit at Reception," *New York Times*, April 22, 1982, p. A22.

[25] Morgan, "Saving Face," p. 142. For a similar view, see McMahon, "Credibility and World Power," p. 469.

SHOULD STATES WORRY ABOUT THEIR REPUTATIONS?

Is it rational for decision-makers to worry about their reputations for resolve? If decision-makers give reputations to other states or actors, then it would be foolish not to be concerned with one's own reputation. Despite its importance to deterrence theory, scholars have uncovered little empirical evidence to support the assumption that commitments are interdependent and that reputations form.

Glenn Snyder and Paul Diesing found only one instance in which a decision-maker gave another state a reputation. From this they concluded that "statesmen are apparently overly concerned about resolve reputation."[26] They speculate that a reputation for resolve may be acquired or lost in specific geographic regions or on similar issues.[27]

Paul Huth and Bruce Russett make a significant contribution to the study of deterrence success and failure by including past behavior as one of their independent variables. Their 1984 study found that past behavior had no impact on the outcome of crises. Their more recent studies suggest that Snyder and Diesing were on the right track. Huth and Russett found that the defender's past behavior and reputation are important only when the two combatants have a continuing rivalry with prior confrontations.[28] These later works suggest that A's past behavior toward B, C, and D is irrelevant to E, which infers A's future behavior only from A's past behavior toward E. Huth's recent case studies provide causal weight to Huth and Russett's 1984 study.[29] Huth found that the defender's reputation affects deterrence outcomes only when the two combatants have a continuing rivalry with prior confrontations. This finding is important, but it has problems.

Huth found that if A retreated from B's challenge in one crisis, B often challenged A in the next crisis. However, Huth also found that if A de-

---

[26] Snyder and Diesing, *Conflict among Nations*, p. 188.

[27] For other scholars who suggest that commitments are context-dependent, see George and Smoke, *Deterrence in American Foreign Policy*, p. 556; Robert Jervis, "Deterrence Theory Revisited," *World Politics* 31 (January 1979): 289–324; Richard Ned Lebow, "Beyond Deterrence," *Journal of Social Issues* 43/4 (1987): 37; Stephen Maxwell, *Rationality in Deterrence*, Adelphi Paper No. 50 (London: International Institute of Strategic Studies, 1968).

[28] Paul Huth and Bruce Russett, "What Makes Deterrence Work?" *World Politics* 35 (July 1984): 496–526; Huth and Russett, "Deterrence Failure and Crisis Escalation," *International Studies Quarterly* 32 (March 1988): 29–46; Huth and Russett, "Extended Deterrence and the Outbreak of War," *American Political Science Review* 82 (June 1988): 423–443; Huth, *Extended Deterrence and the Prevention of War* (New Haven: Yale University Press, 1988).

[29] See Huth, *Extended Deterrence*.

feated B's challenge in one crisis, B often challenged A again in the next crisis. The only way to prevent another challenge by B is to end the crisis in stalemate. If a history of prevailing *or* backing down prompts a challenge, then a state's reputation cannot be the cause of these outcomes.[30] The answer may be to examine what reputations decision-makers give to their adversaries.

Huth presents four crises that examine explicitly the role of past behavior. These cases provide evidence that reputations for resolve affected outcomes only in World War I.[31] He offers some evidence that the Germans believed past Russian behavior showed that the Russians were irresolute. For example, the undersecretary of state for foreign affairs, Alfred Zimmermann, said: "Bluffing constitutes one of the favorite weapons of Russian policy, and while the Russian likes to threaten with the sword, yet he does not willingly draw it for the sake of others at the critical moment."[32] Huth provides other evidence, however, that suggests Russia's reputation was not determinant. For example, the German foreign minister thought that Russia lacked the capability to fight a major war: "at bottom Russia is not now ready to strike." Huth notes that the German chancellor was uncertain that Russia could be deterred and that the German General Staff thought that the balance of capability would soon shift to Russia's advantage.[33]

Even if the shifting balance of power from Germany to Russia convinced the chancellor to challenge Russia, did a Russian reputation for irresolution tip the balance in favor of a challenge? As I argue in Chapter 4, Austrian and German policy-makers used situational attributions to explain Russia's defeat in the Bosnian Crisis. As a result, they could not sensibly believe that the Russians would be irresolute in 1914 because of 1909.

Ted Hopf's work also casts doubt on deterrence's interdependence assumption. It appears that Soviet decision-makers continued to view the United States as a highly credible adversary even after U.S. defeats in the Third World. The Soviets reasoned that the United States would

[30] James Fearon argues that his statistical reevaluation of Huth and Russett's cases shows that the evidence does not support the assumption that challengers perceive commitments as interdependent. James Fearon, "Signaling versus the Balance of Power and Interests," *Journal of Conflict Resolution* 38 (June 1994): 261–265.

[31] Huth does not show in the other three cases that reputations for resolve formed. Note that Huth suggests Russia's Balkan retreats in both 1909 and 1912 were the basis of its reputation for lacking resolve.

[32] Huth, *Extended Deterrence*, p. 186.

[33] Ibid.

continue to respond vigorously to roll back Soviet gains.[34] Hopf's findings of Soviet perceptions of American resolve may be generalizable to American policy-makers' perceptions of Soviet resolve.

Like their Soviet counterparts, American decision-makers did not seem to infer that behavior in one area results in similar behavior in another area. For example, it does not appear that the Reagan administration inferred from the Soviet withdrawal from Afghanistan that Gorbachev would behave similarly in Eastern Europe. Indeed, Gorbachev's actions in Afghanistan were taken to be those of a wily Leninist who would rather retreat in an unimportant area in order to fight in an important one. According to one Reagan administration official: "If they do get out, we'd have to applaud. But we'd also say, 'Watch out—this Kremlin rug salesman is going to try to parlay the new situation into a denuclearization of Europe, a new role for the Soviet Union in the Middle East, and so on.' "[35] This anecdote suggests that behavior may not be interdependent and that it may be hard for an adversary to lose its threatening reputation.

It appears that actors base their predictions on the specifics of the situation or perhaps the history of a continuing relationship, and not on a state's aggregate behavior. Yet, much of the logic of deterrence theory and practice rests on the assumption that states draw general conclusions about future behavior based on another's aggregate behavior. We unfortunately lack the evidence to determine if, or to what extent, actors perceive commitments interdependently.

Why has there been so little research on deterrence theory's interdependence assumption? First, it might seem that since reputation clearly matters in domestic politics it ought to matter in international politics. Second, because deterrence theory developed deductively, its assumptions were posited rather than tested. For example, the interdependence assumption was treated as a useful premise for theory construction rather than a testable hypothesis.[36] Finally, the absence of psychological theories made it difficult to test assumptions concerning reputation. As Arnold Wolfers observed, the ability to deter requires "an examina-

[34] See Ted Hopf, *Peripheral Visions: Deterrence Theory and American Foreign Policy in the Third World* (Ann Arbor: University of Michigan Press, 1994), pp. 37–40, 45–46, 62–69, 118–123, 129–130.

[35] Quoted in Craig Whitney, "Does Tumult Imperil Gorbachev's Goals?" *New York Times*, March 2, 1988, p. A12.

[36] George and Smoke, *Deterrence in American Foreign Policy*, pp. 66–71; Jervis, "Deterrence Theory Revisited," p. 302; Paul Huth and Bruce Russett, "Testing Deterrence Theory: Rigor Makes a Difference," *World Politics* 42 (July 1990): 472–473.

tion of the psychology of individuals."[37] Although deterrence theory posits a psychological relationship, it remains firmly embedded in the Realist tradition which emphasizes power and assumes rational actors. Realism is not readily adaptable to the study of perceptions.

What empirical evidence we have suggests that reputation may be less important than deterrence theory expects. However, this evidence is insufficient to determine whether decision-makers ought to be concerned about their reputation. As noted above, the problem is not just with evidence, but also with theory. In the next two sections, I critique the theoretical contributions to the study of reputation.

It should be noted that the question of whether history is diagnostic of future behavior is different from the question of whether it is used. What evidence we have suggests that history is not diagnostic. This suggestion does not mean that history is unimportant. Robert Jervis has demonstrated that decision-makers are "strongly influenced by where they have been."[38] But this does not mean that decision-makers are strongly influenced by where *others* have been.

REPUTATION IN TRADITIONAL DETERRENCE THEORY

According to the dictionary, a reputation is a "recognition by other people of some characteristic or ability." So people can have many different reputations. The same, it seems, is true for states. States can have reputations for being bold, resolute, demanding, reckless, unreliable, flexible, trustworthy, irrational, or predictable, fighters, bullies, or bluffers.[39] States can also acquire more subtle reputations. For example, Schelling suggests states acquire a "reputation for being occasionally unreasonable."[40] No one spells out exactly how to get one of these reputations. Presumably, a state will be given the appropriate reputation for behaving demandingly, recklessly, or unreliably.

There is an air of unreality to all this. Schelling and others have focused on how to manipulate one's reputation without ever considering

---

[37] Arnold Wolfers, *Discord and Collaboration: Essays on International Politics* (Baltimore: Johns Hopkins University Press, 1962), p. 9.

[38] Robert Jervis, "Realism, Game Theory, and Cooperation," *World Politics* (April 1988): 321. See also Robert Jervis, *Perception and Misperception in International Politics* (Princeton: Princeton University Press, 1976), esp. chap. 6.

[39] For these references, see Schelling, *Arms and Influence*; Snyder and Diesing, *Conflict among Nations*; Jervis, "Deterrence and Perception."

[40] Schelling, *Arms and Influence*, p. 68.

how a state would actually get such a reputation. It is difficult enough to convince adversaries of one's genuine interests and intentions.[41] It is doubly difficult to trick adversaries into attributing particular behavioral peculiarities to oneself. President Nixon supposedly tried to convince the North Vietnamese that he was a madman who would stop at nothing to win the war.[42] This tactic may have worked for some segments of his domestic audience, but it does not appear to have affected the North Vietnamese.

Who actually gets these reputations—the state, the decision-maker(s), or the different bureaucracies? Or do all three acquire reputations? If state leaders acquire reputations, then a change in the leadership of state B may mean a change in the reputation B has, as well as a change in the reputations that B ascribes to others. For example, President Eisenhower and Secretary of State Dulles tried both accommodation and coercion to change Indonesia's foreign policy, but Indonesian president Sukarno remained staunchly opposed to U.S. policies. One observer noted that "Dulles couldn't understand or approve of Sukarno, in any way, shape, or form. . . . Sukarno was repugnant to him." A change in U.S. administration led to a changed view of Sukarno. President Kennedy reportedly said: "When you consider things like the CIA's support of the 1958 rebellion, Sukarno's frequently anti-American attitude was understandable."[43] Sukarno's policy remained the same.

If it is true that a change in leader of state B can result in a changed reputation for B and for the reputation B gives to other states, then reputations may be in constant flux. To the extent that reputations are given to states (e.g., Israel is tough on terrorists) then a change in leadership will not affect reputation. The only way to determine who (if anyone) acquires reputations is by reference to the perceptions actors have about adversaries and allies.

In searching for evidence concerning reputation, it is easy to confuse self-perceptions with reputations. As mentioned earlier, A's reputation

---

[41] When Schelling was asked to put some of his ideas into practice and devise a strategy to send the right signals to the North Vietnamese, he was stumped. "In the end," writes Fred Kaplan, "he failed to come up with a single plausible answer to the most basic of questions." See Kaplan, *Wizards of Armageddon*, p. 335.

[42] See Seymour Hersh, *The Price of Power: Kissinger in the Nixon White House* (New York: Simon and Schuster, 1983), pp. 53, 75, 119, 126, 568.

[43] John Allison and Kennedy, quoted in Richard H. Moss, "The Limits of Policy: An Investigation of the Spiral Model, the Deterrence Model, and Miscalculations in U.S. Third World Relations" (Ph.D. diss., Princeton University, 1987), pp. 293, 240.

is the perception that B, C, and D have of A. If A acts out of concern for A's reputation, then it is self-perceptions that matter, not reputation. For example, Robert Jervis suggests that England's reputation was damaged after it appeared to break its promise to assist Denmark against Prussia and Austria in 1864; Britain was thereafter more cautious in making promises.[44] It is true that Britain believed its reputation was damaged and that this belief probably led it to be more cautious. It does not appear that any of the other major players—France, Prussia, or Austria—assumed Britain would behave similarly in the future.[45] Britain's self-image took a beating, not its reputation.

States may be given reputations, but they do not own them: a reputation is not the same as a self-image. Nor is a state's reputation a piece of property that it owns. As F. G. Bailey remarked, "A man's reputation is not a quality that he possesses, but rather the opinions which other people have about him."[46] A reputation is not a "property" concept but a "relational" concept. A property concept can be defined and measured without reference to another actor. A relational concept refers to "an actual or potential relationship between two or more actors."[47] Here are some pairs of property and relational concepts: foreign policy and international politics, lever and leverage, policy and power, intentions and capabilities.

"Credibility" is a relational concept. It implies the existence of other actors. Whether a threat or promise is credible depends entirely on the perceptions of others. It makes no more sense to speak of "inherent credibility" than it does to speak of inherent leverage, inherent power, or inherent capability.[48] Nonetheless, it is commonplace to refer to "inherent credibility."

Reputation is also a relational concept. It requires the existence of other actors. My reputation is whatever others think of me. My friends may think I have a reputation for keeping my promises, my enemies may think I have a reputation for breaking my promises—whatever I think of my promise-keeping propensity is irrelevant to my reputation.

[44] Jervis, *Logic of Images*, p. 89.

[45] Jonathan Mercer, "The Villafranca Armistice and the Schleswig-Holstein Crisis" (unpublished MS, Columbia University, 1988).

[46] F. G. Bailey, *Gifts and Poisons: The Politics of Reputation* (Oxford: Basil Blackwell, 1971), p. 4.

[47] David Baldwin, *Economic Statecraft* (Princeton: Princeton University Press, 1985), p. 22; see also David Baldwin, "Interdependence and Power," *International Organization* 34 (Autumn 1980): 496.

[48] It is sensible to talk about inherent capability when referring to nuclear war.

For a reputation to be a property concept, we would need a commonly recognized institution to make authoritative judgments about another's character. This is what a credit bureau does. Although it might be desirable to have a "credibility bureau" in international politics, such an institution is unlikely, in part because no state would surrender its ability to interpret whether another state's threat was credible. More important, would we really want a world in which states could be officially branded irresolute?

Nonetheless, reputation is usually thought of as a property concept. For example, Schelling contends that "Soviet expectations about the behavior of the United States are one of the most valuable assets we possess in world affairs." William Kaufmann refers to recent U.S. behavior and notes: "This then is the record—the credit, as it were—that we have at our disposal in making credible any policy of deterrence." Snyder and Diesing make the same mistake: "As 'resolve credit' with adversaries can be earned and 'banked' by repeated instances of firmness, so 'loyalty credit' with present or potential allies can be generated and drawn upon in the future by repeated demonstrations of support."[49]

This is no mere semantic quibble. Treating reputation as a property concept leads scholars and decision-makers to think of it as a tool that can be readily controlled and manipulated. It fosters the misconception that others view our behavior as we do. When we understand that reputation is a relational concept, it becomes obvious why we must study others' perceptions to understand our reputation. To the extent that state B may think about A's reputation, such thinking is done from B's perspective and B may have very different concerns and interests than does A. As the three empirical chapters demonstrate repeatedly, what you see depends on where you stand; this point is missed by those who treat reputation as a property concept.

GAME THEORY, REPUTATION, AND DETERRENCE

There has recently been an enormous amount of work on reputation by economists.[50] Using advanced game theoretic techniques to handle

---

[49] Schelling, *Arms and Influence*, pp. 124–125; Kaufmann, *Requirements of Deterrence*, p. 10; Snyder and Diesing, *Conflict among Nations*, p. 432.

[50] Using backward induction, Reinhard Selten showed that rational actors would not try to develop reputations in finite complete information games. Kreps and Wilson resolved the paradox by adding a small amount of incomplete information and developing

[28]

incomplete information, economists have offered sophisticated models showing why rational actors will choose to develop reputations. Rational-choice scholars generally assume that reputations form; the task they set for themselves is determining how to manipulate a reputation to obtain the desired results.[51]

Although the formal work on reputation has focused mainly on economic situations, such as when a monopolist might seek to develop a reputation as a tough competitor to deter other firms from entering its market, this approach may also yield more general insights into how reputations form in international politics. For example, in the classic article in this tradition, David Kreps and Robert Wilson suggested applying their approach to international diplomacy. Peter Ordeshook suggests that Kreps and Wilson's formal approach to reputation is well suited to study the issue of reputation for resolve in international politics. James Alt, Randall Calvert, and Brian Humes apply Kreps's sequential equilibrium approach to Saudi Arabia's decision to flood the oil market in 1985 and suggest applying their reputation model to security policy. John Scott uses the approach to argue for using reputation to deter terrorists. Barry Nalebuff uses sequential equilibrium approaches in order to develop a model of reputations for strength among states in international politics. And R. Harrison Wagner uses a sequential equilibrium model to show that "it is consistent with rational behavior for statesmen to act contrary to their apparent interests in unimportant matters in order to influence their adversaries' expectations of how they might act in more important situations." Even scholars who do not use game theory have referred to

---

a sequential equilibrium. Models using sequential equilibria to address reputation issues are at the frontier of current game theory. See Selten, "The Chain Store Paradox," *Theory and Decision* 9 (April 1978): 127–159, and David M. Kreps and Robert Wilson, "Reputation and Imperfect Information," *Journal of Economic Theory* 27 (August 1982): 253–279. For reviews of this literature, see Robert Wilson, "Deterrence in Oligopolistic Competition," in *Perspectives on Deterrence*, ed. Paul Stern, Robert Axelrod, Robert Jervis, and Roy Radner (New York: Oxford University Press, 1989), pp. 157–190; Bruce Clark, "Deterrence, Reputations and Competitive Cognitions" (Ph.D. diss., Stanford University, 1993); Keith Weigelt and Colin Camerer, "Reputation and Corporate Strategy: A Review of Recent Theory and Applications," *Strategic Management Journal* 9 (September/October 1988): 443–454.

[51] Alt, Calvert, and Humes note that their model "accords a major role in international relations to reputation and threat, as any student of diplomacy would want" (James Alt, Randall Calvert, Brian Humes, "Reputation and Hegemonic Stability: A Game-Theoretic Analysis," *American Political Science Review* 82 [June 1988]: 446).

this work to support arguments on reputation's importance in international politics.[52]

These formal approaches rely on three assumptions in their efforts to create a model of reputation. Reviewing these assumptions serves two purposes. First, it should help the theorists of rational deterrence to construct better models of reputation. Second, reviewing these assumptions will show that the deterrence hypothesis I test in subsequent chapters is consistent with both traditional deterrence theory and rational-choice approaches to reputation. Given the requirement that a hypothesis on reputation be generalizable and falsifiable, and generate testable predictions, this discussion helps to demonstrate that the deterrence hypothesis presented at the end of this chapter is properly deduced from deterrence theory.

The First Assumption: Observed Behavior Is Self-evident

Existing formal models of reputation assume that an actor knows its own type—strong or weak, honest or dishonest, resolute or irresolute—but nobody else knows the actor's type.[53] Because this information is incomplete, in some circumstances an actor that is irresolute can imitate the behavior of a resolute actor and fool observers into thinking it is resolute. It can thereby get a reputation for being resolute and this reputation can act as a deterrent.

Although an actor's type constitutes incomplete information in these models, an actor's behavior and the inferences that should be drawn from that behavior are common knowledge. Because an actor's preferences or type cannot be directly observed, game theorists rely on ob-

---

[52] Kreps and Wilson, "Reputation and Imperfect Information," p. 275; Peter Ordeshook, *Game Theory and Political Theory* (New York: Cambridge University Press, 1986), p. 454; Alt, Calvert, and Humes, "Reputation and Hegemonic Stability," p. 461; John L. Scott, "Deterring Terrorism through Reputation Building," *Defense Spending and Economic Growth*, ed. James E. Payne and Anandi P. Sahu (Boulder, Colo.: Westview, 1993); Barry Nalebuff, "Rational Deterrence in an Imperfect World," *World Politics* 43 (April 1991): 313–335; R. Harrison Wagner, "Rationality and Misperception in Deterrence Theory," *Journal of Theoretical Politics* 4/2 (1992): 134; Robert McElroy, *Morality and American Foreign Policy: The Role of Ethics in International Affairs* (Princeton: Princeton University Press, 1992), pp. 46–53.

[53] Most models of international crises allow only two types. See Michael D. McGinnis, "Deterrence Theory Discussion: 1, Bridging or Broadening the Gap? A Comment on Wagner's 'Rationality and Misperception in Deterrence Theory,'" *Journal of Theoretical Politics* 4/4 (1992): 444.

served behavior to infer an actor's type.[54] Observers treat behavior as a signal that helps to reveal a target's type. If actors were to disagree over the meaning of a target's behavior, it would be impossible to signal one's probable type effectively.[55] That is, if we do not know how observers will interpret our behavior, or if observers will offer different explanations for our behavior, then effective signaling becomes impossible. The existing formal literature on reputation insists, therefore, that a target's behavior must be self-evident—everyone (including the target) must know how the target behaved and must draw the same inference from that behavior. As David Kreps put it: "Reputations must be based on observables in order to work. Ambiguity and uncertainty cause problems."[56]

The more ambiguous a state's behavior, the less information the state conveys about its probable type. How a state can credibly signal information to others is an important and growing area of game theory. For example, a signal is thought to be credible when it entails costly behavior.[57] Much of the formal work on reputation in economics assumes that "weak" behavior is costly, so that a "strong" actor would not behave in a weak way. As a result, any "weak" behavior will be taken as proof that the monopolist is weak; and any "strong" behavior will be used to update beliefs about the probability that the actor is strong.[58]

The existing formal work on reputation generally assumes that observers will infer weakness from weak behavior and strength from strong behavior. For example, Wagner assumes that a state that yields is irresolute and a state that stands firm is (with some probability) resolute. Scott assumes that a state that negotiates with terrorists reveals a weak type and a state that counterattacks reveals a strong type. Alt,

---

[54] For further discussion, see McGinnis, "Deterrence Theory Discussion," p. 449; and James D. Morrow, *Game Theory for Political Scientists* (Princeton: Princeton University Press, 1994), pp. 17–19.

[55] Morrow, *Game Theory for Political Scientists*, pp. 19, 307.

[56] David Kreps, "Corporate Culture and Economic Theory," in *Perspectives on Positive Political Economy*, ed. James Alt and Kenneth Shepsle (Cambridge: Cambridge University Press, 1990), p. 108.

[57] For a good discussion of credibility and costly signals, see James Fearon, "Threats to Use Force: Costly Signals and Bargaining in International Crises" (Ph.D. diss., University of California at Berkeley, 1992). Also see Nalebuff, "Rational Deterrence," pp. 323–324.

[58] Kreps and Wilson, "Reputation and Imperfect Information," p. 260. Note that some models allow for the possibility that one "weak" act does not ensure an irrevocable reputation for weakness. See Alt, Calvert, and Humes, "Reputation and Hegemonic Stability," p. 454.

Calvert, and Humes assume that coercive behavior elicits a reputation for a willingness to use coercion and that noncoercive behavior elicits the opposite reputation.[59] It is also possible to assume the opposite. In one of Nalebuff's models, he assumes "that a country that intervenes is *weak*, not strong."[60] However, existing models do not allow "weak" behavior to elicit a reputation for weakness from one observer and a reputation for strength from a different observer.

For reasons of tractability and simplicity, existing formal work on reputation generally assumes that all actors have perfect observability and common interpretations—that is, when actors observe a target's past behavior, they update their prior beliefs in the same way. Because everyone must interpret the target's behavior similarly, that behavior must speak for itself; it must be self-evident.[61] For example, if a monopolist keeps its promise, observers will update their beliefs about the likelihood that the monopolist is a promise-keeper. But if observers are uncertain how a monopolist behaved—did it keep its promise, break its promise, or keep only part of its promise—then the behavior does not unambiguously reveal the monopolist's probable type. Even if observers agree that the monopolist probably kept its promise, they may disagree over why it did so—is it an honest type or did the particular situation compel it to be honest?[62] Assessing an actor's probable type is a complex inference problem. Reputation models need to overcome the assumption of perfect observability and common interpretation of behavior to capture the complexity of the formation of reputations.[63]

Existing reputation models assume that while information about another's type is unknown, how one should interpret behavior is known. Because empirical tests of these reputation models are rare in economics and nonexistent in political science, it is hard to know how one

---

[59] Wagner, "Rationality and Misperception"; Scott, "Deterring Terrorism"; Alt, Calvert, and Humes, "Reputation and Hegemonic Stability."

[60] Nalebuff, "Rational Deterrence," p. 327.

[61] Kreps makes a related point when he notes that any invocation of a Nash equilibrium means there is a self-evident way to play the game. See David Kreps, *Game Theory and Economic Modelling* (Oxford: Clarendon Press, 1990), pp. 31–32, 136.

[62] If the situation is always identical, then how one explains the behavior is irrelevant. Both situational and dispositional attributions can be used to predict future behavior in the same situation. However, observers must make dispositional explanations if their attributions are to have cross-situational validity.

[63] Kreps notes that "imperfect observability and its impact on reputation have been an important area of research" (*Game Theory and Economic Modelling*, p. 72).

should infer preferences from behavior.[64] In other words, if we observe a state yielding in a crisis, how should we determine how observers will explain that behavior? Should we assume that everyone will view it in dispositional terms, in which case a reputation for being irresolute might form? Or should we assume that everyone will view it in situational terms, in which case no information has been gained about another's resolve? James Morrow pointed out the difficulty of inferring type from behavior when he observed that the standard game theoretical story about reputation "requires the ability to make heroic inferences about intentions."[65]

Without an explicit theory to tell us how people will interpret behavior, we have no basis on which to determine whether or not a state's retreat furnishes information about its resolve. As discussed above, most reputation models resolve this dilemma by assumption: a state that yields reveals its irresolution.[66] This is also the solution for scholars in the large N or quantitative tradition. For example, Huth and Russett code a state that stands firm as resolute and a state that yields as irresolute.[67] Because traditionalists such as Schelling, formal theorists such as Wagner, and quantitative scholars such as Huth and Russett all assume that when a state backs down it will be viewed as irresolute and when a state stands firm it will be viewed as resolute, this assumption will be a central part of the deterrence hypothesis I test later.

---

[64] The novelty of the approach can explain the absence of empirical work in political science, but not the absence of empirical tests in economics. After reviewing the formal literature in economics, Wilson noted that "game theory suffers from extreme rationality and informational assumptions, and little has been done to establish an empirical basis for these assumptions" ("Deterrence in Oligopolistic Competition," p. 172). Economists have conducted a few tests of reputation models in artificial settings; the results were mixed. For a review, see Clark, "Deterrence, Reputations and Competitive Cognitions." Also see Yun Joo Jung, John H. Kagel, and Dan Levin, "On the Existence of Predatory Pricing: An Experimental Study of Reputation and Entry Deterrence in the Chain-store Game," *RAND Journal of Economics* 25 (Spring 1994): 72–93.

[65] James Morrow, "Alliances, Credibility, and Peacetime Costs," *Journal of Conflict Resolution* 38 (June 1994): 270.

[66] One could also assume that a state that yields in a crisis reveals its resolution or acknowledge a more complex relationship between a target's behavior and an observer's inference. Existing game theoretical approaches generally attribute a particular value to standing firm or to intervening in a conflict. For example, in one of Nalebuff's models, "Intervention is observed to be worth an amount x" ("Rational Deterrence," p. 322). Nalebuff does not attempt to solve for the value of reputation; instead, he assumes this value in order to offer numerical illustrations of reputational effects.

[67] Huth and Russett, "What Makes Deterrence Work?"

The Second Assumption: Reputation Is a Property Concept

Like traditional deterrence theorists, the authors of existing formal work treat reputation as a property rather than as a relational concept. Viewing reputation as a property concept fits with the earlier assumption that behavior is self-evident. Because everyone has perfect observability and interprets behavior similarly, only one reputation will form. For example, if we assume that everyone knows resolute behavior when they see it, that everyone attributes that behavior to the actor's disposition (rather than to a transient situation), and that everybody then uses that explanation to update their beliefs about an actor's type, then resolute behavior generates a reputation for being resolute. In that case we can concentrate on building this reputation by being resolute. But if some observers interpret resolute behavior as irresolute, then our behavior can generate multiple reputations.[68]

Assuming that behavior is self-evident permits an actor to build up or draw down its reputation as if it were a bank account. Indeed, existing formal work on reputation explicitly treats reputation as a property to be manipulated. Drew Fudenberg and Jean Tirole suggest that "intuitively . . . reputations are like assets." Keith Weigelt and Colin Camerer note that game theorists have recently formalized "the idea that a firm's reputation is an asset which can generate future rents." Bruce Bueno de Mesquita and David Lalman construct a model that permits actors "to build reputations" by "enforcing or backing down from their initial demands."[69]

Although game theorists recognize that a target's reputation is what others think of it, existing models assume that the target can make others think it is resolute by behaving in a resolute way. Observers are like accountants who carefully tabulate the target's behavior and collectively give the target one reputation. As Fudenberg and Tirole put it, "Each player's reputation is . . . summarized by his opponents' current beliefs

---

[68] Nothing in rational-choice theory requires that everyone explain the same behavior similarly. However, as Green and Shapiro note in reference to game theory's homogeneity assumption, "in practice to allow interpersonal variation may generate insuperable problems of tractability" (Donald Green and Ian Shapiro, *Pathologies of Rational Choice Theory: A Critique of Applications in Political Science* [New Haven: Yale University Press, 1994], p. 17).

[69] Drew Fudenberg and Jean Tirole, "Reputation Effects," in *Game Theory* (Cambridge: MIT Press, 1991), p. 367; Weigelt and Camerer, "Reputation and Corporate Strategy," p. 443; Bruce Bueno de Mesquita and David Lalman, *War and Reason: Domestic and International Imperatives* (New Haven: Yale University Press, 1992), p. 38.

about his type."[70] Because a state knows how each act will be interpreted, it can act strategically to manipulate the perceptions of others.

Because behavior is self-evident, an actor knows what behavior will elicit what reputation. This means an actor has "an incentive to invest in her reputation by acting reliably, because her reputation is an intangible asset that earns her rents."[71] If I break a promise, or if I back down in a crisis, I know that everyone else will think I am a promise-breaker or that I am irresolute. This knowledge allows me to manipulate my reputation by changing my behavior. It means I can build up my reputation and save it for a rainy day.

There are two disadvantages to viewing reputation as a property concept. First, if we think of reputation as property, then we are likely to believe that by manipulating our behavior we can create the desired reputation. Because we know how others ought to explain our behavior, we know what type of behavior will elicit a particular reputation. But this is right only if everyone explains behavior the same, rational, way.[72] We can only know how we should behave (to get a particular reputation) if we know how others tend to explain behavior. Because the rational course depends upon the perceptions of observers, whether the observers' perceptions are rational is irrelevant. For example, if our adversary irrationally believes that our failure to defend President Rosebud in Xanadu reveals us to be an irresolute state, the rational course might be to defend our ally in order to avoid a reputation for irresolution.

From this logic it follows that psychological explanations do not necessarily require a rational baseline.[73] We do not need to know how actors should explain each other's behavior to determine whether it is rational to worry about one's reputation. In this case, what matters is not whether others' beliefs are rational, but whether they are systematic. Idiosyncratic explanations would defeat any generalizations or predictions. Chapter 2 discusses how people tend to explain behavior without drawing conclusions about its rationality.

The second disadvantage of viewing reputation as a property concept is that it is a bad empirical fit. Because we know that people often

---

[70] Fudenberg and Tirole, *Game Theory*, p. 367.

[71] Weigelt and Camerer, "Reputation and Corporate Strategy," p. 444.

[72] Because game theory assumes optimizing behavior it addresses how people should behave, not how they do behave. See Ken Binmore, *Essays on the Foundations of Game Theory* (Cambridge, Mass: Basil Blackwell, 1990), p. 14.

[73] For the argument that psychology is useful only to explain "erroneous beliefs," which imply a deviation from a rational baseline, see Fearon, "Threats to Use Force," pp. 36–37, 103–104.

explain the same behavior differently, we also know that reputation cannot be a property concept. Even unambiguous behavior—such as backing down in a conflict—can generate different interpretations, some of which may yield information about the target's resolve and some may not. There is not a simple correlation between behavior and reputation. Viewing reputation as a relational concept shifts our attention from how a target behaves to how observers interpret that behavior, and makes it possible for observers to hold opposite views of another's reputation for resolve.

Game theoretic work on reputation in international politics needs to allow for different observers to hold different, even competing, opinions about a state's resolve. It needs to recognize that because people can explain the same behavior differently, a state cannot invest in its reputation by standing firm, for example, because different observers may explain that behavior differently. By turning their attention to these issues game theorists may devise a solution. Until they do, a deterrence hypothesis on reputation must assume that an actor can invest in her reputation—not reputations—by manipulating her behavior and thus manipulating the perceptions of others.

The Third Assumption: Commitments Are Interdependent

Reputations form only if people believe that past behavior can be used to predict future behavior. Because the existing formal work on reputation seeks to demonstrate how reputations can be used, rather than test the assumption that reputations form, this work assumes interdependence. If players did not use the past to predict the future, then reputations would not form; if players use the past to predict the future, then reputations form. These models assume that past behavior will be used to predict similar behavior in the future. For example, Kreps notes that for reputations to form "there must be a mechanism that ties B's opportunities in future rounds to past behavior. It is critical to our story that the As are able to observe B's past actions and that they condition their behavior on B's actions." Weigelt and Camerer observe that "actions, such as imitating the behavior of another type, work because players infer types from past observed behavior." And Wagner notes that in the second iteration of a repeated game, "A will use his updated estimate of the likelihood that B will punish, given B's behavior in Game 1."[74]

[74] Kreps, "Corporate Culture," p. 107; Weigelt and Camerer, "Reputation and Corporate Strategy," p. 446; Wagner, "Rationality and Misperception," p. 132.

With interdependence comes the assumption that the game will be repeated. For example, in Kreps's model the players know there is a 90 percent chance that the game will be repeated.[75] In these repeated games everything remains constant except the players' knowledge of how others played in past games (which is updated after each round). Wagner's model also varies the payoffs between the first and second game. In short, formal models of reputation assume that everyone knows the situation will be repeated, that everyone knows how everyone else played in the last game, and that everyone will use this information in the same way to make identical predictions of future behavior.[76]

There are three reasons why game theorists who apply their model of reputation to international politics should reconsider the interdependence assumption. The first reason is that international politics rarely resembles an iterated game. Morrow nicely summarizes the problem:

> In formal models of reputations, the players know the situation is the same across all rounds. They can easily draw inferences about the other players' future actions from some histories of the game. . . . Even when the cost of punishment varies across rounds, the other factors that influence the leader's willingness to carry out costly actions do not. But in international crises, these other factors always vary across cases.[77]

Because situations rarely repeat themselves exactly, using this assumption to describe the effect of reputation in international politics may obscure more than it reveals.

The requirement that the situation be repeated leads to a second problem with the interdependence assumption. There are two different types of reputation for resolve—general and specific. A *general* reputation means someone has an enduring character trait that reappears in different types of situations. In this case, a dispositional attribution has cross-situational validity. A *specific* reputation applies not across types of situations, but within specific types of situations, such as over specific issues or in specific regions. (Note that even specific reputations—

---

[75] Kreps, "Corporate Culture," p. 106.

[76] These games also assume perfect recall. See Morrow, *Game Theory for Political Scientists*, p. 65.

[77] Morrow, "Alliances, Credibility, and Peacetime Costs," pp. 270–271.

such as being funny only at funerals—are based on dispositional attributions).[78]

Because international crises are always somewhat different, even specific reputations must be valid in somewhat different situations. I refer to reputations as having cross-situational validity. Chapter 5, which examines the second Moroccan crisis, offers an easy test for the argument that reputations form over specific issues or in particular regions. In this case, the same countries confronted one another five years later over the same issues in the same region with many of the same actors.

Game theorists have addressed how specific reputations for resolve form; they have yet to address general reputations, for two reasons. First, if we define resolve as a function of things that vary according to the situation, then resolve cannot have cross-situational validity. For example, if we define resolve as some composite of capability, interests, and value for the status quo, this mix is likely to yield a different "resolve" in different situations.[79] Of course, if the identical situation is repeated, then we can use this mix to generate a specific reputation for resolve.

Second, formal work has not addressed general reputations because those models assume the game is always repeated, which means the situation is always similar. Thus existing models assume that past behavior is a "useful guide to future behavior *in similar situations.*"[80] This observation is not new. Formal theorists such as Wagner and James Fearon recognize that their models capture specific but not general reputations.[81] Although existing formal work on reputation assumes that the actor's type is "perfectly correlated across games," in principle there is no reason why an actor's type in a new situation could not be imperfectly correlated with its type in previous situations.[82] This would be a step toward a formal understanding of general reputations.

[78] Although we cannot use situational attributions to give someone a reputation, someone can get a reputation for behaving a particular way in a particular situation. This subtle distinction becomes clearer when we understand that a reputation can form whenever situation alone does not explain behavior. Just as someone would not get a reputation for fleeing a burning building, someone could get a reputation for being funny at funerals (because situation alone cannot explain this behavior). Thus even situation-specific reputations require dispositional attributions. This observation explains why a dispositional attribution—either within or across situations—is necessary for a reputation to form.
[79] Scholars commonly define resolve as a function of other things, such as interests and capabilities. For examples, see Fearon, "Threats to Use Force," pp. 116–117.
[80] Paul Milgrom and John Roberts, "Predation, Reputation, and Entry Deterrence," *Journal of Economic Theory* 27 (August 1982): 283 (my emphasis).
[81] See Wagner, "Rationality and Misperception," p. 134; and Fearon, "Threats to Use Force," p. 132.
[82] Fudenberg and Tirole, *Game Theory*, p. 389. According to Fudenberg and Tirole, "An open question in this field is what happens when the incumbent's type need not be the

By addressing specific but not general reputations, game theorists miss an aspect of reputation that has preoccupied decision-makers and traditional deterrence theorists: the possibility that observers draw general conclusions about our likely future behavior based on past behavior. For example, because many strategists and decision-makers believe it is difficult to make a threat to use nuclear weapons credible, they sometimes try to bolster their reputation for resolve at one level by being resolute in lower levels of conflict. For example, Americans did not fight and die in Vietnam simply to avoid future challenges in the same region or over similar issues, but to keep the United States from getting a general reputation as an unreliable ally or an irresolute adversary. John McNaughton advocated sending more ground troops to Vietnam in part "to show [the] world [the] lengths to which [the] U.S. will go to fulfill commitments" and to "firm up U.S. commitment in [the] eyes of all Reds, allies and neutrals."[83] By defining a reputation as having validity only in the same situation, formal approaches so truncate the concept that it misses most of what we are interested in.

The third and most serious problem with assuming interdependence is its indeterminacy. Simply put, even if identical repeated games characterized international politics and we were uninterested in general reputations, the interdependence assumption yields indeterminate outcomes. Game theorists recognize that this is a problem. Sequential equilibrium models usually have many different ways to play the game; an actor can only know which equilibrium to play if it knows everybody's subjective beliefs before they started the game and the complete preference schedules of all the players.[84] As Barry O'Neill put it, "If the game has several equilibria, players must know which one others intend to play."[85] Although this formal literature has many strengths, generating determinate, empirically testable hypotheses is not one of them.

To illustrate the indeterminacy problem, I turn not to sophisticated sequential equilibrium models, but instead to the simple game of Chicken.

---

same in each contest, so that the incumbent can be tough in some contests and weak in others" (p. 391). I thank Robert Powell for this point.

[83] "McNaughton Draft for McNamara on 'Proposed Course of Action,'" *Pentagon Papers*, March 24, 1965, No. 96, p. 436.

[84] McGinnis, "Deterrence Theory Discussion," p. 447.

[85] Barry O'Neill, "Deterrence Theory Discussion: 2, Are Game Models of Deterrence Biased towards Arms-Building? Wagner on Rationality and Misperception," *Journal of Theoretical Politics* 4/4 (1992): 469. O'Neill notes that Wagner's model has multiple equilibria; had he chosen a different way to play the game, one could conclude that the pursuit of reputation was a "tragic error" (pp. 472–473).

Traditional deterrence theorists typically use the game of Chicken to give theoretical weight to the interdependence assumption.[86] They generally assume that to back down in one crisis means the vanquished acquires a reputation for lacking resolve and the victor a reputation for resolve. For example, Glenn Snyder stresses the consequences of repeated plays of Chicken: "to yield on one occasion . . . creates an expectation that one will yield again on future occasions, which will encourage 'toughness' in the adversary and put oneself at a disadvantage in future plays."[87] Snyder qualifies this assumption by noting that the defeated state may become resolved to resist any future challenges because of its earlier retreat. Russia and Austria in 1914 are typically used to illustrate the "Never again!" phenomenon. In this case, the Russians vowed to stand firm in part because of their past retreats, whereas the Austrians assumed the Russians would yield as they had before.

While this is a sensible interpretation of potential consequences from repeated plays of Chicken, it is equally plausible that the victor in the first Chicken game will fear that the defeated state will vow "Never again!" This means the victor may expect the loser to be resolute in the next crisis. Although this game is usually invoked to show the dangers of capitulation, it could just as easily show the dangers of winning: beware a state that is defeated for it will seek revenge. In this case, the victor assumes the vanquished will be more, not less, resolute in the future and will seek to avenge its earlier defeat.[88]

When deterrence theorists recognize the possibility of the "Never again!" reaction, they nevertheless contend that the victorious state blithely assumes its defeated adversary will not seek revenge. By doing so, deterrence theorists tap only part of the logic of Chicken. The game of Chicken has no dominant strategy and no determinant outcome. Since defeat may result in a reputation for either resolution or irresolution, it pro-

---

[86] O'Neill points out that most of the basic tenets of nuclear deterrence theory predate game theoretic applications to deterrence. For example, deterrence theorists advanced arguments for the importance of having a reputation for resolve before using the game of Chicken to illustrate it. See Barry O'Neill, "Game Theory Models of Peace and War," in *Handbook of Game Theory with Economic Applications* 2, ed. Robert J. Aumann and Sergiu Hart (New York: Elsevier Science, 1992), esp. pp. 1010–1013.

[87] Glenn Snyder, " 'Prisoners Dilemma' and 'Chicken' Models in International Politics," *International Studies Quarterly* 15 (March 1971): 86.

[88] Jervis raises this possibility in "Deterrence and Perception," pp. 12–13. There is yet another possibility. Instead of thinking the victor is resolute, the loser may expect the victor next time to bluff. This is because the loser may think that the victor believes the loser is irresolute. For illustrations, see Holstein's explanations of the British victory in 1906 (Chapter 3), or Grey's views after the Russian defeat in 1909 (Chapter 4).

vides a shaky foundation on which to build assumptions about resolve. Indeed, there is no theoretical explanation, by economists, deterrence theorists, or critics of deterrence, of why commitments should be viewed as either independent or interdependent.[89] We do not know whether people use the past to predict the future, or if they do, how they do it. Assuming the answer to these questions is useful for some purposes, but it does not help us construct a determinate hypothesis on reputation formation.

Formal models of reputation assume that everyone has perfect observability, that everyone interprets behavior similarly (which means only one reputation forms), and that everyone then uses these past common interpretations in the same way to predict the same future behavior. It is not surprising that scholars who build these assumptions into their models conclude that reputation building is consistent with rational behavior. "Both theory and conventional wisdom," concludes Wagner, "suggest that a state's behavior in one conflict can influence its adversaries' expectations of its behavior in subsequent conflicts."[90] But his theory is indeterminate, conventional wisdom might be wrong, and he offers no evidence.

Wagner constructs a model around the assumption that reputations form and then claims that building reputations is rational. Indeed, the task he set himself was to show that the conventional wisdom of traditional deterrence theorists about reputation could be formalized and that this is consistent with rational behavior.[91] While testing the internal logic of an argument by making it formal has its merits, it is also true that almost any behavior can be explained as rational given a sufficiently elaborate model.[92]

---

[89] See for example Lebow and Stein, "Deterrence," p. 355. Also see Fearon, "Threats to Use Force," p. 129.

[90] Wagner, "Rationality and Misperception," p. 134.

[91] "My aim," says Wagner, "was only to show how the reasoning of earlier deterrence theorists such as Ellsberg could now be formalized, or, in other places, to show that policy-makers' pronouncements cannot be dismissed as inconsistent with rational behavior, as some critics have suggested" ("Deterrence Theory Discussion: 4, Reply to Comments by McGinnis, O'Neill, and Rapaport," *Journal of Theoretical Politics* 4/4 [1992]: 485).

[92] For further discussion, see Kreps, *Game Theory and Economic Modelling*, p. 104. For an illustration of a game theorist explicitly reworking his assumptions to obtain the desired finding, see Thomas Schelling, "The Reciprocal Fear of Surprise Attack," in *Strategy of Conflict*. I thank Robert Powell for this point. For a discussion of how slight changes in a game's parameters can generate results opposite of those originally predicted, see John Neral and Jack Ochs, "The Sequential Equilibrium Theory of Reputation Building: A Further Test," *Econometrica* 60/5 (1992): 1151–1169; and Jung, Kagel, and Levin, "On the Existence of Predatory Pricing." The ability to generate an equilibrium for virtually any desired outcome given incomplete information in a repeated game is known as the folk theorem. For further discussion, see Drew Fudenberg and Eric Maskin, "The Folk Theorem in Repeated Games with Discounting or with Incomplete Information," *Econometrica* 54 (May 1986): 533–554.

Although game theory has contributed to our understanding of different aspects of deterrence, the formal work on reputation has not been as successful.[93] Economists and rational deterrence theorists have built into their models assumptions which ensure that reputations form, that reputations can be manipulated, and that they work as intended. They have shown that traditional arguments about the importance of reputation can be made formal. Until the formal work on reputation goes beyond writing down models to verify "common sense" and abandons or modifies the assumptions discussed above, game theory's contribution to the debate on reputation in international politics will remain modest.

REPUTATION AND DETERRENCE THEORY: CONSTRUCTING A HYPOTHESIS

We have thus gone full circle, beginning with the intuitive arguments about reputation commonly made since Thucydides, then moving to examine the most recent scholarship in the rational-choice literature, only to return without amendment to arguments made by traditional deterrence theorists. The task remains of deducing from the deterrence literature a generalizable, falsifiable, and predictive hypothesis on when either general or specific reputations for resolve form.

This deductive effort could be made easily were it not for the assumption in deterrence theorists' formal and informal work that commitments are interdependent. The interdependence assumption hinders the creation of a testable argument about reputation. For example, imagine a state that gives in, then stands firm, then backs down again. What explanations would the deterrence hypothesis expect? Specifically, how should we expect the British to view the Germans after their Agadir defeat: as irresolute because they backed down in Agadir (immediate behavior); as irresolute because of their earlier defeat in Morocco (same issue and region); or as still resolute because of their victory in Bosnia-Herzegovina (most recent past behavior)?

This indeterminacy creates a problem. Keeping the interdependence assumption in the deterrence hypothesis yields indeterminate predictions. Dropping this assumption is fatal to the argument that reputa-

---

[93] Recent game theoretical contributions include Powell's work on the reciprocal fear of surprise attack and Fearon's study of selection effects. See Powell, *Nuclear Deterrence Theory* and Fearon, "Signaling versus the Balance of Power and Interests." For a comprehensive review of this literature, see O'Neill, "Game Theory Models of Peace and War."

tions for resolve matter. Only by restricting this assumption is it possible for deterrence theory to generate determinate hypotheses. The most we can say is that past behavior governs *expectations* of future behavior. Once the target "acts," immediate behavior, not past behavior, governs explanations. For example, a state that backs down will be viewed as irresolute and others will expect it to be irresolute in the future; if in the next round it stands firm, observers will view it as resolute and will expect it to be resolute the next time. We can, therefore, change our reputation for irresolution by being resolute in the next crisis, or we can lose our good reputation by one irresolute act. Narrowing the scope of the deterrence hypothesis to a specific region or over a specific issue does not resolve the indeterminacy problem.

I make deterrence's hypothesis on reputation determinate by simplifying it: a state that yields should be viewed as irresolute and a state that stands firm should be viewed as resolute; however a state behaved in the last crisis should govern others' expectations of that state. (Chapter 5 examines the hypotheses specific to region and issue.) This formulation makes the deterrence hypothesis on reputation determinate, captures its core assumptions, and avoids the problems associated with "rigorous testing of vague theory."[94]

This hypothesis fits with the beliefs of deterrence theorists (and of decision-makers) about how reputations form, as well as with the formal work on reputation done by game theorists. By excluding other factors from the hypothesis, such as capability or interests, we can evaluate the importance of a reputation for resolve vis-à-vis these other factors. This hypothesis is also practical. Decision-makers have available to them what little information the hypothesis demands. Finally, it is a fair hypothesis; it has but two objectives: first, to determine when observers infer character from behavior; second, to see if observers use past behavior to draw general inferences about future resolution either in a different area, in the same area, or over the same issue. I ask it to do no more than I ask of my own argument, which is equally spare.

[94] Kenneth Waltz, *Theory of International Politics* (New York: Random House, 1979), p. 16.

[2]

Reputation and Psychology

If after we got a dozen guys killed on Sunday, we pull out, it tells people wherever we go—the Golan Heights, Bosnia, Syria, Haiti, wherever—that all they have to do is give us double-digit casualties and they can get rid of us.

—Secretary of Defense Les Aspin

When a state abandons a commitment, how will its allies and adversaries explain this behavior? Will they think it reveals an irresolution certain to reappear; will they explain it away by referring to unique circumstances; or will their explanations differ? To understand when reputations form we need to know how people tend to explain one another's behavior. Rational-actor theories do not address perceptions of cause. Social psychological theories do.

Social psychology is the study of how the "actual, imagined, or implied presence of others" influences our thoughts, feelings, and behavior.[1] It is the study of how people make sense of themselves and of others. Among the most powerful theories in social psychology are causal attribution theories. Attributions are inferences made to explain events. For example, why was Buck Helm rescued after being trapped for eighty-nine hours in the earthquake-wrecked Nimitz Freeway in California? Some say that he survived because he was lucky and dubbed him "lucky Bucky"; others, such as Mrs. Helm, say he survived because "he's really strong and he's got a lot of strong will and he isn't ready to die."[2] When we seek to explain an event, we make inferences about the situation, the person, or both.

---

[1] G. W. Allport, "The Historical Background of Modern Social Psychology," *Handbook of Social Psychology* 1, ed. Gardner Lindzey and Elliot Aronson (Reading, Mass.: Addison-Wesley, 1968), p. 3.

[2] Quoted in Timothy Egan, " 'Nobody's Tougher,' " *New York Times*, October 23, 1989, p. B10.

By understanding when decision-makers are likely to make what sort of attribution we will be able to determine the conditions under which reputations for resolve form. Because a reputation is a judgment of another's character, a dispositional (or character-based) attribution is necessary to generate a reputation. If others believe that a state backed down because of the balance of capability, this is a situational rather than a dispositional attribution. A situational attribution implies that anyone in the same situation would behave similarly. A state that yielded when the balance of capability was against it might stand firm in a different situation. Because the explanation does not bear on the character of the state's decision-makers, no reputation forms.

A reputation for resolve forms if two conditions are met. First, an observer must explain the target's behavior as a function of its character (or disposition). Second, the observer must use this explanation to predict or explain the target's future behavior. A dispositional attribution is not the same as a reputation. A reputation forms only if the observer uses a dispositional attribution to predict or explain later behavior. For example, if we explain another's retreat in dispositional terms—they were irresolute—and because of this we expect them to be irresolute in the future, then we have given them a reputation for irresolution. This logic is exactly what John Foster Dulles worried about: "If our conduct indicates a continuing disposition to fall back and allow doubtful areas to fall under Soviet Communist control, then many nations will feel confirmed in the impression . . . that we do not expect to stand firm short of the North Atlantic area."[3] If we know when decision-makers are most likely to make either a situational or dispositional attribution, then we can begin to understand when reputations form.

When do we explain behavior more in terms of the transient situation, or more in terms of an enduring character? Social psychologists have found that our beliefs, expectations, and desires drive our explanations of others' behavior. A central tenet of intergroup relations is that we tend to use character-based attributions to explain an out-group's *undesirable* behavior. Yet, we will explain away with situational attributions an out-group's *desirable* behavior. For example, we are likely to think that our adversary's retreats reflect not an irresolute character, but its untenable situation; whereas we are likely to think our adversary's challenges reflect not its difficult situation but its aggressive, revisionist nature.

---

[3] Quoted in John Lewis Gaddis, *Strategies of Containment: A Critical Appraisal of Postwar National Security Policy* (New York: Oxford University Press, 1982), p. 103.

The out-group therefore cannot win. While we tend to explain away with situational attributions desirable out-group behavior, we tend to accept as characteristic out-group behavior that we find undesirable. The following hypothesis can be formulated: *Desirable out-group behavior elicits situational explanations, and undesirable out-group behavior elicits dispositional explanations.* This hypothesis addresses the first of reputation's two parts: when will decision-makers use dispositional attributions to explain another's behavior? Only dispositional attributions can generate reputations. Because I assume that allies are part of the out-group, this hypothesis applies to both allies and adversaries.

The second aspect of reputation formation is the interdependence of commitments: do people use past demonstrations of resolution (or ir-resolution) to predict the same type of behavior in the future? Reputations can form only if commitments are interdependent. In contrast to deterrence theorists, I expect commitments to be more independent than interdependent. If observers believe that the transient situation explains a target's behavior, then that explanation cannot be used to predict or explain future behavior in a different situation. By definition, situational attributions do not have cross-situational validity; they cannot be used to generate reputations. Whenever observers use situational attributions to explain behavior, a reputation cannot form.

If situational attributions must be independent, can dispositional attributions be interdependent? Although I will discuss later why dispositional attributions are likely to be more independent than interdependent, note that dispositional attributions can be used to predict or explain future behavior in different situations. If I believe my adversary demonstrated resolve in one place, this belief may influence my expectations or explanations of its future behavior. Since dispositional attributions are valid across situations, every dispositional attribution can generate a reputation.

Because situational attributions do not address another's character, they cannot be used to predict behavior in different situations. I argue that observers use dispositional attributions to explain an out-group's undesirable behavior, and situational attributions to account for an out-group's desirable behavior. As a result, only undesirable behavior elicits dispositional attributions; and so only undesirable behavior can generate a reputation. Therefore we can establish the conditions under which reputations for resolve might form:

First, *adversaries can get reputations for having resolve.* An adversary that stands firm is scorned, not welcomed. Because this behavior is undesirable, an observer will make dispositional explanations which can generate a reputation.

Second, *allies can get reputations for lacking resolve.* If an observer is disappointed that its ally backed down, then the observer will explain its ally's behavior in dispositional terms. This attribution can generate a reputation.

Third, *adversaries rarely get reputations for lacking resolve.* An adversary who backs down is welcomed, not scorned; those who desired that the threat not be kept will view it in situational terms. Situational attributions cannot generate a reputation.

Fourth, *allies rarely get reputations for having resolve.* If an ally stands firm, as desired by the observer, then the observer will use the situation to explain this behavior. Situational attributions cannot generate a reputation, as Table 1 summarizes.

The hypothesis that the desirability of another's behavior determines type of attribution yields these four propositions. Because the desires hypothesis predicts only the type of attribution (either situational or dispositional), these propositions assume the content of an attribution. For example, these propositions assume that decision-makers will find it desirable either when their adversaries back down, or when their allies stand firm; they will view it as undesirable either when their adversaries stand firm, or when their allies back down. These four propositions also assume that each dispositional attribution bears on

Table 1. Attributions and their consequences for reputations

	Attribution	Reputation
Target's undesirable behavior	If adversary stands firm, observer makes dispositional attributions.	Adversary can get reputation for having resolve.
	If ally backs down, observer makes dispositional attributions.	Ally can get reputation for lacking resolve.
Target's desirable behavior	If adversary backs down, observer makes situational attributions.	Adversary cannot get reputation for lacking resolve.*
	If ally stands firm, observer makes situational attributions.	Ally cannot get reputation for having resolve.*

*Note: Although situational attributions *cannot* generate reputations, my argument is probabilistic; this means observers will sometimes use disposition when I expect situation. Therefore, in the text I replace *cannot* with *rarely.*

[47]

the other's resolve, and will then be used to predict future resolution. In other words, they assume interdependence between dispositional attributions. As a result, reputations for resolve can form in two of these four situations. It does not mean that they will form.

To many readers this hypothesis and its propositions may seem suspiciously counterintuitive or wrong. My object in the rest of this chapter is to allay some of these concerns. The next three sections explain the theoretical basis of the argument and present some of the experimental work behind it. The fourth section reviews the deterrence and the desires hypotheses and discusses the extent to which they are competing explanations. The last section discusses theoretical and methodological problems with applying psychology to international politics.

Why should our desires have anything to do with how we explain another's behavior? There are several complementary theories which suggest that how we view another's behavior, whether desirable or undesirable, affects how we interpret that behavior. These explanations include the effects of saliency, the self-serving bias, and the egocentric bias. A related theoretical approach which uses "expectations" to predict attributions also supports the desires hypothesis. I use the research on expectations to support my argument for the way adversaries explain each other's behavior. However, I choose desires over expectations to explain how reputations form for two reasons: the expectations hypothesis could be circular, and its propositions on allies seems wrong. I devote a section to the role of expectations and adversaries.

Before the sections on "desires" and "expectations," I discuss basic concepts and theory needed to understand these later sections. Two points are particularly important to my argument. First, people are not idiosyncratic in their causal attributions. Second, saliency (or vividness) strongly influences our causal explanations. I address these issues next.

CORRESPONDENT INFERENCE THEORY AND OVERATTRIBUTION

Fritz Heider developed the distinction between situational and dispositional attributions as the key to understanding how people explain behavior. He viewed people as naive scientists searching to understand the links between various effects and possible causes. Heider believed that observers explain cause either by pointing to situational factors external and out of the control of the actor, or by pointing to dispositional factors such as the actor's own beliefs, character traits, or motives.[4] The research agenda in social psychology was thus set: do people explain behavior as a product of enduring dispositions or of transient situational context? In other words, when is responsibility for an action assigned to people, and when is it assigned to the environment?

Edward Jones and Keith Davis used Fritz Heider's seminal work, *The Psychology of Interpersonal Relations*, to create testable hypotheses for determining how people attribute cause. Heider argued that people tend to use dispositional attributions to explain others' behavior. In our efforts to understand and control our social environment, we tend to explain even transient and variable behavior as a product of relatively unchanging conditions. Heider's insights provide the basis for virtually all subsequent work on attribution: "It seems that behavior in particular has such salient properties it tends to engulf the total field rather than be confined to its proper position as a local stimulus whose interpretation requires the additional data of a surrounding field—the situation in social perception."[5] Based on Heider's observations, Jones and Davis hypothesized that people infer disposition directly from behavior and called this correspondent inference theory.[6] According to this theory, we will perceive someone who performs an act that benefits others as a kind person.

The tendency to perceive correspondence between disposition and act proved to be robust. A series of experiments showed that even when situational factors clearly determined behavior, observers still inferred dispositions that corresponded with behavior. For example, even when observers were informed that an actor was asked to write a pro-Castro speech, observers, after seeing the actor read the speech, inferred the actor was pro-Castro.[7] The tendency to discount overwhelming situational constraints on behavior and exaggerate the importance of disposition was dubbed the fundamental attribution error by Lee Ross and

[4] Fritz Heider, *The Psychology of Interpersonal Relations* (London: Lawrence Erlbaum Associates, 1958).

[5] Ibid., p. 54.

[6] Edward E. Jones and Keith E. Davis, "From Acts to Dispositions: the Attribution Process in Person Perception," *Advances in Experimental Social Psychology* 2, ed. L. Berkowitz (New York: Academic Press, 1965), pp. 219–266.

[7] Edward E. Jones and Victor A. Harris, "The Attribution of Attitudes," *Journal of Experimental Social Psychology* 3 (January 1967): 1–24. For an equally surprising study, see Martin A. Safer, "Attributing Evil to the Subject, Not the Situation: Student Reaction to Milgram's Film on Obedience," *Personality and Social Psychology Bulletin* 6 (June 1980): 205–209.

the overattribution effect by Edward Jones.[8] As Philip Tetlock observed, overattribution is "remarkably difficult to eliminate" and "one of social psychology's better-replicated phenomena."[9]

Exactly why people tend to overattribute disposition and discount situational factors is debatable. The best explanation combines Heider's notion of "behavior engulfing the field" and Amos Tversky and Daniel Kahneman's anchor-adjustment bias. For the observer, the actor's behavior is more salient or figural than the colorless background of the actor's situation. We naturally tend to see actors causing acts. As Edward Jones remarks, situation is hard to see: "The notion that situations can cause action is abstract and derivative, almost metaphoric in its implications."[10]

People tend to attribute cause to whatever they notice most. One study that illustrates this tendency had subjects observe two actors in a scripted conversation. When one actor was seated in a bright light, or rocked in a rocking chair, or even wore a more complexly patterned shirt, observers made more dispositional attributions to the more "figural" actor, and more situational ones to the other actor.[11] The finding that "what you *attend* to is what you *attribute* to" is one of the best supported generalizations in attribution theory.[12] Consequently, an observer will view salient or "available" information as the probable cause of behavior.[13]

Tversky and Kahneman found that once we make an initial attribution we are remarkably resistant to adjusting the view to accommodate new information.[14] This tendency explains why experimental subjects

[8] Lee Ross, "The Intuitive Psychologist and His Shortcomings: Distortions in the Attribution Process," *Advances in Experimental Social Psychology* 10, ed. L. Berkowitz (New York: Academic Press, 1977): 173–220; Edward E. Jones, "The Rocky Road from Acts to Dispositions," *American Psychologist* 34/2 (1979): 107–117.

[9] Philip Tetlock, "Accountability: A Social Check on the Fundamental Attribution Error," *Social Psychology Quarterly* 48/3 (1985): 227–228. Several other psychologists concluded that overattribution was "perhaps the preeminent bias in the attribution literature." See Arthur Miller, William Ashton, and Mark Mishal, "Beliefs concerning the Features of Constrained Behavior: A Basis for the Fundamental Attribution Error," *Journal of Personality and Social Psychology* 59/4 (1990): 635.

[10] Jones, "The Rocky Road," p. 114.

[11] Leslie Zebrowitz McArthur and David L. Post, "Figural Emphasis and Person Perception," *Journal of Experimental Social Psychology* 13 (November 1977): 520–535.

[12] Lee Ross and Richard Nisbett, *The Person and the Situation: Perspectives of Social Psychology* (Philadelphia: Temple University Press, 1991), p. 140.

[13] Amos Tversky and Daniel Kahneman, "Availability: A Heuristic for Judging Frequency and Probability," *Judgment under Uncertainty: Heuristics and Biases*, ed. Daniel Kahneman, Paul Slovic, and Amos Tversky (Cambridge: Cambridge University Press, 1982) pp. 163–178; M. Ross and F. Sicoly, "Egocentric Biases in Availability and Attribution," *Journal of Personality and Social Psychology* 37/3 (1979): 322–337.

[14] Tversky and Kahneman, "Judgment under Uncertainty: Heuristics and Biases," *Judgment under Uncertainty*, pp. 4–20.

continue to make dispositional attributions even when they know that situation explains behavior.[15] Jones reasoned that once we make an initial correspondent inference, it serves as an anchor or baseline which we inadequately modify according to new information.

Madison Avenue is aware of this tendency. A recent television commercial uses a man dressed as a doctor to make a pitch for a brand of aspirin after saying, "I'm not a doctor, but I play one on T.V." In general, people fail to adjust adequately to situational constraints (the man is an actor) after making an initial correspondent inference (we see a doctor). Substantial experimental evidence supports this explanation. Johnson, Jemmott, and Pettigrew found that the more people are made aware of determining situational factors, the more they adjust for these factors (although these adjustments remain insufficient).[16]

Because subjects tend to attribute causality to whatever is most salient, it should be possible to change their explanations by changing what they notice. For example, if salience explains overattribution, and situation is made salient, then people ought to overattribute to situation and discount disposition. It follows that if the initial correspondent inference can be shifted from "actor-action" to "situation-action," then people should overattribute to situation and fail to adjust adequately to determining dispositional factors. George Quattrone tested and confirmed these expectations.[17]

When altered perspectives produce a shift in salience, a corresponding change in inferences results. Consequently, actors should perceive their own behavior differently than observers do. Whereas observers view an actor as driven by his disposition, an actor "tends to attribute his own reactions to the object world."[18] For actors, situation is more salient than their own behavior. This is the actor-observer difference.[19]

A number of studies have demonstrated that changing an actor's perspective—for example by videotaping the actor's behavior and then replaying it for her—results in corresponding changes in attributions.

---

[15] For a review of the overattribution effect in the face of blatant and overwhelming situational causes, see Jones, "The Rocky Road."

[16] For a review of the evidence, see Joel T. Johnson, John B. Jemmott III, and Thomas F. Pettigrew, "Causal Attribution and Dispositional Inference: Evidence of Inconsistent Judgments," *Journal of Experimental Social Psychology* 20/6 (1984): 567–585.

[17] George A. Quattrone, "Overattribution and Unit Formation: When Behavior Engulfs the Person," *Journal of Personality and Social Psychology* 42/4 (1982): 593–607. See also Robert M. Arkin and Shelly Duval, "Focus of Attention and Causal Attribution of Actors and Observers," *Journal of Experimental Social Psychology* 11 (September 1975): 427–438.

[18] Heider, *Psychology of Interpersonal Relations*, p. 157.

[19] E. E. Jones and R. E. Nisbett, *The Actor and the Observer: Divergent Perceptions of the Causes of Behavior* (Morristown, N.J.: General Learning Press, 1971).

An actor who explained her behavior in situational terms will, after viewing her performance on video-tape (and having the perspective of an observer), explain this behavior in more dispositional terms.[20] While we see our own behavior as highly dependent on the context, we see others' behavior as a product of stable dispositional qualities. As with overattribution, the existence of the actor-observer difference is generally accepted, but the questions of "why," "when," and "with what implications" remain.[21]

There are three qualifications to the general phenomenon of overattribution and actor-observer difference. The first is a study by Tetlock which found that accountability can wipe out overattribution.[22] Tetlock found that when subjects were not made accountable, they overattributed to disposition as they had in previous experiments. However, when the subjects were told *before* making their evaluations that they would have to defend their views they were considerably more sensitive to situational constraints. Consistent with the anchor-adjustment hypothesis, when subjects were told *after* they made their evaluations that they would be accountable, it had no affect on their attributions.

Second, Garth Fletcher and his colleagues reasoned that just as people vary in the level of their attributional complexity, they will also vary in their susceptibility to overattribution.[23] This means that attributionally complex people are less prone to overattribution than are people who use simpler causal schema. This finding, taken together with Tetlock's finding on accountability, suggests that policy-makers may not be subject to overattribution errors: decision-makers are often publicly accountable for their attributions, are strongly motivated to make accurate attributions, and are usually complex thinkers. It should be noted, however, that neither increasing complexity nor accountability necessarily means more valid or accurate causal judgments. In fact, Tetlock found that people who are held accountable for their explanations often

[20] See M. D. Storms, "Videotape and the Attribution Process: Reversing Actors' and Observers' Points of View," *Journal of Personality and Social Psychology* 27 (August 1973): 165–175; Michael Ross and Garth Fletcher, "Attribution and Social Perception," *Handbook of Social Psychology* 2, ed. G. Lindzey and E. Aronson (New York: Random House, 1985).

[21] Gifford Weary, Melinda A. Stanley, John H. Harvey, *Attribution* (New York: Springer-Verlag, 1989), pp. 38–39. Also see Miller, Ashton, and Mishal, "Beliefs concerning the Features of Constrained Behavior," p. 635.

[22] Tetlock, "Accountability."

[23] Garth Fletcher, Paula Danilovics, Guadalupe Fernandez, Dena Peterson, Glenn Reeder, "Attributional Complexity: An Individual Differences Measure," *Journal of Personality and Social Psychology* 51/4 (1986): 875–884.

attempt to use non-diagnostic information and engage in "interpretive overkill."[24]

Third, there are systematic exceptions to overattribution and the actor-observer effect. Three exceptions bear directly on my hypothesis: the self-serving bias, the egocentric bias, and the positivity and negativity bias. I examine later the first two biases when discussing my hypothesis. I consider now only the positivity and negativity bias.

There is an abundance of evidence that people make dispositional attributions for behavior they view positively, while using situational attributions for behavior they view negatively. It is generally believed that people cause positively valued behavior while situational factors cause negatively valued behavior. This is true for actor and observer alike.[25] This positivity bias was found to be strongest among intimate others, and weakest for strangers or disliked others. Consequently, as Taylor and Koivumaki suggest, "a person who is disliked or hated may well be viewed as responsible for bad behaviors and not responsible for good ones. In other words, we may find a corresponding 'negativity' effect for disliked others."[26] We can now see that decision-makers may explain behavior differently depending upon whose behavior they are explaining—an enemy's, a friend's, or their own behavior.

EXPECTATIONS AND ADVERSARIES

Neither the fundamental attribution error nor the actor-observer difference considers the effect that preconceptions (or expectations) have on attributions. Since people are driven more by theory than by data, these preconceptions ought to influence how we interpret behavior.[27]

---

[24] Philip Tetlock and Richard Boettger, "Accountability: A Social Magnifier of the Dilution Effect," *Journal of Personality and Social Psychology* 57 (September 1989): 397.

[25] See Joop Van der Plight and J. Richard Eiser, "Actors' and Observers' Attributions, Self-serving Bias and Positivity Bias," *European Journal of Social Psychology* 13 (January–March 1983): 95–104; Wayne Tillman and Charles Carver, "Actors' and Observers' Attributions for Success and Failure," *Journal of Experimental Social Psychology* 16/1 (1980): 18–32.

[26] Shelley Taylor and Judith Hall Koivumaki, "The Perception of Self and Others," *Journal of Personality and Social Psychology* 33/4 (1976): 408.

[27] See Robert Jervis, *Perception and Misperception in International Politics* (Princeton: Princeton University Press, 1976), esp. pp. 153, 163–165; Charles G. Lord, Lee Ross, and Mark R. Lepper, "Biased Assimilation and Attitude Polarization: The Effects of Prior Theories on Subsequently Considered Evidence," *Journal of Personality and Social Psychology* 37/11 (1979): 2098–2109.

James Kulik argues that the relative importance of situation or disposition depends on one's prior conceptions of the target.[28] If the target behaves as expected, then this behavior will be seen as reflecting the target's disposition even in situations in which neutral observers would attribute that behavior to compelling situational factors. In contrast, an observer will seize upon incidental situational factors to explain an actor's unexpected behavior.

An observer's efforts to explain behavior that is not congruent with expectations leads to such intense scrutiny of situational pressures that situational factors that normally might be viewed as inhibiting that behavior, may instead be viewed as compelling it. When behavior contradicts prior beliefs, Kulik found that "subjects were, contrary to the fundamental attribution error, so sensitive to potential situational causes that factors normally unnoticed or judged implausible were then perceived as important causes."[29]

The overattribution effect predicts that observers will infer disposition from behavior. For example, if Mary gives money to charity, then Mary is perceived to be a generous person:

behavior ⟶ dispositional attribution

In contrast, Kulik proposes that people infer disposition from behavior only when that behavior is expected. Rather than being led by behavior, we are led by our expectations of that behavior. If we think Mary is a generous person, and we see her give money to charity, we will correspondingly view her as generous. However, if we think Mary is generous, and we observe her behave in an ungenerous way, we will not make the inference that she is stingy; instead, we will look for situational constraints on her behavior:

expected behavior ⟶ dispositional attribution
unexpected behavior ⟶ situational attribution

[28] James Kulik, "Confirmatory Attribution and the Perpetuation of Social Beliefs," *Journal of Personality and Social Psychology* 44/6 (1983): 1171–1181.
[29] Kulik, "Confirmatory Attribution," p. 1179. For another study that found that people prefer situational attributions for unexpected behavior, and dispositional attributions for expected behavior, see Jennifer Crocker, Darlene Hannah, and Renee Weber, "Person Memory and Causal Attributions," *Journal of Personality and Social Psychology* 44/1 (1983): 55–66.

Observers are able to "explain away" supposedly out-of-character behavior by finding the cause of the unexpected behavior in the situation.

The more situational the attribution, the less that behavior is judged to correspond with disposition. The result is what Kulik calls a "confirmatory attribution pattern" that perpetuates our beliefs about others. Confirmatory attribution is not necessarily an error nor does it represent some sort of cognitive failure. It generally makes more sense to discount a disconfirming bit of evidence than to junk one's theory or belief. When our beliefs or theories are well founded, a confirmatory attribution pattern may enhance our inferential accuracy.[30] When our beliefs are wrong or induced by non-content-based categories, such confirmatory attributions can be harmful. For example, it is astonishingly easy to trigger intergroup discrimination. Even when people are placed in an imaginary group based on some trivial guessing game, and when they have no idea who is in their group or the other group, there is a strong tendency to show in-group favoritism and out-group discrimination.[31] When the categories are not arbitrary, but instead clear, systematic, and infused with racial, religious, or national distrust, confirmatory attribution patterns become pernicious.

If decision-makers are subject to this bias, then they may explain their allies' and adversaries' behavior in predictable ways. For example, if they expect their adversaries to behave in an undesirable way, they will use dispositional attributions to explain that behavior. However, if their adversaries behave, unexpectedly, in a desirable way, they may use situational attributions to explain away this behavior. Thomas Pettigrew developed hypotheses consistent with the assumptions of in-group / out-group dynamics and confirmatory attributions and applied them to race relations.

Pettigrew noted that one of the most systematic exceptions to overattribution was the tendency to use situational attributions to explain away the positive behavior of disliked out-groups.[32] More concretely, there is a tendency in racists' causal attributions of African-Americans "to assign transitory factors to explain positive performance and permanent factors to explain negative performance."[33] This bias, which

---

[30] Kulik, "Confirmatory Attribution," p. 1178.

[31] For a review of Henri Tajfel's minimal group paradigm, see Jonathan Mercer, "Anarchy and Identity," *International Organization* 49 (Spring 1995): 229–252.

[32] Thomas Pettigrew, "The Ultimate Attribution Error: Extending Allport's Cognitive Analysis of Prejudice," *Personality and Social Psychology Bulletin* 5/4 (1979): 461–476.

[33] Thomas Pettigrew and Joanne Martin, "Shaping the Organizational Context for Black American Inclusion," *Journal of Social Issues* 43/1 (1987): 44.

Pettigrew dubbed the "ultimate attribution error," is an extension of overattribution to include positive and negative preconceptions of targets. Pettigrew hypothesized that observers will view antisocial behavior within their group as situationally caused, but will often view that same behavior when committed by out-groups in dispositional terms.

For example, imagine an observer who believes that Scotland is full of "cheapskates." Mary is Scottish. The observer expects Mary not to give to charity. If Mary gives to charity, the observer searches for and finds some situational explanation to salvage his conception of the cheap Scot; if Mary does not give to charity, this reflects a Scottish disposition and no alternative explanations are believed needed. Conversely, a Scottish observer, who believes that his countrymen are kind and generous people, will make opposite attributions. If Mary gives to charity, this action reflects Scottish generosity; if she does not give to charity, this choice reflects external constraints that make charity difficult or impossible.

Confirmatory attributions are strongest where there are strong beliefs. While racists certainly fall into the trap of confirmatory attributions, this bias is quite general. The experiments that confirmed the existence of this bias did not focus on highly prejudiced or uneducated subjects.[34] The stronger our expectations or prejudices, the greater the influence on our interpretations. However, even arbitrary categories, where there are no expectations or beliefs of the other, can provoke biases for the in-group and against the out-group.[35]

Donald Taylor and Vaishna Jaggi's research supports Pettigrew's hypothesis and the view that the bias is not unique to Americans.[36] Taylor and Jaggi examined Hindus' attributions of other Hindus and of Moslems. The Hindu subjects were asked to assess the cause of either Hindus' or Moslems' behavior after reading a one-paragraph description of their behavior. As expected, Hindus viewed positive Hindu behavior as dispositional, and the identical behavior by Moslems as situational. Conversely, Hindus attributed negative Hindu behavior to situation and negative Moslem behavior to disposition. Confirmatory attributions put the out-group in a no-win situation. Daniel Heradstveit has documented similar findings among Arabs and Jews in the Middle

---

[34] For a review of relevant studies, see Pettigrew and Martin, "Shaping the Organizational Context."

[35] See Mercer, "Anarchy and Identity."

[36] Donald Taylor and Vaishna Jaggi, "Ethnocentrism and Causal Attribution in a South Indian Context," *Journal of Cross-Cultural Psychology* 5/2 (1974): 162–171. For further discussion of how culture may affect attributions, see Chapter 6.

East.[37] Marilynn Brewer also found support for Pettigrew's ultimate attribution error in her study of thirty ethnic groups in Kenya, Uganda, and Tanzania.[38]

Because confirmatory attribution is appropriate for studying intergroup behavior, it ought to be appropriate for studying interstate relations. The logic leads to the following hypothesis: when an adversary behaves, contrary to expectations, in a positive way, we explain away this seemingly aberrant behavior with situational attributions. However, when an adversary behaves congruent with our negative expectations, we make corresponding dispositional attributions (even though we would judge our own similar behavior as situational).

President Reagan's initial comments on the U.S. Navy's downing of the Iranian airbus and the Soviet Air Force's attack on the Korean Airlines Jet 007 illustrate the expectations hypothesis. When speaking of the Iranian airbus, Reagan said: "I won't minimize the tragedy. We all know it was a tragedy. But we're talking about an incident in which a plane on radar was observed coming in the direction of a ship in combat and the plane began lowering its altitude. And so, I think it was an understandable accident to shoot and think that they were under attack from that plane."[39]

When the Soviets shot down KAL 007, President Reagan assumed it was intentional; he called it "an act of barbarism born of a society which wantonly disregards individual rights and the value of human life and seeks constantly to expand and dominate other nations."[40] The American attack on a civilian aircraft was inconsistent with Reagan's prior beliefs about the American military and judged situational; the Soviet action was consistent with Reagan's prior beliefs about the Soviet military and judged dispositional.

---

[37] Daniel Heradstveit found that the "respondents are overwhelmingly dispositional when observing their own praiseworthy behavior and their opponent's blameworthy behavior, and overwhelmingly situational when observing their own blameworthy behavior and their opponent's praiseworthy behavior." See Heradstveit, *The Arab-Israeli Conflict: Psychological Obstacles to Peace* (Oslo: Universitetsförlaget, 1979), p. 57.

[38] Marilynn B. Brewer, "The Role of Ethnocentrism in Intergroup Conflict," in *Psychology of Intergroup Relations*, ed. Stephen Worchel and William G. Austin, 2d ed. (Chicago: Nelson-Hall, 1986), pp. 98–100.

[39] Quoted in Julie Johnson, "U.S. Pushes Inquiry on Downing of Jet," *New York Times*, July 5, 1988, p. A1.

[40] Quoted in Philip Taubman, "Soviets Urge a U.S. Pullout of Force in the Persian Gulf," *New York Times*, July 5, 1988, p. A9. For an alternative explanation, see Richard Witkin, "Downing of KAL 007 Laid to Russian Error," *New York Times*, June 16, 1993, p. A14.

The point is not that Reagan made an error in attribution, but that he would systematically discount situational factors in favor of dispositional ones to explain negative (or expected) Soviet behavior. Indeed, confirmatory attributions often appear correct. In explaining U.S. policy toward the Soviet Union, Secretary of State James Baker made this assessment of positive (or unexpected) Soviet behavior: "Nevertheless, having said all that, there seems to me a genuine desire on their part to move positively across a variety of areas. In some, they are doing better than others. I am not saying it comes from any good feeling toward the United States. They are basically forced into this posture by the situation of their economy and the problems they face at home."[41] It is possible that Soviet beliefs caused perestroika more than the need for perestroika caused a change in Soviet beliefs. What matters, however, is not the accuracy of the explanation, but the pattern of attributions.

Were the Soviets pushing perestroika more for dispositional or situational reasons? We cannot know for sure. We do know, based on in-group/out-group dynamics and confirmatory attribution patterns, that adversaries of the Soviet Union will tend to view positive Soviet behavior—such as perestroika—in situational terms, and negative Soviet behavior—such as shooting down civilian airliners—in dispositional terms. Consequently, adversaries will generally be blamed for their negative behavior, and rarely be credited for their positive behavior.

Intergroup dynamics and confirmatory attribution patterns provide intuitively satisfying and compelling explanations and predictions for how adversaries will explain each other's behavior. If negative behavior always elicits dispositional attributions, and positive behavior always elicits situational explanations, then adversaries can get reputations only when they behave negatively. Dispositional attributions are necessary for reputations to form.

Similarly, if adversaries use situational attributions to explain away each other's positive behavior, then adversaries cannot get reputations for their positive behavior, because situational attributions cannot generate a reputation. The next section examines the problem with extending the expectations hypothesis to cover allies and points out a potential methodological problem with using expectations as an independent variable.

[41] Quoted in Thomas Friedman, "How Washington Shifted to Embracing Gorbachev," *New York Times*, October 22, 1989, p. A18.

DESIRES, ALLIES, AND ADVERSARIES

Based on in-group/out-group dynamics and confirmatory attribution patterns, it could be argued that positive behavior by adversaries elicits situational attributions (because it is unexpected), and negative behavior by adversaries elicits dispositional attributions (because it is expected). When this logic is extended to alliance attributions, one reaches the bizarre conclusion that allies can do no wrong. Because we expect positive behavior from our allies, we should explain away undesirable (or unexpected) behavior. In other words, allies will get credit for positive behavior, but receive no blame for negative behavior. Since dispositional attributions are necessary for a reputation, the above logic means that allies can only acquire reputations for positive behavior, and adversaries can only acquire reputations for negative behavior.

Although the expectations hypothesis is logical, it also seems wrong. Allies do not always give one another the benefit of the doubt and often say nasty things about one another. In one colorful example, the French decided to stop importing British beef because British cows suffered from a deadly nerve disease. The British were indignant; they said the disease posed no danger to humans. London cried protectionism and the British tabloid *The Sun* screamed in a headline: "Shop Off You Selfish Frogs."[42] Actors often explain negative ally behavior in dispositional terms; the expectations hypothesis does not predict this.

Possible circularity in the hypothesis poses an additional problem with using expectations as an independent variable to determine when reputations form. We may expect a state to behave aggressively if we believe that state is aggressive. In other words, a reputation may influence an expectation. This introduces some circularity into the argument. It is difficult to know where an expectation comes from. A reputation may help generate an expectation, but it does not determine an expectation; beliefs about the other's situation are also important in determining expectations. As discussed above, intergroup biases can generate expectations. Even arbitrary or non-content-based groupings elicit attributions for the in-group and against the out-group. In this case, categories (rather than past behavior) produce expectations.

Expectations may also operate at higher levels of generality than reputations for particular types of behavior. For example, because Presi-

---

[42] Steven Greenhouse, "Anger in Britain Growing over France's Ban on Beef," *New York Times*, June 2, 1990, p. A9.

dent Reagan expected the Soviets to act aggressively in general, he used this expectation to explain their behavior. The Soviets did not have a reputation for shooting down civilian airplanes, but, when they did, this action fit his general belief about Soviet behavior. The general expectation that an adversary is aggressive does not necessarily mean that an adversary has a specific reputation.

Expectations may be based on situation, intergroup biases, or general beliefs, rather than specific reputations. These alternative sources of expectations may reduce concerns about possible circularity, but do not eliminate them. The possibility remains that reputations may influence expectations. Because of this possibility, and the problem of extending the expectations hypothesis to allies, I use desirability of behavior to determine attributions. This switch from expectations to desires permits me to exploit the general findings of confirmatory attributions without the risk of tautology.

By using the success or failure of policy, that is, desires, as my independent variable, I avoid the risk of circular reasoning. I determine desires based on the success of a decision-maker's policy. Policy success is desirable; policy failure is undesirable. By deriving my independent variable from policy success (or desirable and undesirable outcome), my causal variable is further removed from the possible reputational taint on expectations.

To clarify this point, consider the hardest case for my argument. Imagine that a defender's reputation for irresolution determines a challenger's policy. Based on the defender's reputation for irresolution, the challenger demands that the defender back down. If the defender yields to the threat, how will the challenger explain this desirable outcome? Because desirable behavior elicits situational attributions, my hypothesis expects the challenger to use transient situation to explain away the defender's retreat. Rather than view the defender's retreat as confirming its reputation for irresolution, the challenger should explain its retreat using other factors, such as the distribution of capability. This example shows that the desires hypothesis is not circular. If we desire our adversary to be irresolute (based on its reputation), and it backs down, then we should explain this retreat as a function of the situation. A situational attribution cannot be used to support our belief in the other's irresolution.[43]

---

[43] In contrast, the expectations hypothesis could be tautologous in this situation. The expectations hypothesis contends that expected behavior elicits dispositional attributions. Imagine that the challenger expects the defender to be irresolute because of its reputation

There are strong theoretical reasons why desires may determine how we explain another's behavior. The first reason stems from efforts to explain correspondent inferences. Experimental research shows that observers use whatever is most salient or vivid to explain another's behavior. People tend to see a correspondence between behavior and disposition because they cannot "see" situation. In other words, they tend to see an actor causing action. As discussed earlier, George Quattrone shows that by making situation more salient than disposition, it is possible to make people use situation more than disposition to explain behavior. Nothing is more important to a decision-maker than the success or failure of her policy. By switching to desires, I suggest that decision-makers view their own policies as most salient. As a result, they will explain behavior based on policy success or failure, that is, the desirability of the outcome.

There are several complementary explanations, both cognitive and motivated, for our tendency to base our attributions on desires. As discussed earlier, we tend to give greater causal weight to whatever we attend to. It appears that people naturally attend to things which have hedonic relevance. This tendency suggests that affect—including like or dislike—influences subsequent perceptions. Our likes and dislikes influence what we "see": "Accessible attitudes orient our attention to objects that have the potential for hedonic consequences and thus ready us to respond appropriately."[44] Because we are likely to attend to whatever has hedonic relevance, and because we are likely attribute to whatever we attend to, our desires are likely to influence our attributions.

The tendency to explain outcome based on its desirability is a well-established phenomenon that social psychologists have dubbed the self-serving bias. People's tendency to accept credit for positive outcomes and deny responsibility for negative outcomes is "one of the best established, most often replicated findings in social psychology."[45] We give seemingly self-serving attributions in part because we expect success more than we

---

for irresolution. If the defender backs down, then the challenger should explain this expected behavior in dispositional terms, i.e., the defender is irresolute. This step completes the circle. A reputation for irresolution generates an expectation; if the expectation is met, this leads to a dispositional attribution which confirms the reputation.

[44] David R. Roskos-Ewoldsen and Russell H. Fazio, "On the Orienting Value of Attitudes: Attitude Accessibility as a Determinant of an Object's Attraction of Visual Attention," *Journal of Personality and Social Psychology* 63/2 (1992): 210.

[45] Ross and Fletcher, "Attribution and Social Perception," p. 12.

expect failure.[46] We expect our policies to succeed and when they fail we do not accept responsibility. For example, a British diplomatic representative to the European Economic Community complained about American exporters: "The Americans think they have a God-given right to the world market. If they're not increasing their share, they think the rules are wrong or that somebody must be cheating."[47]

The cause of the self-serving bias is debatable. It may be rooted in the twin motivations to enhance and protect one's ego. Plausibility serves as a check for this bias.[48] These biases may also be rooted in cognitions. People are driven more by theory than by data, so we tend to see co-variation where we expect it—sort of "believing is seeing," to paraphrase Robert Jervis.[49] Because we adopt strategies that we think will succeed, we generally expect success more than failure. As a result of our expectation to see covariation between our actions and success, we are more inclined to assume responsibility for desirable outcomes.

By taking credit ourselves for desirable behavior, we do not credit the other for his desirable behavior. And yet, we are quick to place blame on the other when his behavior is undesirable. When a decision-maker's policies work (meaning that an ally or adversary behaves "desirably"), this response only shows these policies caused that behavior. When his policies fail to elicit desirable behavior, this failure is taken not as a weakness of his policy, but as a reflection on whomever is messing up his plans. This tendency is compounded by an egocentric bias that leads us to exaggerate our influence when we get what we want and to minimize the influence of third parties or other situational forces. We do this in part because we generally know more about our efforts than the efforts of others, and in part to gratify our ego.[50]

The tendency to exaggerate our influence leads to a tendency to exaggerate our own importance in the calculations of other states. When we are harmed by the actions of another, we tend to view the injury not as an unintended consequence of a policy directed toward a third party, but as an action intended to harm us. When a state acts in a way that threatens us, we assume the act was intended to threaten us and was

[46] Philip Tetlock and Ariel Levi, "Attribution Bias: On the Inconclusiveness of the Cognition-Motivation Debate," *Journal of Experimental Psychology* 18 (January 1982): 75.

[47] Quoted in Peter Kilborn, "Allies Faltering in Effort to End Aid for Farmers," *New York Times*, May 17, 1988, p. A1.

[48] Tetlock and Levi, "Attribution Bias."

[49] Jervis, *Perception and Misperception*, p. 170.

[50] See Jervis, "Overestimating One's Importance as Influence or Target," *Perception and Misperception*, pp. 343–355.

taken in spite of our policy (never because of it); the act reflects on the state's disposition.[51]

As a result of the above biases, we are likely to view the cause of undesirable behavior to be the other's disposition, and the cause of desirable behavior to be the situation our policy either created or exploited:

Undesirable behavior —→ dispositional attribution
Desirable behavior —→ situational attribution

Because a decision-maker's policy is so important, his perceptual focus is on that policy. As Robert Jervis observed: "When the other behaves in accord with the actor's desires, he will overestimate the degree to which his policies are responsible for the outcome. . . . When the other's behavior is undesired, the actor is likely to see it as derived from internal sources rather than as being a response to his own actions."[52] These findings on the importance of salience and hedonic relevance, as well as the influence of self-serving and egocentric biases, support a switch to desires from expectations.

Using desires as my independent variable has a considerable payoff. First, it offers similar and plausible explanations for adversaries' behavior as does the expectations hypothesis, but eliminates the risk of tautology. For example, an adversary's unexpected (or positive) behavior is also desirable behavior, both of which elicit situational attributions; an adversary's expected (or negative) behavior is also undesirable behavior, both of which yield dispositional explanations. As a result, adversaries never credit each other for good behavior, but instead use situational attributions to explain away this behavior. However, adversaries hold one another responsible for their bad behavior and use dispositional explanations. Because only dispositional attributions can generate a reputation, adversaries can get reputations only when their behavior is undesirable.

The desires hypothesis also offers plausible explanations of the behavior of an ally. As noted above, the expectations hypothesis predicts that allies cannot get reputations for lacking resolve. Because observers do not expect negative behavior from their ally, they explain away this behavior with situational attributions. In this case, allies could never get reputations for negative behavior, such as breaking promises. The switch to de-

---

[51] Ibid., pp. 350–351; Susan T. Fiske and Shelley E. Taylor, *Social Cognition* (Reading, Mass.: Addison-Wesley, 1984), p. 86.

[52] Jervis, *Perception and Misperception*, p. 343.

sires makes the hypothesis more intuitively satisfying. Observers use situational attributions to explain the desirable behavior of an ally, and dispositional attributions to explain the undesirable behavior of an ally.

In short, the switch to desires from expectations captures the same powerful findings of expectations, eliminates the risk of tautology, and better addresses ally attributions. For these reasons, I choose desires as my independent variable and propose the following hypothesis: decision-makers view behavior that helps their policy in situational terms, and they view behavior that harms their policy in dispositional terms.

Let me briefly review the logic behind my hypothesis. Because decision-makers care most about the success or failure of their policies, they find their own policy most salient. As a result, the success or failure of their policy shapes their interpretations of an outcome. In addition to saliency, there are cognitive and motivated biases at work. The motivated part is obvious. Decision-makers do not want to blame themselves when their policies fail; instead they tend to blame the "misbehaving" state. When their policy succeeds, they are quick to take credit. Their policy forced the other state to behave as it did; had it not been for the situation created by one's policy, the state would have behaved differently. There is also a cognitive side to my hypothesis. Decision-makers expect their policies to succeed and, when they succeed, they see covariation between policy and outcome.

For example, consider British and German explanations of the Russian capitulation to German threats in the 1909 Bosnian Crisis. The British wanted the Russians to stand firm and were bitterly disappointed in their ally's retreat. They viewed Russia's behavior as undesirable. As a result, they used dispositional explanations, such as the Russians' lack of resolve, to explain St. Petersburg's defeat. In contrast, the Germans were thrilled with the Russian capitulation. They took credit for creating a situation that gave the Russians no choice but to yield. They did not infer that the Russians were irresolute, but that any sensible person in the same situation would have behaved similarly. In this case, desirable behavior led to situational explanations. Because the Germans used the situation to explain Russian behavior, they made no inference about Russian resolve. The Germans believed the Russians had no choice but to yield, like the child who wears glasses and so cannot fight; as a result, there were "no enduring costs in refusing to compete."[53] Of course, if the Germans believed they could later recreate the situation, they might expect the same outcome.

---

[53] Thomas Schelling, *Arms and Influence* (New Haven: Yale University Press, 1966), p. 120.

More generally, what sort of attributions would we expect Cuban, Rumanian, and Chinese communists to make of Soviet perestroika and revolution in Eastern Europe? Fidel Castro opposed perestroika as a betrayal of socialism and expressed contempt for the East European "apprentices of capitalism."[54] Nicolas Ceauşescu declared that the communist leaders allowing reform never wanted or worked for socialism anyway.[55] According to one Chinese official, an internal Chinese Communist Party memorandum "says the changes in Eastern Europe were a subversion of socialism, and it says Gorbachev is responsible for them." The Chinese leadership reportedly viewed Gorbachev "as something of a dangerous madman."[56] The undesirable policies and events in the Soviet Union and Eastern Europe resulted not in a keen analysis of the material forces and conditions that may have caused this turmoil—which one might expect from Marxists—but instead the cause was rooted in the "dangerous madman" Gorbachev and his ideologically perverted allies.

It is sensible to use desires rather than expectations to explain how reputations form. Whereas expectations and desires offer similar predictions for adversaries, they differ in their predictions for how allies will explain each other's behavior. The undesirable behavior of both allies and adversaries, I argue, results in dispositional attributions; their desirable behavior elicits situational attributions. The distinction between ally and adversary is nonetheless important. As I discuss in the next section, the type of behavior that needs explaining differs between friends and enemies.

HYPOTHESES AND PROPOSITIONS

A reputation forms if it passes two tests. First, an observer must explain a target's behavior in dispositional terms. Second, this attribution must then be used to explain or predict future behavior. This section re-

---

[54] Larry Rohter, "For Castro, More Isolation and Economic Trouble," *New York Times*, November 14, 1989, p. A20; Larry Rohter, "Castro Says He'll Resist Changes Like Those Sweeping Soviet Bloc," *New York Times*, December 9, 1989, p. A9.

[55] Alan Riding, "Rumanian Leader Refuses Changes," *New York Times*, November 21, 1989, p. A1; Rone Tempest, "'The Helmsman Who Guides' Stays His Course," *Los Angeles Times*, December 17, 1989.

[56] "Worried Chinese Leadership Says Gorbachev Subverts Communism," (Reuters) *New York Times*, December 28, 1989, p. A1; Steven Erlanger, "China Line: No Thawing," *New York Times*, December 29, 1989, p. A9; Erlanger, "Beijing View of the Furor," *New York Times*, December 13, 1989, p. A8.

views the way that the deterrence and desires hypotheses address reputation's two parts.

How will decision-makers interpret each other's behavior? The deterrence hypothesis on resolve assumes that behavior reveals disposition. (Although ignored by deterrence theorists, the best theoretical support for this belief is correspondent inference theory.) Observers will use dispositional attributions to explain a state's behavior. Table 2 illustrates the deterrence hypothesis.

In contrast, the desires hypothesis allows for distinctions between ally and adversary. Because the kind of behavior we find desirable differs between friend and foe—we usually prefer our adversaries to yield in a crisis and our allies to stand firm—our explanations of that behavior will also differ. Observers tend to explain an ally's (desirable) resolution in situational terms and an adversary's (undesirable) resolution in dispositional terms. Table 3 illustrates the desires hypothesis.

I argue that desirable behavior—such as when an ally stands firm or an adversary backs down—elicits situational attributions. However, undesirable behavior—such as when an ally backs down or an adversary stands firm—elicits dispositional attributions. Where my argument predicts situational attributions, it differs with the deterrence argument; where my argument predicts dispositional attributions, so does the deterrence argument.

Interdependence is the second aspect of reputation. In this instance, interdependence means using past behavior to predict or explain future behavior. The deterrence hypothesis assumes a tight interdependence between commitments. Interdependence means every dispositional attribution generates a corresponding reputation: a state that yields to a threat gets a reputation for irresolution, a state that stands firm gets a reputation for resolution. For the deterrence argument, an attribution is a reputation.

Unlike the deterrence hypothesis, which uses past behavior to determine type of attribution, my argument uses desires as an independent variable. As a result, if my hypothesis successfully predicts attributions, then commitments are *independent* rather than *interdependent*. If past be-

Table 2. Deterrence hypothesis: How observers explain another's behavior

	Ally	Adversary
Stand firm	Dispositional	Dispositional
Back down	Dispositional	Dispositional

Table 3. Desires hypothesis: How observers explain another's behavior

	Ally	**Adversary**
Stand firm	Situational	Dispositional
Back down	Dispositional	Situational

havior determines how people predict or explain behavior, then my argument would often be wrong. For example, if (as I argue) undesirable behavior always yields dispositional attributions, and desirable behavior always yields situational attributions, then past behavior cannot be governing these explanations. When the link with the past is severed, commitments become independent. Since interdependence is necessary for reputations to form, consistently correct predictions mean commitments are independent and reputations do not form.

However, my hypothesis cannot adequately test for interdependence when a state continually acts in an undesirable way. An observer that views another's behavior as continually undesirable should continue to make dispositional attributions. In this case, we cannot tell whether past behavior or immediate behavior causes these attributions. Even though each attribution may not be dependent on the preceding one, a reputation can form.

Because a reputation can form when an observer uses disposition to explain another's behavior, it is possible that some observers will use these attributions to predict or explain future behavior. In other words, it is possible that decision-makers will use past dispositional attributions to predict future behavior. Although I expect commitments to be more independent than interdependent, it is possible for the reverse to be true. If we assume that every dispositional attribution generates a corresponding reputation, then we arrive at the four propositions discussed earlier: adversaries can get reputations for having resolve, but rarely for lacking resolve; allies can get reputations for lacking resolve, but rarely for having it. See Table 4.

Table 4. Four propositions on reputation formation

	Ally	**Adversary**
Stand firm	No reputation	Reputation for resolve
Back down	Reputation for irresolution	No reputation

If we assume that commitments are interdependent, then the desires and the deterrence hypotheses yield both competing and complimentary predictions. The deterrence hypothesis predicts that a reputation always forms because behavior is always attributed to the target's character. In contrast, the desires hypothesis recognizes that sometimes observers make situational explanations for another's behavior. In these cases, a reputation cannot form. Thus, whenever I predict "no reputation," deterrence predicts "reputation." The demanding assumption that dispositional attributions are interdependent generates the four propositions in Table 4; of these propositions, the ones in the upper right and lower left quadrants are also held by deterrence theory.

There are three points to make about the distinction between situation and disposition. First, these two types of attributions are not dichotomies. People often make both situational and dispositional attributions to explain an event. For example, the man pulled from the earthquake rubble in Oakland was called both lucky (a situational attribution) and a man with a fighting spirit and a great will to live (a dispositional attribution). There is no reason why both explanations cannot be right. Rather than treating these two explanations as opposites on a continuum, we ought to judge each independently of the other.[57] For example, a reputation can form whenever observers use disposition to explain someone's behavior, even if they simultaneously make a situational explanation.

Second, it is often difficult to distinguish between situational and dispositional attributions. For example, does the attribution, "he did it for the money," reflect the disposition of greed or the situation of opportunity? In the absence of a greater context, the attribution is ambiguous and should not be used as evidence for either kind of attribution. There is a difference between ambiguous attributions and ambiguous cause. For example, the answer to the question, "does poverty result more from situational or dispositional factors?", is important to public policy. For my purposes, however, the appropriate question is: "When people seek to explain poverty, do they make more situational or more dispositional attributions and what explains this tendency?" My immediate concern is not with how people should see the world, but how and why they see the world as they do.

[57] Sheldon Solomon, "Measuring Dispositional and Situational Attributions," *Personality and Social Psychology Bulletin* 4/4 (1978): 589–594.

Third, it is important, however, that people draw the right inferences from their attributions. There is some evidence that even when an observer thinks situational factors were responsible for an actor's behavior, the observer may nonetheless attribute a disposition that corresponds with the situationally induced behavior.[58] For example, the German kaiser was disappointed with the Italians' failure to support Germany in the first Moroccan Crisis. He understood the situational reasons for that behavior, but nonetheless spoke of the "miserable and degenerate Latin peoples."[59] In most cases, I find that actors do not infer disposition from behavior they recognize as situationally induced.

COMMON CRITIQUES

A common criticism of social psychological approaches to international politics centers on the distinction between individuals and groups. What is true for interpersonal relations may not be true for intergroup relations. Psychological theories that work wonderfully for individuals may work poorly or not at all for groups.[60]

We know that strong in-group identity affects causal attributions in favor of the in-group. There are different explanations for in-group favoritism. It may be functional, it may stem from a need for a positive social identity, it may stem from categorization.[61] Whatever the explanation, people behave differently toward members of their group than toward people not in their group. Many scholars have drawn on attribution theories to understand how an individual in a group explains the behavior of out-group members. For example, earlier I discussed how Pettigrew and Kulik use expectations—often created by intergroup biases—to explain causal attributions. Scholars commonly use attribution theory to explain intergroup attributions. After warning against

[58] Glenn Reeder, "Implicit Relations between Dispositions and Behaviors," *Attribution: Basic Issues and Applications*, ed. John H. Harvey and Gifford Weary (New York: Academic Press, 1985), pp. 87–116.

[59] Quoted in G. P. Gooch, *Before the War: Studies in Diplomacy*, vol. 1: *The Grouping of the Powers* (New York: Longmans, Green, 1936), p. 263.

[60] Philip E. Tetlock, "Testing Deterrence Theory: Some Conceptual and Methodological Issues," *Journal of Social Issues* 43/4 (1987): 85; Robert Jervis, "Hypotheses on Misperception," *World Politics* 20/3 (1968): 455.

[61] Muzafer Sherif, *Group Conflict and Cooperation: Their Social Psychology* (London: Routledge and Kegan Paul, 1966); Henri Tajfel and John Turner, "The Social Identity Theory of Intergroup Behavior," in *Psychology of Intergroup Relations*, pp. 7–24; John Turner, *Rediscovering the Social Group: A Self-categorization Theory* (New York: Basil Blackwell, 1987).

"naive extrapolations from the interpersonal to the intergroup level of analysis," Miles Hewstone observed that "intergroup attribution seems to be one case in which extrapolation is justifiable."[62] Like these scholars, I am interested in how individuals in groups explain an out-group's behavior.

Of course, I am not interested in just any individuals, but in how skilled, intelligent, and accountable people explain behavior that matters enormously to them. The experimental basis for attribution theories usually comes from American college sophomores in an introduction to psychology class. Not only is the population for these experiments narrow, but the experiments are artificial and do not resemble the kind of situation decision-makers are often in.

These are sound criticisms. Bismarck was not an American college sophomore. Nevertheless, the problems may not be so severe. First, the experimental basis was narrow, but is constantly expanding. Cross-cultural psychologists are hard at work testing the validity of attribution theories in different cultures on adults, teenagers, and children.[63] Note that even if the theories are ethnocentric, the differences between cultures may mean that other cultures are more likely to explain behavior in ways that diminish the importance of reputation.[64]

It is true that an experimenter's lab and a crisis between states are different situations, but this objection is beside the point. As Herbert Kelman argued, what matters is not the difference in settings, but the relevance of the isolated variable.[65] To develop a cognitive or motivated argument it is sensible first to strip away the noise, which can best be done in a controlled, experimental setting. The test for these theories is how well they explain intergroup attributions in natural settings, not whether the experimental setting resembles international politics. Indeed, using theory confirmed in the lab to test hy-

[62] Miles Hewstone, *Causal Attribution: From Cognitive Processes to Collective Beliefs* (Oxford: Basil Blackwell, 1989), p. 203.

[63] See John W. Berry, Ype H. Poortinga, Marshall H. Segall, Pierre R. Dasen, *Cross-Cultural Psychology: Research and Applications* (Cambridge: Cambridge University Press, 1992); Garth Fletcher and Colleen Ward, "Attribution Theory and Processes: A Cross-Cultural Perspective," in *The Cross-Cultural Challenge to Social Psychology*, ed. Michael Harris Bond (London: Sage, 1988).

[64] For more on this question, see Chapter 6.

[65] Herbert Kelman, "Social-Psychological Approaches to the Study of International Relations: The Question of Relevance," in *International Behavior: A Social-Psychological Analysis* (New York: Holt, Rinehart, and Winston, 1966), pp. 597–598.

potheses against historical cases is a methodological strength, not a weakness.[66]

It is possible that decision-makers, though subject to the same biases as everyone else, may be influenced by other, more important factors that lead them away from the attributions I expect. Although organizational factors (such as bureaucratic politics or an organization's culture) may affect what an individual finds desirable, they do not affect how people make causal attributions.[67] For example, if the Pentagon views an ally's military intervention as undesirable, but the State Department views it as desirable, these organizationally based desires should lead to attributions that fit my hypothesis. Although the issue does not arise in my cases, it is easy to imagine situations where different individuals or organizations within the state have opposite views of an outcome's desirability. The point is that people—even within the same government—sometimes explain the same behavior differently. The more perceptions differ, the more complicated become efforts to manipulate reputations.

It is also true that decision-makers, like everyone else, can learn. But what we learn depends upon how we understand events. If we believe someone's behavior was situationally induced, we cannot know how that person will behave in a different situation. If we think her behavior revealed her disposition, then we might think she will behave similarly in different situations. (We might also think she will behave differently in the future because of the way she behaved in the past.)

Strategic reassessment might be an example of learning. Policy-makers will sometimes reevaluate past policies and reach different conclusions. Although the effect of strategic reassessment on my argument will vary, it is likely to strengthen it. Strategic reassessment is most likely to occur when a policy has failed—that is, when the outcome was undesirable.[68] For example, if an adversary stood firm, and an observer

---

[66] Philip Tetlock makes this point in "Methodological Themes and Variations," *Behavior, Society, and Nuclear War*, ed. Philip Tetlock, Jo L. Husbands, Robert Jervis, Paul Stern, Charles Tilly (New York: Oxford University Press, 1989), pp. 342–343.

[67] The best discussions of bureaucratic politics and organizational culture can be found, respectively, in Robert Art, "Bureaucratic Politics and American Foreign Policy: A Critique," *Policy Sciences* 4 (December 1973): 467–490, and Elizabeth Kier, *Imagining War: French and British Military Doctrine between the Wars* (Princeton: Princeton University Press, forthcoming).

[68] Robert Jervis points out that decision-makers are less likely to engage in strategic reassessment when their policy succeeds. This pattern is captured by the expression: "Nothing fails like success." See Jervis, *Perception and Misperception*, pp. 278–279.

initially attributed this response to its resolve, strategic reassessment suggests that now the observer will attribute the adversary's behavior to the situation. Or, if an ally backed down, and this behavior was initially attributed to the ally's irresolution, strategic reassessment implies that the situation will now be used to explain the ally's behavior. If decision-makers are most likely to change their minds about another's behavior in those situations where I expect them to make dispositional attributions initially, then the chances are increased that even undesirable behavior will eventually result in situational attributions.

Because policy-makers can learn, might my argument be self-invalidating? It is a common problem with psychological theories that once we are made aware of certain biases or tendencies, we can change our behavior accordingly and invalidate the theory. Although having my argument accepted and acted upon by policy-makers is hardly an immediate concern, the possibility poses an interesting question. If the way we tend to explain behavior became common knowledge, then no one would worry about their reputation. This development would make my argument irrelevant, not invalid. My argument would be invalid only if actors changed the way they explain behavior. Because I discuss only how people tend to explain behavior, not how people should explain behavior, my argument should not be self-invalidating.

The final criticism is the most sweeping. It could be suggested that my argument requires decision-makers to behave in an irrational, simplistic, and mechanistic way. Such profoundly irrational and inefficient behavior would eventually be replaced by more efficient, rational behavior. I have three responses.

First, keeping in mind the objective of a generalizable and falsifiable argument, compare my hypothetical decision-maker to the one assumed by deterrence theorists. Deterrence theory's decision-maker believes that behavior generates a corresponding disposition which in turn generates a reputation. My decision-maker is more complex. She views behavior as either dispositionally or situationally induced. Her explanations differ depending upon whether she is explaining an ally's or an adversary's behavior. And she generally recognizes that past behavior does not determine future behavior. Compared to the simpleton assumed by deterrence theorists, my decision-maker is a genius.

Second, although the decision-making process does not adhere to classic standards of rationality, the result is sensible and intuitive. Decision-makers tend to behave as if they lived in a self-help system. Policy-makers are more likely to worry that their adversaries might challenge or their allies might defect, than to be confident that their adversaries are irresolute and their allies are resolute. Policy-makers lean more toward "worst-case" than "best-case" thinking. As a result, they sometimes think their adversary is resolute, but rarely assume it is irresolute; and they sometimes think their ally is irresolute, but rarely assume it is resolute. These are also the four propositions derived from my hypothesis. A decision-making process that uses desires to explain attributions survives because it is easy, efficient, and well suited to international politics.

Third, the test of an argument is not whether it is rational, but how well it explains or predicts behavior. My question is empirical: when do reputations form? We can address this question by understanding the two parts of reputation formation. Deterrence theory has one set of expectations, I offer another. I use the following three empirical chapters to see which hypothesis works better. While my argument is sometimes wrong, it is almost always better than the deterrence argument.

[3]

The First Moroccan Crisis

"If Russia keeps her hands free in Europe and if I conclude my agreements with England, Italy and Spain, you will see Morocco fall into our garden like ripe fruit," wrote the French foreign minister to a colleague in early 1904.[1] Morocco did wind up in the French garden, but only partially and only after a bruising diplomatic campaign. The French planned to strengthen their position on the continent and obtain a chunk of North Africa through a series of colonial agreements with Italy, Spain, and England. The Germans thought otherwise and were not going to allow France to do to Morocco what England had done to Egypt. Primarily out of concern for his country's reputation, Chancellor Bernard Bülow sent Kaiser Wilhelm to Tangier to demonstrate German interest in Morocco. "Under the circumstances," said Bülow, "Your Majesty may await the outcome of the Moroccan question with a quiet mind."[2]

Both sides confidently executed their plans; the issues at hand were minor. What at first appeared to be a trivial colonial dispute quickly spiraled into a major confrontation. Although the apparent stakes in the Moroccan Crisis concerned German political and economic rights in Morocco, the real stakes concerned future deterrence (or reputation) and the future configuration of international alliances.

I use a two-part test to examine how the leading decision-makers in England, France, Russia, Germany, and Austria explained one another's

[1] Delcassé to Maurice Paléologue, quoted in G. P. Gooch, *Before the War: Studies in Diplomacy*, vol. 1: *The Grouping of the Powers* (New York: Longmans, Green, 1936), p. 153.

[2] Quoted in Raymond J. Sontag, "German Foreign Policy, 1904–1906," *American Historical Review* 33 (January 1928): 289.

behavior in the Moroccan Crisis. First, when will policy-makers use more situational or dispositional attributions to explain another's behavior? Second, will policy-makers use earlier demonstrations of resolve to predict or explain another's behavior? Based on the evidence found in this chapter, it appears that decision-makers give neither allies nor adversaries reputations for resolve. This is chronologically the first case I examine, however, and so possible interdependence with previous crises cannot be fully tested. I work around this difficulty by examining how policy-makers explained one another's behavior at two different points in the same crisis. First, how did observers explain French foreign minister Théophile Delcassé's forced resignation in June 1905? Second, how did observers explain the German retreat at the Algeciras Conference in March 1906? This chapter also examines the influence that the 1898 Fashoda Crisis may have had on subsequent German perceptions of French resolve. The crises examined in Chapters 4 and 5 offer better tests of interdependence and reputation.

BACKGROUND TO THE FIRST MOROCCAN CRISIS

Théophile Delcassé became head of the French Foreign Ministry in June 1898 and remained in office until his resignation on June 6, 1905. He saw France as a Mediterranean power with an African empire—from Algeria and Tunisia to the French Congo. The acquisition of Morocco was part of this view. Delcassé also used colonial policy to strengthen his continental policy.[3] For example, he recognized Italian rights in Tripoli in exchange for both Italian recognition of French rights in Morocco and a secret Italian promise that the renewed Triple Alliance (of Germany, Austria-Hungary, and Italy) contained nothing hostile to France. This promise weakened Italian allegiance to the Triple Alliance. The rapprochement between France and Italy became more significant after the Anglo-French Entente. Italy, with its long vulnerable coast, would not dare fight a war against these two great Mediterranean powers.[4]

---

[3] John F. V. Keiger, *France and the Origins of the First World War* (London: Macmillan, 1983), p. 18; Bertha R. Leaman, "The Influence of Domestic Policy on Foreign Affairs in France, 1889–1905," *Journal of Modern History* 15 (December 1942): 453.

[4] Eugene N. Anderson, *The First Moroccan Crisis, 1904–1906* (Chicago: University of Chicago Press, 1930), p. 26; Gooch, *Grouping of the Powers*, p. 127; Barbara Jelavich, *The Habsburg Empire in European Affairs, 1814–1918* (Hamden, Conn.: Archon Books, 1969, 1975), pp. 141–42; Paul Kennedy, *The Rise of the Anglo-German Antagonism, 1860–1914* (Boston: George Allen and Unwin, 1980), p. 269.

The Russo-Japanese war, which found England allied with Japan and France with Russia, prompted France to pursue further negotiations with Britain for a colonial agreement. In spite of Delcassé's humiliating defeat at the hands of the British at Fashoda, he engineered the April 1904 agreement which resolved the major sources of friction in Anglo-French relations: the British obtained Egypt and the French acquired Morocco. Each promised the other diplomatic support in the execution of these rights. Delcassé then settled with Spain over the partition of Morocco.[5]

In short, Delcassé made agreements with all the interested great powers, except Germany, in order to allow France to control Morocco. The omission of Germany was not an oversight. Delcassé refused to negotiate with the Germans because he believed they would insist on confirmation of the French losses of 1871. He also distrusted German ambitions in the Mediterranean. Delcassé's advisers urged him to negotiate with Germany. His closest adviser on Moroccan affairs (and later French representative to the Algeciras Conference) complained: "The great misfortune is that he finds it repugnant to have talks with Germany. 'The Germans are swindlers,' he says. But, in heaven's name, I'm not asking for an exchange of romantic words or lovers' rings but for a business discussion!"[6] Delcassé's failure to give sufficient weight to German interests, slight as they were, led the Germans to demand recognition of those interests and begin the Moroccan Crisis.

The Germans were not going to allow France to control Morocco without compensation. Germany's minor economic interests in Morocco were guaranteed by the 1880 Madrid Convention; any change in the status of Morocco required consultation with the signatories to that convention.[7] The Germans correctly believed that Delcassé was step-

---

[5] C. J. Lowe and M. L. Dockrill, *The Mirage of Power*, vol. 1: *British Foreign Policy, 1902–1914* (Boston: Routledge and Kegan Paul, 1972), pp. 7–9; Anderson, *First Moroccan Crisis*, pp. 81–109.

[6] Paul Révoil to President Loubet's secretary general, Able Combarieu (March 1902), quoted in Christopher Andrew, *Théophile Delcassé and the Making of the Entente Cordiale: A Reappraisal of French Foreign Policy* (New York: St. Martin's Press, 1968), p. 270.

[7] According to Raymond Poidevin, the Wilhelmstrasse manufactured German economic interests in Morocco to advance its political objectives: "Until the beginning of 1905, the Wilhelmstrasse did not worry about the French financial penetration of Morocco. . . . The 'coup de Tanger' profoundly changed this attitude." Poidevin argues that "the Franco-German financial rivalry in Morocco was thus above all a political question. . . . Starting from nothing, German financial interest grew in a few weeks, lending an important political arm to diplomacy." See Raymond Poidevin, *Les relations économiques et financières entre la France et l'Allemagne de 1898 à 1914* (Paris: Armand Colin, 1969), pp. 277–278, 285.

ping on their rights.[8] By opposing France in the name of the Open Door, they felt assured of American and English support.[9]

The German leadership was uninterested in imperial gains and did not seek territory in the Moroccan challenge. Friedrich von Holstein, an important adviser at the Wilhelmstrasse, wrote in a letter to Bülow: "You know better than anyone that we defended the Moroccan position not because we were out for acquisitions . . . but merely in order to uphold His Majesty's prestige."[10] Holstein and Bülow launched the Moroccan Crisis not for reasons of trade or territory, but primarily to preserve and strengthen Germany's reputation.

Holstein, Chancellor Bülow, and the kaiser believed that threats and intimidation were more effective in disarming adversaries than promises and conciliation. They were all believers in the "big stick": the French would turn to Germany once they realized that nothing could be gained without German consent. For example, before the kaiser went to Tangier to demonstrate German interests, Holstein wrote: "The French will only consider approaching us when they see that English friendship is not enough to obtain Germany's consent to the French seizure of Morocco."[11]

Less than two months after the signing of the April 1904 Anglo-French Entente, Holstein worried about Germany's international position: "We stand here before a test of strength; a German retreat in the face of Anglo-French resistance would in no way be conducive to bringing about better German-English relations, but would on the contrary give the English, the French, and the rest of the world practical proof that one gets most from Germany by treating her badly."[12]

[8] Ima Christina Barlow, *The Agadir Crisis* (Chapel Hill: University of North Carolina Press, 1940), p. 26; Gooch, *Grouping of the Powers*, p. 171; Kennedy, *Rise of Anglo-German Antagonism*, p. 276.

[9] Sontag, "German Foreign Policy," p. 289.

[10] Holstein to Bülow (September 19, 1905), *The Holstein Papers: The Memoirs, Diaries, and Correspondence of Friedrich von Holstein, 1837–1909,* vol. 4: *Correspondence, 1897–1909,* ed. Norman Rich and M. H. Fisher (Cambridge: Cambridge University Press, 1963), No. 913, p. 373. See also Dwight E. Lee, *Europe's Crucial Years: The Diplomatic Background of World War I, 1902–1914* (Hanover, N.H.: University Press of New England, 1974), p. 115; A. J. P. Taylor, *The Struggle for Mastery in Europe, 1848–1918* (New York: Oxford University Press, 1971), p. 428.

[11] Quoted in Andrew, *Théophile Delcassé*, p. 269. See also Chaim D. Kaufmann, "Out of the Lab and into the Archives: A Method for Testing Psychological Explanations of Political Decision Making," *International Studies Quarterly* 38 (December 1994): 537–574; and Stephen Van Evera, "Why Cooperation Failed in 1914," *Cooperation under Anarchy*, ed. Kenneth A. Oye (Princeton: Princeton University Press, 1986), pp. 80–117.

[12] Quoted in Norman Rich, *Friedrich von Holstein: Politics and Diplomacy in the Era of Bismarck and Wilhelm II*, vol. 2 (Cambridge: Cambridge University Press, 1965), p. 683.

Holstein and Bülow pressured the British to recognize trivial German interests in Egypt. They obtained the recognition they desired, but at the cost of a further deterioration in Anglo-German relations. They were now to apply the same "big stick" policy toward France and teach it a lesson as well.[13]

Although the primary objective of German policy-makers was to protect Berlin's reputation, their policy was not coherent and it evolved with the situation. For example, removing Delcassé from office became an objective only after it became apparent that he was vulnerable. Norman Rich nicely summarized German policy in this crisis: "Neither the Kaiser's nor Holstein's policy was a war policy, it was merely a stupid policy."[14]

Bülow and Holstein thought their policy would prevent a war, not almost start one.[15] With this in mind, Bülow convinced his reluctant sovereign to visit Tangier and express German interests in Morocco. Bülow and the German Foreign Office gave the kaiser extensive directions on what to say when he landed in Tangier. Kaiser Wilhelm chafed at what he saw as their distrust of his diplomatic abilities: "The foreign office treats me as if I were a secretary of legation. I know best what I have to say!"[16] Indeed, he was so pleased with his Tangier reception that he made a considerably greater commitment to Morocco than Bülow and Holstein intended. Upon reading the kaiser's speech, Holstein became ill with anger and took refuge in bed.[17]

The German demonstration at Tangier was the beginning of the end for Delcassé. Wrongly believing he had an English offer of alliance, he was confident in his ability to ride out the German storm. In late April, he assured a friend: "Germany cannot want war. Her present attitude is no more than bluff; she knows that she would have England against her. I repeat that England would back us to the hilt and would not sign peace without us. Do you think that the Emperor William can calmly envisage the prospect of seeing his battle fleet destroyed, his naval commerce ruined, and his ports bombarded by the English fleet?"[18]

---

[13] Ibid., pp. 683, 700.

[14] Ibid., p. 745.

[15] S. L. Mayer, "Anglo-German Rivalry at the Algeciras Conference," in *Britain and Germany in Africa: Imperial Rivalry and Colonial Rule*, ed. Prosser Gifford and William Roger Louis (New Haven: Yale University Press, 1967), p. 219.

[16] Quoted in Oron J. Hale, *Germany and the Diplomatic Revolution: A Study in Diplomacy and the Press, 1904–1906* (Philadelphia: University of Pennsylvania Press, 1931), p. 102.

[17] Lee, *Europe's Crucial Years*, p. 115; Hale, *Germany and Diplomatic Revolution*, p. 103.

[18] Delcassé to Paléologue, quoted in Andrew, *Théophile Delcassé*, p. 279.

Delcassé's confidence was not matched among his cabinet colleagues and the parliament or by public opinion. Confronted with united opposition to his Moroccan policy, he offered his resignation on April 22, but withdrew it the next day upon the request of President Emile Loubet. An intercepted telegram, sent on April 26, alerted Delcassé that Prime Minister Maurice Rouvier had offered the Germans his dismissal in order to make peace.[19]

Sensing an opportunity to oust their archrival—the man who weakened Italian allegiance to the Triple Alliance and strengthened French-Russian and French-English relations—the Germans turned on the pressure. They warned Rouvier: "We sincerely wish for peace but we cannot wait any longer to settle our account, if necessary by force of arms." And again in June, the German ambassador to France threatened: "We can wait no longer: either an agreement or an open breach."[20] At a dramatic cabinet meeting in early June 1905, Delcassé and Rouvier had their final showdown. Delcassé was forced to resign.

Having ousted Delcassé, both the Germans and the French anticipated better relations. But the Germans continued to demand a conference and Rouvier continued to resist. The French yielded and the Germans got their conference. It was held at Algeciras in early 1906. At the Algeciras Conference Berlin found itself confronted by France, Russia, and England. With only Austria at its side, Germany appeared to retreat and accept compromise.

EXPLANATIONS FOR DELCASSÉ'S RESIGNATION

At this point in the account of the Moroccan Crisis, deterrence theory can predict the ways that policy-makers will explain Delcassé's resignation. Because the French bowed to German threats of war everyone should view the French as irresolute. Conversely, because the Germans held firm and forced the French humiliation, everyone should view the Germans as resolute. Furthermore, because the French demonstrated a similar lack of resolve at Fashoda, there will be, at a minimum, snide references to this earlier French defeat.

[19] Leaman, "Influence of Domestic Policy," p. 472; Christopher Andrew, "France and the German Menace," in *Knowing One's Enemies: Intelligence Assessment before the Two World Wars*, ed. Ernest May (Princeton: Princeton University Press, 1984), p. 130.
[20] Hugo von Radolin, quoted in Andrew, *Théophile Delcassé*, p. 297.

My hypothesis offers some similar and some different predictions in this case. First, decision-makers who opposed Delcassé's resignation ought to view it in dispositional terms. My argument predicts type of attribution—either situational or dispositional—but cannot predict, for example, what kind of dispositional attribution someone will make. Because I cannot specify the content of a dispositional attribution, I assume that allies' undesirable behavior elicits attributions for lacking resolve, and adversaries' undesirable behavior elicits attributions for possessing resolve. Deterrence theory would make the same predictions. Second, those who support the resignation ought to view it in situational terms; this explanation opposes the deterrence prediction. For example, the British viewed Delcassé's resignation as undesirable. The Entente was weakened, their interests jeopardized, and their support dismissed as either insufficient or provocative. I expect them to make dispositional attributions asserting that the French lacked resolve. In contrast, the Germans viewed Delcassé's resignation as desirable. They should have credited their policy with the success and viewed French behavior in situational terms: the French did not lack resolve, they simply had no choice given the situation.

British and German Explanations of Delcassé's Resignation

The deterrence and desires hypotheses correctly predicted that most key British decision-makers would believe that Delcassé's resignation revealed French irresolution. Lord Lansdowne, the British foreign minister, thought the resignation "disgusting."[21] To his ambassador in Paris, Francis Bertie, he wrote:

> Delcassé's resignation has, as you may well suppose, produced a very painful impression here. What people say is that if one of our Ministers had had a dead set made at him by a foreign Power the country and the Government would not only have stood by him but probably have supported him more vigorously than ever, whereas France has apparently thrown Delcassé overboard in a mere fit of panic. Of course the result is that the 'entente' is quoted at a much lower price than it was a fortnight ago.[22]

[21] Quoted in Thomas Newton, *Lord Lansdowne: A Biography* (London: Macmillan, 1929), p. 341.
[22] Lansdowne to Bertie (June 12, 1905), quoted in C. J. Lowe and M. L. Dockrill, *The Mirage of Power*, vol. 3: *The Documents* (Boston: Routledge and Kegan Paul, 1972), p. 426.

Lansdowne later complained: "Recent events have, I am afraid, undoubtedly shaken peoples' confidence in the steadfastness of the French nation."[23] Prime Minister Arthur Balfour also thought the event showed France "could no longer be trusted not to yield to threats at the critical moment of a negotiation."[24]

Unlike the prime minister and the foreign minister, the British ambassador to France offered a more situational explanation. In responding to Lansdowne's views, Bertie wrote: "Delcassé would have fallen even if Germany had not been menacing, but he might not have fallen so soon. His elimination from the Cabinet was in great part due to his treatment of his colleagues. He did not keep them fully informed of what he did and proposed to do. . . . Several of his *chers collègues* disliked him and it ended by his being set aside."[25] This attribution by Bertie does not accord with my expectations or with deterrence theory's predictions. I discuss this and other evidence that contradicts my hypothesis in Chapter 6.

It is not surprising, except to deterrence theory, that the Germans explained Delcassé's resignation differently from the British. The Germans were pleased at their policy's success. To express his gratitude to Bülow, Kaiser Wilhelm made him a prince on the day of Delcassé's resignation. Holstein wrote to his cousin that "our cleverest and most dangerous enemy has fallen."[26]

The Germans disliked Delcassé, and they certainly should not have viewed him as lacking resolve; in their view, Delcassé was forced to resign because he pursued an unpopular anti-German policy and was outmaneuvered by the "clever" tactics of Rouvier.[27] The Germans might view Prime Minister Rouvier as an irresolute man. Not only did he bow to German threats, he even negotiated Delcassé's dismissal with the Germans behind Delcassé's back. Contrary to the expectations of the deterrence argument, my hypothesis predicts the Germans will view Rouvier's behavior in situational terms and not believe that he lacks resolve.

---

[23] Lansdowne to Sir Reginald Lister (July 10, 1905), quoted in Lowe and Dockrill, *Documents*, p. 426.

[24] Balfour to the king (June 8, 1905), quoted in Sir Sidney Lee, *King Edward VII: A Biography*, vol. 2: *The Reign: 22nd January to 6th May 1910* (New York: Macmillan, 1927), p. 344.

[25] Quoted in Hale, *Germany and Diplomatic Revolution*, p. 136.

[26] Quoted in Rich, *Friedrich von Holstein*, p. 707.

[27] Flotow, chargé d'affaires in Paris to Bülow (June 7, 1905), *German Diplomatic Documents, 1871–1914*, vol. 3: *The Growing Antagonism, 1898–1910*, trans. and ed. E. T. S. Dugdale (New York: Harper and Brothers, 1930), pp. 228–229.

The Germans thought the whole affair was Delcassé's fault. Had he not followed his foolish, anti-German, "stormy and brutal" policy, relations between France and Germany would be wonderful.[28] Now that the unreasonable Delcassé was gone, good relations with Rouvier and France were possible. The day after Delcassé's resignation, Holstein wrote to Hugo von Radolin, the German ambassador to France, that the problem between the two countries was "now a matter of form; for we don't want to upset France's future." Holstein regretted that Rouvier did not plan to remain foreign minister and instructed his ambassador: "You can tell Rouvier and his confidants in all sincerity that we would very much like to get out of the impossible situation in which Delcassé has placed us and arrive at a better relationship with France, but Rouvier must show us a decent way out."[29] Bülow also blamed Delcassé for the lamentable state of Franco-German relations.

Rouvier now sought bilateral talks to end the crisis, but Bülow felt that a conference had to be held. He explained the situation to the German embassy in Paris: "A year ago we were free to have negotiated with France from a position which would have led to a definitive result immediately. Since then M. Delcassé has forced us to seek another standpoint. We cannot leave the Sultan [of Morocco] in the lurch at the very moment when, at our advice, he has sent off invitations to the conference."[30]

The Germans continued to demand a conference to settle Moroccan affairs; Rouvier—like Delcassé—refused. Rouvier was puzzled that the Germans refused to settle now that Delcassé was gone, and the Germans were puzzled that Rouvier should adopt the Delcassé program. German explanations of Rouvier's behavior changed as he assumed an increasingly uncompromising position—but they did not change in the direction that deterrence theory would expect.

By the end of June, the German leaders were becoming impatient. From Paris, Radolin preached patience and reported that Rouvier's uncompromising position was a product of the influence of Delcassé's adherents in the French Foreign Ministry. In time, Rouvier would understand he had no choice but to compromise, Radolin maintained. "But I do feel that when [Rouvier] sees that he can do nothing else

[28] Bülow to Radolin (May 22, 1905), quoted in Hale, *Germany and Diplomatic Revolution*, p. 127.
[29] Holstein to Radolin (June 7, 1905), *Holstein Papers*, No. 890, p. 343.
[30] Bülow to the German embassy (June 6, 1905), quoted in Rich, *Friedrich von Holstein*, pp. 707–708.

[than] to accept the conference and that *he will get no far-reaching concessions from us . . .* , he will finally yield to the inevitable and formally accept the conference as desired."[31] Like Radolin, Bülow and Holstein could attribute Rouvier's refusal to attend a conference only to the pernicious influence of the remaining pockets of "Delcasséism."[32]

As Rouvier continued to refuse any concessions to the Germans, they began to speak of him in disparaging terms. Holstein thought that Rouvier must be a weak man because he submitted to Delcassé's policy, which subverted France's and Rouvier's position:

> It is definitely a great weakness of Rouvier's and shows a lack of logical reflection that he has not realized how, by adopting the Delcassé program, he is helping Delcassé back to his feet, the man who is now probably his worst enemy. . . . I still have the hope that Rouvier will come to his senses before it is too late and adopt a reasonable policy again instead of wrapping himself in the prophet's cloak of Delcassé.[33]

And later, Holstein writes that Rouvier "is really a weak man and allows himself to be terrorized by the Delcassé group."[34] "However, who knows?" thought Holstein, "Perhaps a few sensible people may yet be found in France."[35]

Like Radolin, Bülow, and Holstein, the kaiser also believed Rouvier nothing more than Delcassé in sheep's clothing. When advised that continued German resistance could result in Rouvier's replacement by Delcassé, the kaiser responded: "It doesn't matter! That would make the situation all the clearer. It is better to have Delcassé conducting his own policy than to have Rouvier doing it for him!"[36]

The German leadership viewed Delcassé's policy as reckless and foolish. They believed that Rouvier did France a great service by removing him. However, Rouvier's refusal to meet the "legitimate" German demands revealed him to be a weak and duplicitous man. When Rouvier showed the greatest resolve, he was reviled by the German leadership and held in contempt as a weak man. This response contradicts deterrence theory's expectations and confirms my hypothesis:

---

[31] Radolin to Holstein (June 22, 1905), *Holstein Papers*, No. 894, p. 345; Rich, *Friedrich von Holstein*, p. 711.

[32] See Sontag, "German Foreign Policy," p. 291.

[33] Holstein to Radolin (June 23, 1905), *Holstein Papers*, No. 896, pp. 346–347.

[34] Holstein to Bülow (July 20, 1905), *Holstein Papers*, No. 903, p. 354.

[35] Holstein to Radolin (February 12, 1906), *Holstein Papers*, No. 934, p. 396.

[36] Quoted in Rich, *Friedrich von Holstein*, p. 736.

German observers used situational attributions to explain Rouvier's desirable behavior, and dispositional attributions to explain his undesirable behavior.

The Aftereffects of Fashoda

One issue remains concerning German views of France before the Algeciras Conference. To what extent did the Germans expect Delcassé to back down because he had yielded to the British at Fashoda? If commitments are interdependent, the French defeat at Fashoda should be viewed as an invitation to challenge the French in Morocco. In both conflicts, Delcassé was foreign minister, the immediate issues at stake were trivial, and Delcassé was viewed as part of the problem.[37]

I found only one reference to the Fashoda Crisis, written after Delcassé resigned and after the Germans realized that Rouvier might not compromise. In a memorandum dated February 22, 1906, Holstein wrote:

> The rapprochement between France and England began immediately after Fashoda when the French saw that they could accomplish nothing *against* England. In the same way, the French will not approach the idea of a rapprochement with Germany until they see that English friendship—which after the last election results can only be platonic—is not enough to gain them the agreement of Germany for their seizure of Morocco, but that Germany wishes to be loved for her own sake.[38]

This statement could be viewed either as an example of reasoning by analogy or as evidence that Holstein expected concessions from the French because they backed down at Fashoda, that is, reputational reasoning.

I contend that in the statement above Holstein makes a situational explanation of French behavior. Just as the British outmaneuvered the French at Fashoda leaving them no choice but to give way to British demands, so the French would be outmaneuvered in Morocco. The French would have no choice but to accept German demands, especially since their ally would do nothing. Holstein believed that the French diplomatic position was weak, not that French decision-makers were irresolute.

---

[37] On Fashoda, see Susan Peterson, *Crisis Bargaining and the State* (Ann Arbor: University of Michigan Press, 1996), chap. 4: "The Fashoda Crisis."
[38] Quoted in Rich, *Friedrich von Holstein*, p. 737.

Holstein uses Fashoda as an analogy not only because he applies it to Rouvier (rather than Delcassé), but more important because he applies the same reasoning to the victor at Fashoda—Britain. The Fashoda analogy is just another name for the "big stick." I mentioned earlier how belief in the big stick encouraged the Moroccan challenge as well as how this same strategy was applied against Britain in Egypt in 1904. Holstein also used big-stick reasoning against Britain in South Africa. He hoped the affair would give Germany "a small diplomatic success and England a small political lesson."[39] He applied the same pressure tactics against Britain in Samoa. According to Norman Rich, Holstein's primary purpose in the Moroccan Crisis remained constant. Rich believes Holstein wanted to make both Britain and France realize that colonial agreements were only possible with German consent: "Britain had been obliged to conclude a separate agreement with Germany over Egypt. Now France too would have to be taught a lesson."[40]

Holstein saw in Fashoda confirmation of the big stick. Since he applied the same tactics to both the winners and the losers at Fashoda, it seems likely that he thought Fashoda a useful analogy and not evidence of a weak-willed France.[41] Even if one rejects this argument and sees in Holstein's statement an example of reputational reasoning, it is still odd that it should be employed so late in the game and against Rouvier. Contrary to deterrence theory's assumption of interdependence, Fashoda was not used by German decision-makers as evidence that the French would yield to German threats in Morocco.

French, Austrian, and Russian Explanations of Delcassé's Resignation

Like the Germans, and unlike the British, the French were generally pleased with the outcome. Delcassé had taken them to the brink of war and for what? As the nationalist press observed, "for thirty-four years we have refrained from a war against Germany for the recovery of Alsace-Lorraine. Does Mr. Delcassé wish to go to war for

---

[39] Ibid., p. 472; see also pp. 590–601.

[40] Ibid., p. 700.

[41] The Fashoda analogy was inappropriate to the situation in Morocco. Whereas France was isolated at Fashoda, it was strongly supported by Britain in Morocco. Additionally, the rapprochement between France and England was made in spite of Fashoda, not because of it. For an analysis of how decision-makers (mis)use analogies, see Yuen Foong Khong, *Analogies at War: Korea, Munich, Dien Bien Phu, and the Vietnam Decisions of 1965* (Princeton: Princeton University Press, 1992).

[85]

Morocco?"[42] Rouvier had delivered France from Delcassé's dangerous adventure.

Delcassé's argument that the Germans were bluffing and the English offering an alliance remained unpersuasive. Rouvier believed the British had offered an alliance, but discounted its value (the British fleet did not have wheels). He did not believe the Germans were bluffing because their grievances were understandable: "[Germany] is disturbed and humiliated by your encirclement of her. In our Morocco dispute she sees an excellent occasion to break the ring, and she is prepared for extremities. . . . Are we in a condition to sustain a war against Germany? No, No! Even with the aid of the British fleet we should be in for a worse catastrophe than in 1870. We should be criminals to indulge in such an adventure. France would not recover."[43]

For Rouvier, most of the high command, and the rest of the cabinet, the issue was capability, not resolve: "Our military situation and the condition of the country would lead us to defeat and to the Commune."[44] With Delcassé gone, Rouvier and his colleagues believed peace was at hand.

Up to this point, Germany and France were engaged in a bilateral dispute. In contrast to the domestic stability in England and Germany, Austria and Russia were consumed by domestic crises. They desired a peaceful end to the Moroccan Crisis, which they wished had never been started; neither strongly desired any particular outcome as long as it was peaceful. The weaker the desires, the more difficult it is to test my hypothesis. At this stage, Austria and Russia may best be viewed as neutrals in the Moroccan Crisis; my hypothesis becomes indeterminate. The deterrence hypothesis expects these states to view the French as irresolute and the Germans as resolute.

Since 1900, Austria had been increasingly viewed as the "sick man" of Europe. Just as all of Europe dreaded the inevitable scramble for territory when the Ottoman Empire collapsed, so all feared a dissolution of the Hapsburg Empire. Hungary increasingly challenged Franz Joseph's authority. The Hungarian parliament resisted the crown's ef-

---

[42] Quoted in Samuel R. Williamson, Jr., *The Politics of Grand Strategy: Britain and France Prepare for War, 1904–1914* (London: Ashfield Press, 1990), p. 33.

[43] Quoted in Gooch, *Grouping of the Powers*, p. 179.

[44] Quoted in Andrew, *Théophile Delcassé*, p. 289. Paul Kennedy believes a German attack against France probably would have had the greatest chance of success in the summer of 1905. Paul Kennedy, *The Rise and Fall of the Great Powers* (New York: Vintage Books, 1989), p. 252.

forts (begun in 1903) to increase the size of the common army with a proportionate increase in Hungarian conscripts. The deadlock degenerated into crisis by 1905. As the emperor of Austria and king of Hungary, Franz Joseph subjected Hungary to virtual martial law and the general staff in Vienna began working on plans for the invasion and occupation of Hungary. The domestic situation in the Dual Monarchy had so deteriorated that in June, Berlin sent out feelers to St. Petersburg for an entente in case the Austro-Hungarian Empire dissolved.[45]

Austria-Hungary seemed stable when compared to Russia. In the midst of a war with Japan (in which the Russians did not win one significant battle), they were confronted with revolution, sparked by "Bloody Sunday" in January 1905. The Russian fleet suffered a crushing defeat at Tsushima days before Delcassé's resignation. In addition to these problems, Russia was on the verge of bankruptcy. The Portsmouth Treaty (which officially ended the war with Japan) was not signed until September 1905.[46]

I found little evidence bearing on Austrian or Russian explanations of Delcassé's resignation. Delcassé had been a good friend of the Russians and, it seems, they were disappointed to see him resign. The only evidence I found was in Serge Sazonov's memoirs. Sazonov, who became the Russian foreign minister in 1909, wrote that "France was compelled to deprive herself, for a time, of the services of her gifted Foreign Minister, under circumstances damaging to her national self-esteem."[47] Events subsequent to Delcassé's resignation may easily have influenced Sazonov's interpretation. In my study, memoirs which do not refer to or cite documents are evidence of last resort. I uncovered no evidence that the Austrians paid attention to Delcassé's resignation.

In the absence of evidence to the contrary, the possibility remains that Austrian and Russian decision-makers viewed Delcassé's resignation as evidence of French irresolution and German resolution. However, giving another state a reputation requires attention to the other's behav-

---

[45] Francis Roy Bridge, *From Sadowa to Sarajevo: The Foreign Policy of Austria-Hungary, 1866–1914* (London: Routledge and Kegan Paul, 1972), pp. 260–271; Arthur J. May, *The Hapsburg Monarchy: 1867–1914* (Cambridge: Harvard University Press, 1951), pp. 352–356, 387–388; Kennedy, *Rise and Fall*, p. 216.

[46] William C. Fuller, Jr., *Civil-Military Conflict in Imperial Russia: 1881–1914* (Princeton: Princeton University Press, 1985), p. 133; Dietrich Geyer, *Russian Imperialism: The Interaction of Domestic and Foreign Policy, 1860–1914*, trans. Bruce Little (New York: Berg, 1987).

[47] Serge Sazonov, *Fateful Years, 1909–1916: The Reminiscences of Serge Sazanov* (London: Jonathan Cape, 1928), p. 24.

ior, which takes time and energy. Given the grave domestic troubles in Austria and Russia, it would be surprising if they paid much attention to a bilateral dispute over issues of little immediate concern.

As the desires hypothesis expected, the British thought the French lacked resolve and the Germans thought nothing of the sort. It was not until Rouvier began to resist German demands that the Germans began to believe he was irresolute. The deterrence hypothesis also expected the British to view the French as irresolute, but it wrongly expected the Germans to view Rouvier as resolute. Finally, deterrence failed an easy test for interdependence: the Germans applied the Fashoda analogy— in the guise of the big stick—to both the winner and the loser at Fashoda. I uncovered no evidence that the Germans thought Delcassé would back down in Morocco because he backed down in Fashoda. The Germans challenged not because they doubted French resolve, but because they doubted French capability. Because German policy-makers expected no objections from London, they believed the French would be isolated and would have to yield.

EXPLAINING THE OUTCOME OF THE ALGECIRAS CONFERENCE

Had the Germans been satisfied with Delcassé's resignation, they might have achieved their own Fashoda. Instead, they continued to press for a conference to resolve the Moroccan affair. After months of negotiations with Rouvier, the Germans finally obtained their coveted conference, which was held at Algeciras from January 16 to April 7. Although the conference confirmed the integrity and independence of Morocco, the Germans found themselves politically isolated and forced to accept an agreement that gave France political and economic predominance in Morocco. German belligerence pushed France and England ever closer, which in turn pulled Italy further from the Triple Alliance, and the Russians sidled up to the Anglo-French Entente. Only Austria remained a steadfast supporter of Germany.

After Algeciras, the deterrence hypothesis expects everyone to view the Germans as irresolute and the French as resolute. The British, Russians, and Austrians ought to be viewed as reliable allies. The desires hypothesis suggests that states satisfied with the outcome of Algeciras will explain others' behavior in situational terms, and those dissatisfied with the outcome will use dispositional explanations.

[88]

German Explanations for Their Defeat at Algeciras

The German leadership did not gracefully accept their defeat at Algeciras. Instead, they blamed Italy, Russia, France, England, and themselves. Only Austria's support spared it from Berlin's acerbic attacks. According to the deterrence hypothesis, the Austrians should win the gratitude and goodwill of Germany by standing fast alongside their beleaguered ally. In contrast, I suggest that the desirable Austrian behavior should lead to situational explanations (which means there will be no reservoir of goodwill in Germany and no assumption of future Austrian support).

While historians have since debated whether the Italians were loyal to their German ally at Algeciras, at the time the Germans were disappointed with Rome's support.[48] Though German policy-makers offered different explanations for the Italians' undesirable behavior, at least one important actor used situational attributions to explain Italian actions. The German ambassador to Italy, Anton Monts, was dissatisfied with Italian support at Algeciras: "If Italy fails us in the relatively unimportant Morocco question, that is a foretaste of what we may expect in really serious times."[49] Italy, he thought, was nothing but a "deadweight" on the Triplice.[50]

As much as Monts disliked and distrusted Italy, he understood its behavior in largely situational terms: "In whatever circumstances and under whatever Government Italy will seek to hold herself aloof from a war against England. The Triplice was concluded under the presupposition of friendly relations with England."[51] In a later memo (June 1906), he observed: "The Italian Minister is not yet born who will refuse to be part of an Anglo-French defensive arrangement, strengthened at need by agreements with Russia."[52] Although this statement could be interpreted as a dispositional explanation, I think it is more situational. Monts believed that Italian security needs prevented any Italian minis-

---

[48] For example, see May, *The Hapsburg Monarchy*, p. 388; Edward Crankshaw, *The Fall of the House of Habsburg* (New York: Viking Press, 1963), p. 327; Luigi Albertini, *The Origins of the War of 1914*, trans. and ed. Isabella M. Massey, vol. 1: *European Relations from the Congress of Berlin to the Eve of the Sarajevo Murder* (New York: Oxford University Press, 1952), pp. 168–174; C. J. Lowe and F. Marzari, *Italian Foreign Policy: 1870–1940* (Boston: Routledge and Kegan Paul, 1975), pp. 93–95.
[49] Quoted in Gooch, *Grouping of the Powers*, p. 258.
[50] Richard Bosworth, *Italy and the Approach of the First World War* (London: Macmillan, 1983), pp. 64–65.
[51] Quoted in Albertini, *Origins of the War*, p. 181.
[52] Ibid.

ter from waging war against the two strongest Mediterranean powers. His explanation had more to do with Italian geography than Italian character. In this case, undesirable behavior elicited a situational attribution and contradicts both the deterrence and desires hypotheses. I address disconfirming evidence in Chapter 6.

At first glance, it appears the Germans were grateful to the Austrians for their support. The kaiser fired off a telegram to the Austrian foreign minister, Count Agenor Goluchowski, publicly thanking him for being "a brilliant second on the duelling-ground" and assuring him of German support in a similar situation.[53] While the kaiser's message was intended to be a public swipe at Italy (since no similar telegram was sent there), the Austrians also took offense at the congratulatory telegram. As the German ambassador to France, Radolin, reported to Holstein: "We are, after all, completely *isolated* in the world, and everybody hates us, even Austria, which is absolutely furious about the Goluchowski telegram."[54] The Austrians perceived themselves as a great power, not a German satellite or a "second" in a Franco-German duel; they were incensed at the German attitude.

Bülow feared that Austria would exploit Berlin's isolation by dragging it into disputes of no consequence to Germany. It was this fear of Austrian exploitation that led Bülow to advise the kaiser on the necessity of deceiving Germany's "loyal" ally:

> Therefore we must not show too great a desire in Vienna for help or act as if we feel isolated in any way. The Austrians must receive the impression that we have perfect faith in ourselves for every eventuality. We must, therefore, portray our relations to Russia, Italy, and England as better perhaps than they really are, and even if we have a reasonable grudge toward Italy we must dissemble. . . . Austria will hold to us more closely if she thinks that our relations with Russia are satisfactory.[55]

Future Austrian support could not be assumed. When Austrian interests diverged from German interests, Austria might not be loyal. As the German ambassador to Austria reported: "Only a war against Italy

---

[53] Quoted in G. P. Gooch, *History of Modern Europe: 1878–1919* (New York: Henry Holt, 1923), p. 368.

[54] Radolin to Holstein (May 8, 1906), *Holstein Papers*, No. 976, p. 421.

[55] Quoted in Oswald Henry Wedel, *Austro-German Diplomatic Relations, 1908–1914* (Stanford: Stanford University Press, 1932), pp. 37–38. Also see Anderson, *First Moroccan Crisis*, pp. 398–399.

would be really popular and that would not help us; on the contrary, it would weaken our entire position."[56]

In short, Austria's support at Algeciras was welcomed, but was not taken by the Germans as an indication of future Austrian support. Holstein, who thought the Austrians "cool and politically reserved" while the Hungarians were "actually hostile," put no stock in future Austrian support.[57] Indeed, he felt the Austrians acted as much to help France as to help Germany: "Goluchowski points out that Austrian mediation was just as much in the interests of France as of Germany."[58] The German leadership did not attribute to the Austrians a character trait of loyalty or resolve. In a different situation the Austrians might behave differently. Fearing isolation, as well as the destabilizing consequences within Germany of a dissolution of the Dual Monarchy, German policymakers adopted support for Austria as a central tenet.[59]

The Russians were French allies and eventually gave France their full diplomatic support. According to the deterrence hypothesis, loyal behavior by an ally ought to be recognized as such by ally and adversary alike. The Germans should have a grudging respect for or at least not open hostility toward Russia for keeping its alliance obligations. In contrast, I argue that because Russian support contributed to the French victory at Algeciras, the Germans should view this undesirable Russian behavior in dispositional terms. That is, the Germans should believe that Russia chose to hurt Germany, not that it was compelled to do so by the situation.

In fact, the Germans were furious with Russian behavior at Algeciras. Toward the end of March, Vladimir Lamsdorff, the Russian foreign minister (from 1900 to 1906), denounced German policy and upheld French policy in an article published by a French newspaper. The article so upset the Germans that Bülow would not show it directly to the kaiser.[60] In their view, they had earned Russian support by virtue of their strong support of Russia during the Russo-Japanese War; they had even provided more support than France. Now they sought to cash those "goodwill" chips in exchange for Russian support—or at least neutrality—at Algeciras.[61] Well before the Moroccan dispute, the kaiser

---

[56] Karl von Wedel to Bülow (February 12, 1906), quoted in Wedel, *Austro-German Relations*, p. 37.

[57] Holstein to Pascal David (May 13, 1906), *Holstein Papers*, No. 980, p. 424.

[58] Holstein to Otto Rose (June 18, 1906), *Holstein Papers*, No. 986, p. 429.

[59] James Joll, *The Origins of the First World War* (New York: Longman, 1984), p. 47.

[60] Anderson, *First Moroccan Crisis*, p. 368; Rich, *Friedrich von Holstein*, p. 741.

[61] Sontag, "German Foreign Policy," p. 289.

considered the value of Russia's goodwill: "The most far-reaching benevolent neutrality towards Russia! She will help us later against the Japs!"[62] The Germans believed, as do some contemporary observers, that Berlin practiced "very benevolent neutrality" toward Russia and had repeatedly "compromised her neutrality" thereby running the risk of armed conflict with Japan.[63]

As far as the Russians were concerned, there were no "goodwill" chips to be cashed. Both Foreign Minister Alexander Izvolsky (1906–1910) and Prime Minister Sergei Witte (1905–1906) interpreted German support not as beneficent, but as malign. In his memoirs, Izvolsky writes that after Algeciras the Germans reverted "to the well-worn subject of the benefits heaped upon Russia by Germany during the war with Japan and Russia's ingratitude therefore." He thinks this nonsense. The Germans wanted the Far East war to continue and that is why they "helped" Russia. Anyway, continues Izvolsky, the Germans had been paid back already "by the signing of a treaty of commerce, extremely advantageous to the Germans and onerous for Russia."[64] Similarly, Witte writes of Germany "dragging us into the war with Japan."[65] At least one contemporary historian shares their view that the Germans did not have Russia's best interests at heart.[66]

The Germans punished Russia for dropping the Björkö treaty and supporting France at Algeciras by refusing to participate in a loan desperately needed by Russia.[67] As far as the kaiser was concerned, the Russians had "grown fat off of us long enough." When he heard of the

---

[62] Quoted in ibid., p. 283.

[63] Bernard F. Oppel, "The Waning of a Traditional Alliance: Russia and Germany after the Portsmouth Peace Conference," *Central European History* 5 (December 1972): 319; Jonathan Steinberg, "Germany and the Russo-Japanese War," *American Historical Review* 75 (December 1970): 1985.

[64] *The Memoirs of Alexander Iswolsky*, trans. and ed. Charles Louis Seeger (London: Hutchinson, 1920), pp. 37, 45.

[65] *The Memoirs of Count Witte*, trans. and ed. Abraham Yarmolinsky (Garden City, N.Y.: Doubleday, Page, 1921), p. 414.

[66] Kennedy, *Rise of the Anglo-German*, p. 268.

[67] The tsar and the kaiser met informally at Björkö (in the Finnish Gulf) on July 25, 1905, to discuss improving German-Russian relations. They signed an agreement that could have resulted in Russia fighting on the side of Germany against France. The tsar did not inform Lamsdorff of the treaty until August 30, 1905. It was so detrimental to Russian interests (as well as violating the treaty of alliance with France) that Lamsdorff forced the tsar to reject it. See Anderson, *First Moroccan Crisis*, esp. chap. 15; Gooch, *History of Modern Europe*, pp. 380–382. For further discussion of the loan, see Olga Crisp, "The Russian Liberals and the 1906 Anglo-French Loan to Russia," *Slavonic and East European Review* 39 (June 1961): 503.

Liberal party's opposition to a Russian loan, the kaiser remarked: "I'm very glad to hear it, they won't get a penny from us!"[68] Holstein also thought Russia should be punished: "It is equally important for us in our ordinary relations with Russia that Witte should have to pay the bill for Lamsdorff's anti-German policy, which hurts him financially and makes him look bad. . . . It is the only way we can get rid of Lamsdorff. But even if he stays he will have learned that Germany must be treated decently."[69] The Germans punished Russia for its loyal behavior toward France.[70]

The Russians, in turn, believed this punishment unjust. Witte wrote of German "treachery" for refusing to participate in the loan, which was inspired as "an act of vengeance for Algeciras and for our rapprochement with England."[71] Lamsdorff also viewed Germany's rebuff as revenge for Algeciras.[72]

Needless to say, the Germans did not credit the Russians for being loyal French allies nor did they offer situational explanations for Russian behavior. Instead, Bülow, Holstein, and Kaiser Wilhelm viewed the Russians as ungrateful back-stabbers who needed to be taught a lesson. This response fits my hypothesis and is contrary to the deterrence hypothesis. Even if the Germans thought they had "goodwill" chips to cash in for Russian support, they had no such illusions regarding France or England.

According to the deterrence hypothesis, the Germans should consider both France and England as resolute for having withstood German pressure. Because the Germans viewed French and British behavior as undesirable, I expect them to make dispositional attributions. Since I cannot specify the content of these attributions, I assume the Germans may think their adversaries resolute.

German views of Rouvier fit the desires hypothesis. The Germans did not view the French as resolved for resisting German pressure. Instead, they offered alternative explanations for French behavior, such as

[68] Quoted by Oppel, "Waning of a Traditional Alliance," pp. 325, 326.

[69] Holstein to Bülow (March 25, 1906), *Holstein Papers*, No. 944, p. 402.

[70] Bülow opposed a Russian loan at least in part because he thought it was a financial risk. He was aware that by not participating, Germany might be driving "Russia into the open arms of England." Bülow to Otto Hammann (April 2, 1906), quoted in Ralph Richard Menning, "The Collapse of 'Global Diplomacy': Germany's Descent into Isolation, 1906–1909" (Ph.D. diss., Brown University, 1986), p. 31. For German bankers' view, see Oppel, "Waning of a Traditional Alliance," p. 328.

[71] *Memoirs of Count Witte*, p. 304.

[72] Oppel, "Waning of a Traditional Alliance," p. 326.

the continuing influence of Delcassé. They understood that France, because of its weak military capability, could withstand German pressure only with English support. For example, early in the crisis the German ambassador to England, Paul Metternich, complained to Lansdowne that France would come to terms "if you didn't stiffen their backs for them."[73] Similarly, Holstein was hopeful that the Liberals' election would result in French concessions: "The beginnings of the English elections indicate a decisive victory for the peace party. As soon as France is no longer sure of having the English fleet at her side in case of war, she will preserve a peaceful attitude."[74] The dominant German explanation was that France lacked the capability—not the resolve—to resist German demands.

It does not appear that the German leadership made disparaging remarks to each other about French resolve. To the British, however, they ridiculed French behavior. The British ambassador to Germany, Charles Hardinge, reported that the kaiser believed France to be a "bundle of nerves, and a female race not a male race like the Anglo-Saxons and Teutons." Hardinge then reminded the kaiser that French nervousness might be better explained by the German army's ability to crush France.[75] This comment is an example of signaling. The Germans aimed to weaken the Anglo-French Entente, so it is not surprising to find them expressing doubt about French resolve to a British representative.[76]

The Germans did not credit the British with having great resolve or being good allies. Rather, they assumed that Britain was encouraging France in order to provoke a war between France and Germany. "I certainly believe one thing quite firmly," wrote Holstein, "that both Bertie and possibly Lansdowne would like to see France involved in war."[77] The Germans thought French policy was so clearly contrary to French interests that it had to be the work of the English.[78]

Germany did not attribute the uncompromising British position to British resolve. The German leadership, like the leadership of other countries, simply did not worry much about other countries' reputa-

[73] Quoted in Kaufmann, "Out of the Lab," p. 567.

[74] Holstein to von Sternburg (January 14, 1906), *Holstein Papers*, No. 925, p. 387.

[75] Hardinge to Grey (August 16, 1906), *British Documents on the Origins of the War, 1898–1914* (henceforth cited as *BD*), vol. 3: *The Testing of the Entente, 1904–1906*, ed. G. P. Gooch and Harold Temperley (London: HMSO 1928), No. 425, p. 369.

[76] Because signaling is common, I avoid using evidence between adversaries either to support or to contradict my argument.

[77] Holstein to Radolin (July 1, 1905), *Holstein Papers*, No. 898, p. 348.

[78] Gooch, *Grouping of the Powers*, p. 178.

tions for resolve. They did, however, worry a great deal about their own reputation. This tendency to pay more attention to one's own than one's adversary's reputation for resolve has surprising results.

Rather than think the British and French were unlikely to bluff in the future because they had demonstrated great resolve, the Germans thought just the opposite: French and British decision-makers were *more* likely to bluff because they now ostensibly thought that the *Germans* lacked resolve. After the German defeat at Algeciras, Holstein wrote: "More than ever we are being subject to bluff, but no one will push things to extremes."[79] In another memo to Bülow, Holstein warned:

> At Algeciras Germany gave in before collective pressure. If she now allows concessions to be pressured out of her in the Triple Alliance question, then the pressure system will have proved its worth a second time, and will then be used more often and will lead us gradually step by step to a revision of the Peace of Frankfurt. . . . We must be prepared for all kinds of bluff—they will be tried out one after the other to see how they work.

Later in the same memo, Holstein makes clearer his expectation that other states would now try to bluff Germany: "I consider the tone [French prime minister Georges] Clemenceau has recently used in dealing with Germany to be bluff. If he wanted to negotiate, he would say nothing until a suitable moment. But he is using threats because he expects the desired results from threats alone. Every concession that Germany now makes in foreign affairs will encourage this bluff."[80]

Decision-makers worry more about their own reputation for resolve than anyone else's. What was most salient to Holstein was the German defeat, not the British victory. He assumed the British and French would view the outcome the way he did. As a result, and contrary to deterrence expectations, he assumed France and Britain were more rather than less likely to bluff.

Holstein was certain that Germany now had a reputation for lacking resolve. He was convinced that all the other countries stood firm "because they hoped . . . that Germany would lose her nerve. . . . Therein lies the danger. This same method will be used again."[81] The danger was not only that Germany would now be challenged more often than before, but that Germany would no longer be believed when it intended

---

[79] Holstein to Bülow (October 25, 1906), *Holstein Papers*, No. 999, p. 442.
[80] Memorandum by Holstein (October 27, 1906), *Holstein Papers*, No. 1000, pp. 442–443.
[81] Holstein to Pascal David (May 13, 1906), *Holstein Papers*, No. 980, p. 424.

to stand firm. Discussing an issue unrelated to the Moroccan Crisis, Holstein captured what is assumed to be the essential problem with bluffing in a repeated game of Chicken: "But to tamper with our land army, that would be the beginning of the end. Yet to stand firm on this question will be more dangerous than on Morocco—*simply because of the fact that people no longer believe we will do so.*"[82] As we will see, Holstein's fears were unfounded.

Holstein blamed the kaiser for this dangerous reputation as a pushover. "I ought to have realized," wrote Holstein, "that it would be difficult to make Bülow, and impossible to make His Majesty, resolve on the last resort."[83] Holstein feared that in time, "it will be noticed abroad that His Majesty gives in to strong pressure."[84] Perhaps not surprisingly, the kaiser pinned much of the blame on Holstein, as well as German capability and German domestic turmoil.[85]

Aside from blaming Holstein, Italy, Russia, France, and England, the kaiser also blamed the king of England, with whom he had a special relationship. He said of the king at various times: "He is an old peacock. . . . He is Satan; you can hardly believe what a Satan he is. . . . Every morning at breakfast the King of England, jealous of his nephew, reads of the Kaiser's doings in the newspapers and seeks how he can get even with him."[86] Here it should be noted that nasty dispositional attributions may not be wrong, just as situational attributions may not be right. In the above case, the kaiser's invective may not have been misplaced. According to Lansdowne: "The King talks and writes about his Royal Brother in terms which make one's flesh creep, and the official papers which go to him, whenever they refer to H. I. M., come back with all sorts of annotations of a most incendiary character."[87] Once again, undesirable behavior elicits dispositional attributions.

---

[82] Holstein to Pascal David (May 29, 1906), *Holstein Papers*, No. 985, p. 429.

[83] Quoted in Taylor, *Struggle for Mastery in Europe*, p. 439.

[84] Private letter (March 17, 1906), quoted in Rich, *Friedrich von Holstein*, p. 741. See also Holstein to Brandt (March 28, 1906), *Holstein Papers*, No. 959, p. 410; Memorandum by Holstein (May 17, 1906), *Holstein Papers*, No. 983, p. 427.

[85] Rich, *Friedrich von Holstein*, pp. 750–753. As for capability, Bülow reported to Holstein that the kaiser ordered retreat "because our artillery and our navy were not in any condition to fight a war" (undated memorandum by Holstein, *Holstein Papers*, note 1, p. 405). For Bülow's concern over the domestic situation, see Michael Balfour, *The Kaiser and His Times* (London: Cresset Press, 1964), p. 262.

[86] Quoted in Balfour, *Kaiser and His Times*, p. 265.

[87] Quoted in Thomas Newton, *Lord Lansdowne*, p. 330. See also Zara S. Steiner, *The Foreign Office and Foreign Policy, 1898–1914* (Cambridge: Cambridge University Press, 1969), pp. 203–206.

The desires hypothesis captured German decision-makers' beliefs about their allies and adversaries. They did not view the Russians as resolute and loyal allies of the French (as the deterrence hypothesis expected), but instead held the Russians in contempt for their undesirable behavior. Similarly, Holstein failed to view the British as resolute adversaries. Instead, he focused on Germany's alleged reputation for lacking resolve. As a result, he assumed the British would be more likely to bluff in the future because London now thought Berlin was irresolute. Finally, and in contrast to the expectations of deterrence theory, German policy-makers did not expect future Austrian support because of past Austrian support.

Austrian Explanations of the Conference Results

The deterrence hypothesis suggests that Holstein was right to worry about Germany's reputation for resolve. Since Germany backed down at Algeciras, Austria should view its ally as lacking resolve; the Austrians should regard France as having demonstrated resolve. In contrast, I expect Austrian decision-makers to explain both German and French behavior at Algeciras in situational terms. They were relieved that the affair was finally over. The Austrian leaders were consumed by domestic turmoil; they had no political, economic, or security interests in Morocco; and they were eager to maintain good relations with all the parties to the conflict.

I found little evidence bearing on Austrian explanations for the German defeat at Algeciras and no evidence regarding the French victory. This is unsurprising given Austria's marginal interests in the outcome of Algeciras and its chaotic domestic situation.

The Hungarians—meaning the Magyars—continued to resist Austrian control by refusing to pay taxes and to supply even the normal number of troops to the common army. In retaliation, Franz Joseph suspended the Hungarian constitution and dissolved their parliament by sending in a cordon of Romanian troops; this action was taken in February while the Algeciras Conference was well under way. To crush the rebellion, Franz Joseph threatened to introduce political democracy into Hungary. Universal manhood suffrage was a direct threat to the ruling Magyar gentry; they would find themselves a minority not only among other nationalities, but also among Magyar peasants and town-workers. A compromise was eventually reached in

April 1906 which preserved the union and avoided the threat of democracy.[88]

Austria-Hungary's internal turmoil made an active foreign policy difficult. As the Austrians struggled to contain the Magyar insurgents, they discovered that Serbia and Bulgaria had concluded a "secret" customs union which the Austrian leadership assumed to be the beginning of the dreaded Balkan League; this conflict would soon lead to the "pig war," which further weakened Austria's position in the Balkans.[89]

The Germans knew their Austrian ally was in the midst of a severe constitutional crisis during the Algeciras Conference and, as the German ambassador to Austria reported to Bülow, used this understanding to predict the limitations of its support: "Personally I have the impression that Austria-Hungary is with us; but we must not overlook the fact that the Dual Monarchy is not inclined or able to act in a military way. This is due to her sorry domestic situation and her reduced circumstances."[90] This weakness may be the best explanation for Austrian support of Germany at Algeciras. The Austrians went to Algeciras as a diminished power aiming to resolve the dispute as quickly as possible without jeopardizing their relations with Germany. Goluchowski, the Austrian foreign minister, made clear to the Germans his belief that "Morocco was not worth a war."[91]

A. J. P. Taylor suggests that it was vulnerability that caused Austria to pursue a course even less independent than Italy's.[92] Toeing the German line at Algeciras was bad enough; the kaiser's congratulatory telegram (which unintentionally belittled Austria's contribution) was an even greater embarrassment. Goluchowski resigned from office in October 1906 after being hounded by hostile Magyars, humiliated by the "brilliant second" telegram, and held responsible for the disastrous "pig war."[93]

[88] May, *Hapsburg Monarchy*, pp. 357–361; Jelavich, *Habsburg Empire*, pp. 144–145; Bridge, *From Sadowa to Sarajevo*, pp. 270–271; Taylor, *Habsburg Monarchy*, pp. 207–211.

[89] Bridge, *From Sadowa to Sarajevo*, pp. 276–280.

[90] Karl von Wedel to Bülow (February 12, 1906), quoted in Wedel, *Austro-German Relations*, p. 37.

[91] Quoted in May, *Hapsburg Monarchy*, p. 388.

[92] Taylor, *Habsburg Monarchy*, pp. 210, 215. The extent to which the Austrians supported Germany at Algeciras is debatable. Lowe and Marzari contend that Italian and Austrian policies were almost identical and Crankshaw writes of Austria's "luke warm support." See Lowe and Marzari, *Italian Foreign Policy*, p. 95; Crankshaw, *Fall of the House of Habsburg*, p. 327.

[93] F. R. Bridge, *Great Britain and Austria-Hungary, 1906–1914: A Diplomatic History* (London: London School of Economics, 1972), p. 41.

During and immediately after the Algeciras Conference, the Austrian leadership, enveloped in domestic crisis, apparently did not attribute a reputation for resolve to either the Germans or the French. As I discuss in Chapter 4, the Austrians counted on German support in their Bosnian adventure because they believed the Germans were isolated and so had no choice but to support Vienna. Beyond this, it does not appear that the Moroccan Crisis made much of an impression on the Austrian leadership.

British Explanations of the Conference Results

The domestic situation in England was calm and the stakes at Algeciras were believed to be high. Like his Conservative predecessor, British foreign minister Edward Grey feared the consequences of a German victory at Algeciras. Although there was a difference of emphasis between the two men—Lansdowne feared a German port in Morocco more than damage to the Entente, Grey feared just the opposite—both were committed to giving France full diplomatic support and both hinted at military support in case of a German attack.[94] As Russia's position was weakened further by the Far East war, Grey began military staff talks with the French in January 1906.[95]

The deterrence argument expects the British to view the Berlin leadership as irresolute (since they bowed before the British fleet) and the Paris leadership as resolute (since they stood firm before the German threat). In contrast, my hypothesis suggests that the English will explain the behavior of both adversary and ally in situational terms: the Germans will not be held irresolute, the French will not be viewed as resolute. Because the British found the outcome desirable, they should make situational attributions.

Recall that the predominant British explanation for Delcassé's resignation was that the French lacked resolve. However, after the Algeciras victory, Grey remembers Delcassé's resignation differently from his predecessor: "After their attempt to be civil to Germany last year by discarding Delcassé they cannot be expected to make advances again till it is clear that German policy has changed."[96] And much later, in his memoirs, Grey writes: "It was in the preceding months in 1905 that France

[94] George W. Monger, *The End of Isolation: British Foreign Policy, 1900–1907* (New York: Thomas Nelson and Sons, 1963), pp. 196–197, 206, 267, 276–277.
[95] See Williamson, *Politics of Grand Strategy*, esp. chap. 3.
[96] Minutes by Grey (September 24, 1906), *BD*, No. 440, p. 390.

had consented, under German pressure, to the humiliation of dismissing M. Delcassé. She had felt compelled to consent because the German armaments were so much more ready for war than her own. The German pressure left her no option but to bring her own forces and equipment up to date."[97] It is not that the French lacked resolve in dismissing Delcassé; they were merely being "civil" to the demanding Germans. Grey did not remember Delcassé's resignation as revealing an absence of French resolve; this response subverts the interdependence assumption of deterrence theory.[98]

Grey also explained French and Russian behavior at Algeciras in situational terms; his explanation of German behavior is ambiguous. In a note to the British representative at Algeciras, Grey thought the Germans would rather have the conference fail if settlement meant a German diplomatic defeat, but he remained hopeful:

> I think [Germany] is a little Morocco sick; but in any case time may be on the side of France; for the recovery of Russia will change the situation in Europe to the advantage of France; and it is the situation in Europe that will in the long run decide the position of France and Germany respectively in Morocco. I am in hopes that when Russia recovers we may get and keep on good terms with her; if so this also will count on the side of France.[99]

Plagued with revolution, military defeat, and bankruptcy, Russia was unable to balance against Germany, and this weakness explains, in part, the French difficulties at Algeciras. A few days later, Grey remarked: "I am impatient to see Russia re-established as a factor in European politics."[100] The Russians and the French lacked capability, not resolve.

Grey believed the Germans were exploiting a situation which found both France and Russia militarily weak. He hoped that once "Russia is re-

---

[97] Lord Grey, *Twenty-Five Years, 1892–1916*, vol. 1 (New York: Frederick A. Stokes, 1925), pp. 90–91.

[98] Eyre Crowe, in reviewing the reasons for Delcassé's fall in 1907, remarked that Delcassé had failed to consider "the want of loyalty characteristic of French statesmen in their attitude to each other." Although this shows there may be interdependence between events, the attribution does not bear on French resolve toward other states. See Memorandum by Eyre Crowe (January 1, 1907), *BD*, No. 397, p. 401.

[99] Grey to Arthur Nicolson (February 12, 1906), *BD*, No. 278, p. 249. The use of the word "situation" in a sentence does not in itself suggest a situational attribution. For example, in a note to Grey, Cecil Spring-Rice wrote: "At the same time the main factor in the situation here—that is, the Emperor's personal disposition—is shrouded in mystery" (February 13, 1906, *BD*, No. 283, p. 253).

[100] Grey to Spring-Rice (February 19, 1906), quoted in Monger, *End of Isolation*, p. 281.

established" a triple entente could be formed which would be "absolutely secure." Germany could then best be checked, but not now: "The present is the most unfavorable moment for attempting to check her."[101]

Given Grey's belief that the balance of capability favored Germany, he might be expected to explain the outcome at Algeciras as revealing the Germans' weak character. Neither Grey nor any other British decision-maker suggested that the Germans lacked resolve. The Germans were a threat and would continue to be one. At various points in the crisis, Grey explained German behavior in situational terms. For example, he thought the German challenge in Morocco was partly motivated by a need for coaling stations; a need consistently blocked by Britain.[102] More common was his belief that the Germans aimed to upset the Anglo-French Entente.

In general, Grey did not understand what the German problem was. After Algeciras, he busily worked to consolidate an entente with Russia to balance against the German threat. There was no reason for Germany to fear Britain; once Germany recognized this, good relations were possible: "All that is necessary is for the Germans to realize that they have got nothing to complain of."[103] The undesirable German challenge elicited from Grey the view of a dangerous and menacing adversary, but the desirable German retreat did not lead Grey to view Germany as irresolute. As a result, he continued to view the Germans as a menace and their claims as unjust.

Grey's views were common among his Foreign Ministry colleagues. For example, reporting on the aftermath of the Algeciras defeat, the British ambassador to Germany observed: "It is evident that the idea that Herr von Holstein had been made the scape-goat for the recent failure of German Diplomacy is not without foundation."[104] The Germans might be incompetent in diplomacy, but they were not weak-willed.

What was salient to British decision-makers was not the German defeat, but the British victory. As the German leaders thought Germany resolute for ousting Delcassé (but not France irresolute), so the British thought London had demonstrated resolve, not that the Germans had shown a lack of it. Eyre Crowe, senior clerk to the British Foreign Office, illustrates this tendency to assume a reputation for one's own state,

[101] Memorandum by Grey (February 20, 1906), *BD*, No. 299, p. 267.
[102] Grey to Prime Minister Henry Campbell-Bannerman (January 9, 1906), quoted in Grey, *Twenty-Five Years*, p. 114.
[103] Minute by Grey (May 28, 1906), *BD*, No. 416, p. 358.
[104] Frank Lascelles to Grey (August 16, 1906), *BD*, No. 424, p. 366.

while in the same breath not giving a reputation to the other—in this case a defeated state. In his now-famous memorandum, Crowe argued that the Germans challenged France because of a German perception that England lacked resolve: "Her [England's] reluctance for extreme measures, even under severe provocation, had only recently been tested on the occasion of the Dogger Bank incident. It was considered practically certain that she would shrink from lending armed assistance to France." Crowe believed the Germans challenged because they thought England was irresolute.

Crowe was wrong. First, as earlier discussed, the Germans believed the British would support their challenge, not cravenly surrender to it. Second, it does not appear that the Dogger Bank episode entered into German calculations of their Moroccan challenge. The Germans did seek in the Dogger Bank affair to exploit the episode by cashing in on Russian hostility toward Britain and bring the Russians into the German orbit. The policy failed and they blamed Delcassé since he mediated the dispute. British resolve was never an issue with the Germans in the Dogger Bank affair.

Nonetheless, Crowe believed that Britain had an image problem. According to Crowe, the history of Anglo-German relations was one of "entirely one-sided aggressiveness" met by British "concession after concession." Somewhat like a "professional blackmailer," the Germans kept exploiting the British because they knew the British lacked resolve. After Algeciras, everything was different:

> The events connected with the Algeciras conference appear to have had on the German Government the effect of an unexpected revelation, clearly showing indications of a new spirit in which England proposes to regulate her own conduct towards France on the one hand and to Germany on the other. . . . The time which has since elapsed has, no doubt, been short. But . . . there is an impression that Germany will think twice before she now gives rise to any fresh disagreement.[105]

Because Crowe believed German behavior was a consequence of a British reputation for lacking resolve, a change in Britain's reputation should mean a change in German behavior. Like a cold splash of water, the British Moroccan victory would change the German image of England and result in more peaceful relations.

---

[105] Memorandum by Crowe (January 1, 1907), *BD*, appendix A, pp. 400, 414, 416, 419.

As the examination of German explanations of the Moroccan Crisis has already shown, Crowe's expectations—and those of deterrence—were wrong. People often view the same event differently. For example, where Crowe saw British resolution, Holstein saw German irresolution, and neither would have believed the views of the other. Just as the British stance at Algeciras failed to elicit from Holstein an attribution for resolve, so the German stance at Algeciras failed to elicit from Crowe an attribution for a lack of resolve. Each focused on what was most salient to themselves. In this case, Crowe had no reason for his optimism and Holstein no reason for his pessimism. As I pointed out in Chapter 1, only by treating reputation as a relational concept can we understand the role it plays in international politics.

A demonstration of resolve does not translate easily into an attribution—let alone a reputation—for resolve. This difficulty is further illustrated by English explanations of French behavior during the Algeciras Conference. By March, the Germans feared diplomatic defeat and accepted an Austrian compromise on March 6. Grey, Arthur Nicolson, and Hardinge were thrilled; the Entente would survive and peace was assured.[106] "The Germans," thought Nicolson, the British representative at the Algeciras Conference, "have been wonderfully conciliatory."[107] The French response was delayed when the French Government fell (for domestic reasons) the day after the German offer. All the major powers supported the Austro-German compromise, except the French.

Grey thought the French committed a major blunder by holding out for a better deal when they obtained everything they needed with the German offer: "It would be a great pity if France sacrificed the substance to the shadow."[108] Nicolson and Hardinge were irritated and thought the French unreasonable.[109] Regardless of the British view (which was shared by the Russians), the French insisted on standing firm.[110] This resolute French behavior was not welcomed by the British. The British viewed the French as stubborn, not resolute. In Grey's view, "the thing will soon become a joke; if only the French would take that view of it."[111]

---

[106] Monger, *End of Isolation*, pp. 276–277.

[107] Quoted in Lowe and Dockrill, *British Foreign Policy*, pp. 23–24.

[108] Grey to Nicolson (March 10, 1906), quoted in S. L. Mayer, "Anglo-German Rivalry," p. 237.

[109] Lowe and Dockrill, *British Foreign Policy*, p. 24.

[110] D. W. Spring, "Russia and the Franco-Russian Alliance, 1905–14: Dependence or Interdependence?" *Slavonic and East European Review* 66 (October 1988): 587.

[111] Minute by Grey, quoted in Mayer, "Anglo-German Rivalry," p. 238.

In general, behavior can be explained in either a negative or positive light. Just as we tend to portray desirable behavior as "frugal," "far-sighted," "assertive," and "clever," we are likely to portray undesirable behavior as "stingy," "plotting," "aggressive," and "cunning." The French were not resolved on a point of principle, but, in the British and Russian view, were being stubborn over a trivial issue.

This type of interpretation is common. When early in the conference the Germans refused to offer concessions, the Russians thought them stubborn (for this posture delayed a badly needed loan).[112] When the Russians considered continuing their losing war with Japan, Hardinge thought them "inveterate gamblers" (for Russian strength was needed to balance Germany).[113] In short, undesirable behavior will often be cast in an unflattering light. Simply being resolved does not ensure an attribution for resolve.

Most of the evidence in this section supports my argument. Contrary to the expectations of deterrence, the Austrians did not think the French demonstrated resolve or the Germans a lack of it. Austrian policy-makers simply did not pay that much attention to an affair in which their interests were not at stake, preferring instead to focus on Austria-Hungary's severe domestic problems. British decision-makers did focus on the crisis and, contrary to deterrence's expectations, used situational attributions to explain the German defeat and the French victory. For this reason, the British could not give the Germans a reputation for lacking resolve, nor could they give the French a reputation for having resolve.

French Explanations of the Conference Results

The desires hypothesis suggests that because French decision-makers viewed the outcome favorably, they should make situational explanations—the Germans should not be viewed as irresolute, the British should not be viewed as resolute. The deterrence hypothesis suggests the French should view the Germans as irresolute and the British as resolute.

French decision-makers were nervous about the future. Their victory at Algeciras was rewarding, but it did not strengthen Russian capability, or put wheels on the British fleet, or change Europe's geography.

---

[112] Spring, "Russia and the Franco-Russian Alliance," p. 586.
[113] Raymond A. Esthus, *Double Eagle and Rising Sun: The Russians and Japanese at Portsmouth in 1905* (Durham: Duke University Press, 1988), p. 165.

German capability remained undiminished and its ambition perhaps only temporarily checked. Prime Minister Clemenceau was concerned with the condition of the British army. Grey advised the French to look to the Russians to balance on land and the British to balance at sea. To this advice, Clemenceau replied: "It was very desirable that Russia should become such a counterpoise. But at present she had no efficient Government and no money, and for an indefinite period she would continue to be weak."[114] Clemenceau insisted that Britain needed an army worthy of the name.

Grey understood that the French position was difficult. Any French doubt about British reliability might lead Paris toward an agreement with Berlin and allow the Germans to keep London on bad terms with both Paris and St. Petersburg.[115] Grey was so concerned with French sensitivity to any demonstration of Anglo-German friendship that he even prevented a military band from visiting Germany because the band had turned down a similar invitation to visit France.[116]

Repeatedly the French queried the British about the state of French-British and Anglo-German relations, and repeatedly the British sought to assure them of British loyalty to the Entente. For example, Grey reassured Paul Cambon, the French ambassador to England: "If a subject like the Algeciras Conference was to arise again, France might depend upon it that our support would be just as strong and our attitude as firm as it had been before."[117] Both France and England were now so suspicious of Germany that any German effort to improve relations was assumed to be an effort to split the Entente. As Eugene Anderson observed, "They saw German intrigues everywhere—in Persia, in Abyssinia, in Paris, in London."[118] Metternich asked Grey if he thought German friendship compatible with the Anglo-French Entente. "That depends on German politics," remarked Grey. "No," countered Metternich, "it rather seems to depend on French interpretation of German politics."[119]

Even if the French viewed the British as resolute allies at Algeciras, it does not appear they assumed similar support in the future. Nor did

[114] Memo of an interview between Grey and Clemenceau (April 28, 1908), quoted in David Robin Watson, *Georges Clemenceau: A Political Biography* (Great Britain: Eyre Methuen, 1974), p. 225.
[115] Williamson, *Politics of Grand Strategy*, p. 60.
[116] Lowe and Dockrill, *British Foreign Policy*, p. 26.
[117] Grey to Bertie (November 8, 1906), BD, No. 442, p. 393.
[118] Anderson, *First Moroccan Crisis*, p. 403.
[119] Quoted in Anderson, *First Moroccan Crisis*, p. 404.

they feel certain of future Russian support. The French understood that the Russians gave them such strong backing because of the urgent Russian need for capital. After meeting with a Russian representative, French finance minister Raymond Poincaré reported that the Russians believed they had been bought off: "It is the payment of a debt which he has come to claim from France. He talked about the services rendered at Algeciras in a tone which was almost embarrassing for me."[120] The Russians received no credit from the French for being reliable allies. At most, the Russians had shown they could be bought. The French desired Russian support; they obtained that support; and they explained it in situational terms.

The French viewed both their Russian allies and their British friends much as the Germans viewed their Austrian ally. Both France and Germany were pleased with the support they received, but neither attributed to their allies a character trait of loyalty or resolve. In both cases, they explained their allies' desirable behavior in situational terms and worried that they might behave differently in the future. These responses illustrate the tendency to worry more about an ally's than an adversary's resolve. The Triplice assumed that the Triple Entente was resolved, the Triple Entente assumed that the Triplice (or at least Germany and Austria) was resolved. Yet, neither assumed their own allies were resolved. These beliefs are consistent with the four propositions on reputation formation.

Russian Explanations of the Conference Results

The peaceful end to the Moroccan Crisis pleased the Russian leadership, but it was costly. They had earned the enmity of Germany, were forced out of the German capital market, and were bound more tightly to France. They had two contradictory objectives: to settle the conference quickly to obtain an internationally sponsored loan and to avoid an open breach with Germany. They achieved the first, but not the second.

The Algeciras outcome was not obviously desirable or undesirable to the Russian leadership. Their explanations show that they viewed Germany as the aggressor and therefore the major reason for the delay in obtaining a loan. Because they found German behavior particularly undesirable, I would expect them to use dispositional attributions to explain German behavior and more situational ones to explain desirable

---

[120] Quoted in Joll, *Origins of the First World War*, p. 130.

French behavior. The deterrence hypothesis suggests that the Russians should be impressed with French resolve and unimpressed with German resolve.

The central role played by the domestic situation in Russian foreign policy explains why the minister of finance, Vladimir Kokovtsov, and the prime minister, Sergei Witte, were such important actors in the crisis.[121] Unlike the case of Austria, the domestic turmoil in Russia forced them to take an active interest in the Algeciras Conference. As Witte observed, they were "vitally concerned in the Algeciras game."[122]

The Russian foreign minister, Vladimir Lamsdorff, originally planned to work for a compromise favorable to the French. As the conference wore on, the French increasingly leaned on the Russians to pressure the Germans to accept French demands. After the Björkö surprise, the French began pushing for unambiguous Russian support. Lamsdorff and Witte begged the Germans to compromise, arguing that without a loan Russia would succumb to revolution which might spill into Austria and Germany. The Germans suggested that Russian pressure be redirected to Paris. It was not until March 21 that Lamsdorff finally sided unambiguously with the French; German "resolve" and French pressure had finally forced the Russians to stand with France and against Germany. On the day that a settlement was reached, Poincaré resumed the suspended loan negotiations; in mid-April, the Russians secured their largest loan yet.[123]

The Russians reacted bitterly to the German refusal to participate in the loan; they were being punished for supporting France. The Russian leadership does not appear to have taken the position either that Germany was irresolute or that France was resolute. Rather, they viewed the event in more situational terms. They realized the importance of Russian support to France because Paris was in a weak position. For example, shortly before the conference began, Tsar Nicholas II instructed Kokovtsov to secure a loan from Paris and added: "France's present position is by no means an easy one, and it is possible that our help might

[121] Spring, "Russia and the Franco-Russian Alliance," p. 571; David M. McDonald, "Autocracy, Bureaucracy, and Change in the Formation of Russia's Foreign Policy, 1895–1914" (Ph.D. diss., Columbia University, 1988), pp. 6–7, 16.

[122] *Memoirs of Count Witte*, p. 429.

[123] Spring, "Russia and the Franco-Russian Alliance," pp. 585–586; Oppel, "Waning of a Traditional Alliance," pp. 323–325; Geyer, *Russian Imperialism*, p. 243. The French supported the loan not only to keep their promise, but also to promote improved Anglo-Russian relations (by getting British participation in the loan) and because the French needed a strong Russia to balance against Germany. See Crisp, "Russian Liberals," p. 506.

be particularly welcome to her."[124] The tsar hoped to exploit the French situation at Algeciras. Similarly, in a report to the tsar during the crisis, Witte cast the crisis in situational terms:

> The international situation is at present such that Germany has an excellent opportunity to push France to the wall. Russia is not in a position at present to render any considerable military assistance to France. Austria and Italy will not stand in Germany's way. As for Great Britain, she is unable to help France on land, and there is no doubt but that from the military standpoint Germany is perfectly able to give France a sound beating.[125]

For Witte, capability was the issue, not resolve.

The Russians believed the Germans were unreasonable, not irresolute. It was because the Germans were so unreasonable, reports Witte in his memoirs, that their allies defected: "Germany's claims [at Algeciras] were so unfair that even representatives of her Allies, Italy and Austria, in some cases voted for France."[126] For Witte, the desirable behavior of the German allies elicited a situational explanation—it's not that Italy and Austria were disloyal, but that Germany was so unreasonable. In short and as expected, the Russians made largely situational explanations of behavior at Algeciras and viewed German behavior as unreasonable.

A review of the first Moroccan Crisis shows that my hypothesis was usually confirmed. The Germans credited no one with resolve. They viewed Rouvier as irresolute only after he became resolved and blamed British machinations for the unreasonable French position. Holstein blamed the kaiser (who blamed Holstein) and believed the French and British more, not less, likely to bluff. The German leaders were furious with the Russians for supporting their French ally. The British made situational explanations across the board, and credited no one (aside from themselves) with being resolute, and no one with lacking resolve. Toward the end of the conference, when the French showed the greatest resolve, the British and Russians thought them merely stubborn. French behavior suggests they counted on neither future British resolution nor

---

[124] Vladimir Kokovtsov, *Out of My Past: The Memoirs of Count Kokovtsov*, trans. Laura Matveev, ed. H. H. Fisher (Stanford: Stanford University Press, 1935), p. 90.
[125] *Memoirs of Count Witte*, p. 298.
[126] Ibid.

German irresolution. Because they explained allied support in terms of the situation, both France and Germany questioned the support they would be given in the future. The Russians made situational explanations for everyone but the Germans, whom they viewed as unreasonable (and worse). The Austrians were consumed by their own domestic problems and were simply glad to have the whole affair over with.

The interdependence assumption of deterrence theory was not supported. Because only the British explained French behavior as irresolute in the first part of the crisis, only the British should have expected the French to be irresolute in the second part of the crisis. They did not. Unlike Lansdowne, the new British foreign minister, Grey, remembered the French defeat in situational terms and similarly explained the French victory at Algeciras.

[4]

The Bosnia-Herzegovina Crisis

By capitulating to an Austro-German threat of war in 1909, the Russians made the First World War all but inevitable—or so many historians and political scientists believe. While the Russians vowed "Never again!" the Germans assumed that they could easily bully the Entente into another retreat.[1] Imanuel Geiss believes the Bosnian Crisis was a "dress rehearsal" for 1914 and James Joll contends that, because the Russians yielded in 1909, they were expected to yield in 1914.[2] It is clear that the two situations were different: in 1909 the Russians had no intention of fighting, in 1914 they had no intention of yielding. It is less clear how other states viewed Russia's reputation for resolve in 1914 and the extent to which Russia's reputation was dependent upon its earlier retreats. By understanding how key decision-makers explained the Russian capitulation in 1909, we can assess the role reputations for resolve played in 1914.

Although the desires hypothesis did a better job than the deterrence hypothesis in predicting attributions in the Moroccan Crisis, the case did not lend itself to a rigorous test for interdependence since it was chronologically the first case examined. Because the Bosnian Crisis followed on the heels of the crisis over Morocco, we can examine the ways

---

[1] Glenn Snyder and Paul Diesing, *Conflict among Nations: Bargaining, Decision-making, and System Structure in International Crises* (Princeton: Princeton University Press, 1977), p. 541.

[2] Imanuel Geiss, *German Foreign Policy, 1871–1914* (London: Routledge and Kegan Paul, 1976), p. 117; James Joll, *The Origins of the First World War* (New York: Longman, 1984), p. 10. See also Paul Huth, *Extended Deterrence and the Prevention of War* (New Haven: Yale University Press, 1988), pp. 183–196.

the 1906 crisis in North Africa affected decision-makers' beliefs and expectations during the 1908–1909 crisis in the Near East.

Based on the German defeat at the Algeciras Conference in 1906, the deterrence hypothesis expects all states in 1908 to view the Germans as irresolute and all states to view the French as resolute. The British, Russians, and Austrians stood by their allies and so all should view them as loyal allies. These reputations do not last long; they should be replaced by their opposites after the Bosnian Crisis. Based on the outcome of the Bosnian Crisis, the deterrence hypothesis expects everyone to view the Triple Alliance as resolute and the Triple Entente as irresolute.

In contrast, cognitive and motivated factors rather than past behavior govern the desires hypothesis. It is desirability of behavior that determines the type of explanation state leaders will make. Because observers can use dispositional attributions to give others reputations, past dispositional attributions may resurface in later crises to explain or predict behavior. For example, while the Triple Entente explained the German defeat at Morocco in situational terms, these nations viewed overall German behavior as menacing. Far from viewing the Germans as irresolute, the Entente Powers feared the Germans were set on revenge. Similarly, because no ally was credited by another with demonstrating resolve or loyalty at Algeciras, no ally should be viewed as having this character trait because of Algeciras. For example, the Germans should not view the Austrians or the British view the French as being resolute or loyal allies.

The events analyzed in this chapter support my hypothesis. Since undesirable behavior tends to elicit dispositional attributions, it is that behavior—rather than previous behavior—which governs a decision-maker's explanation. As a result, commitments appear to be more independent than interdependent. There is nevertheless enough interdependence between commitments to support the four propositions presented in Chapter 2 that determine when reputations for resolve can form: adversaries can get reputations for having resolve, but rarely for lacking it; allies can get reputations for lacking resolve, but rarely for having it.

The first part of this chapter presents some background to the crisis. The second part considers the initial reactions of the British, French, and Germans to the Austrian annexation. The third part examines policymakers' explanations of each other's behavior during the crisis and the influence of the Algeciras Conference on those explanations. The fourth part reviews how the key actors in England, France, Russia, Germany and Austria explained the outcome of the Bosnian Crisis.

BACKGROUND TO THE BOSNIAN CRISIS

The Austrians feared that Serbian aspirations for a Greater Serbia would further weaken the already crumbling Dual Monarchy. The Serbs, hankering for a Greater Serbia, hoped to unite eventually with Croatia and grab Bosnia and Herzegovina from the moribund Ottoman Empire (which had de jure control) and from the Austrians (who had de facto control). There was little the Serbs could do by themselves. They needed a backer and, after their revolution in 1903, the Serbs believed their Slav brothers in Russia would be their patron.

No one was terribly happy with the situation in the Balkans, but no one was terribly unhappy either. Afraid of war and of one another, and confronted with irreconcilable interests, the Russians and Austrians agreed to an entente in 1897 to support the status quo in the Balkans. The Russians longed for control of the Dardanelles and Bosphorus Straits to the Black Sea, which were economically vital and militarily important to their empire. Russia needed to control Romania and Bulgaria because they were believed to be stepping stones to the straits. There was also constant pressure from Russian pan-Slavs to check Austrian domination over the Slavs in the western Balkans. Unfortunately, Russian control from the Black Sea to the Adriatic posed a strategic threat to the Austro-Hungarian Empire. Equally important, it would unite Russia with small irredentist states whose ambitions required the destruction of the Dual Monarchy.[3]

The Austrians had long been interested in formally annexing Bosnia and Herzegovina. At the 1878 Berlin Conference, Britain had suggested Austrian annexation of this territory and the Russians did not object; Austrian foreign minister Julius Andrássy preferred occupation to annexation. In 1908, Austrian foreign minister Alois Aehrenthal decided it was time to annex it formally. The Austrians often referred to Serbia as "a bone in the throat" and considered it a continuing threat to the terri-

---

[3] Francis Roy Bridge, *From Sadowa to Sarajevo: The Foreign Policy of Austria-Hungary, 1866–1914* (London: Routledge and Kegan Paul, 1972), pp. 225–227; Barbara Jelavich, *The Habsburg Empire in European Affairs, 1814–1918* (Hamden, Conn.: Archon Books, 1975), pp. 139–140; Francis Roy Bridge, "Izvolsky, Aehrenthal, and the End of the Austro-Russian Entente, 1906–1908," *Mitteilungen des Österreichischen Staatsarchivs* 29 (1976): 316–318.

torial integrity of the Dual Monarchy.[4] Annexing Bosnia and supporting the independence of Bulgaria (which would swallow up parts of Serbia and act as a check against Russia) was a limited gambit to ensure Austrian security. An additional incentive to annex Bosnia was the fear that the new regime in Turkey would seek to regain control over Bosnia and Herzegovina.

Russian foreign minister Alexander Izvolsky sought to profit by Austria's intention to annex Bosnia. In exchange for his promise to give up Serbian aspirations and support the annexation, he obtained an Austrian promise to support Russian ambitions in the straits. Izvolsky and Aehrenthal arranged this in a meeting at Buchlau in September 1908.

The announcement of the Austrian annexation of Bosnia and the simultaneous announcement of Bulgarian independence created a sensation in Europe. Izvolsky denied complicity and the Russians, supported by the French and British, challenged the Austrians, who were supported by the Germans. Whereas the British and French offered St. Petersburg only diplomatic support, the Germans gave Vienna a blank check. "I have complete confidence in your judgment," Chancellor Bernard Bülow reported to Aehrenthal. "For that reason I will view whatever decision you eventually arrive at, as the one warranted by the circumstances."[5]

The crisis wore on for six months. First Austria settled with Turkey; then Bulgaria settled with Turkey; the last issue to be addressed was compensation for Serbia. The Austrians, backed by Germany, pressed the Russians to force Serbia to abandon its hope of territorial gain and to accept the annexation without compensation. The Russians delayed. At the end of March 1909, the Germans delivered a note to the Russians—some call it an ultimatum—demanding that the Russians accept the Austrian proposals or risk war. Izvolsky yielded to the demand and the crisis ended.

The Russians were humiliated and the Austrians and Germans triumphant. While the British gave only diplomatic support and the French not even that, the Austrians obtained a blank check from their German ally. After the Triple Entente's victory in the Moroccan Crisis, the Triple Alliance now tied the score.

---

[4] Luigi Albertini, *The Origins of the War of 1914*, trans. and ed. Isabella M. Massey, vol. 1: *European Relations from the Congress of Berlin to the Eve of the Sarajevo Murder* (New York: Oxford University Press, 1952), pp. 144–145.

[5] Bülow to Aehrenthal (October 30, 1908), cited by Oswald Henry Wedel, *Austro-German Diplomatic Relations, 1908–1914* (Stanford: Stanford University Press, 1932), p. 70.

Izvolsky's Strategy and Its Collapse

The Russian and Austrian foreign ministers, Izvolsky and Aehren-thal, had exchanged notes concerning the future of the Balkans and met at Buchlau to hammer out the details. Because no records were kept of the meeting we cannot be sure who promised what to whom. The standard account of the affair portrays Aehrenthal as the deceitful villain and Izvolsky as the complicitous dunce. In this rendering, Aehrenthal led Izvolsky to believe that a great-power conference would be called to permit both Austrian annexation of Bosnia-Herzegovina and greater Russian control over the straits. After the Buchlau meeting, Izvolsky began a leisurely tour of European capitals to gather support for the agreement. Much to Izvolsky's horror, Aehrenthal jumped the gun, announced his intentions, made the annexation a fait accompli, and left Russia with nothing.[6]

Although the above account captures the essence of what happened, Izvolsky was not so naive; he aimed to trick Aehrenthal but events sabotaged his plans. Izvolsky knew of Austrian intentions to annex Bosnia-Herzegovina and he believed there was no way to prevent it. It was an article of faith among the Russian leaders that any war would bring about the collapse of the empire. Peter Stolypin, the Russian prime minister, warned Izvolsky (in February 1908) that he would get no support for an adventurous foreign policy: "Any other policy than a strictly defensive one would, at the present moment, be the evil dream of an abnormal government and would spell disaster for the dynasty."[7] Stolypin was convinced that Russia "needs a breathing space" before it would be strong enough to become a great power again.[8]

Izvolsky shared Stolypin's view. After arranging the deal with Aehrenthal, Izvolsky instructed the acting foreign minister, N. V. Charykov, to inform the ministers of finance, war, and the navy of the plan: "All of them will, of course, agree with us that to strain our relations with Austria (and hence with Germany too) and to risk a war on account of Bosnia and the Herzegovina would be madness, and that we

[6] For general accounts along these lines, see Gordon Craig, *Europe, 1815–1914* (Hinsdale, Ill.: Dryden Press, 1972), pp. 438–440; Snyder and Diesing, *Conflict among Nations*, pp. 538–539; Albertini, *Origins of the War*, pp. 202–210.

[7] Quoted in William Langer, *Explorations in Crisis: Papers on International History* (Cambridge, Mass.: Belknap Press, 1969), p. 59.

[8] Quoted in D. W. Spring, "Russia and the Franco-Russian Alliance, 1905–1914: Dependence or Interdependence?" *Slavonic and East European Review* 66 (October 1988): 588–589.

are proposing the only practical way out."[9] Izvolsky thought the way out was to get compensation in the straits for the annexation which they could not prevent. Opposition to the annexation meant either "futile protest" or "threats which might lead subsequently to hostilities." Instead, Izvolsky sought a policy of "compensations and guarantees."[10]

Not only would this policy get something for nothing, but it would strengthen the Russian position in the Balkans by making Russia appear as the great defender of the Balkan states. Since "futile protest" would harm Russian prestige, Izvolsky planned to exploit anti-Austrian feelings in the Balkans and capitalize on Europe's dismay over the violation of the Berlin treaty. There would be no risk of war, Izvolsky thought, because the "Balkan governments will of course understand that we shall not go to war on account of Bosnia."[11]

His plan would work only if Russia appeared ignorant of Austrian intentions. Once Russia discovered Austrian intentions, he would claim that Russian pressure pushed the Austrians to evacuate a narrow strip of territory separating Serbia and Montenegro, but beyond this his hands were tied: "But what more can be done? To confine ourselves to a futile protest? Not, indeed, to declare war. From here there is a direct transition to compensations and guarantees in favor of Russia and the Balkan states."[12] Izvolsky wanted a conference held after the annexation in order that Austria appear "in the character of the accused, as it were, and we indeed will come forward in the role of defenders of the interests of the Balkan states, and even of Turkey herself."[13] Izvolsky wanted the annexation to occur before a congress could be held and he had a very good idea of when Aehrenthal would make his announcement.[14]

Izvolsky's policy collapsed for two reasons. First, he failed to anticipate the Bulgarian declaration of independence; it was another blow to Turkey and complicated Russian efforts to appear as the benefactor of the Balkan states. Second, he underestimated the strength of pan-Slav

[9] Izvolsky to Charykov (September 24, 1908), quoted in Bridge, "Izvolsky, Aehrenthal, and the End," p. 356.

[10] Izvolsky to Charykov (September 16, 1908), ibid.," p. 350.

[11] Ibid., p. 350.

[12] Ibid., pp. 350–351.

[13] Izvolsky to Charykov (September 24, 1908), in Bridge, "Izvolsky, Aehrenthal, and the End," p. 355.

[14] See the Russian ambassador at Vienna, Prince Urussov, to N. V. Charykov (September 17, 1908), and Izvolsky to Charykov (September 16, 1908), in Bridge, "Izvolsky, Aehrenthal, and the End," p. 348.

sympathies in Russia. When finally informed of the policy, the prime minister and the minister of finance vigorously objected to accepting the Austrian annexation. According to Charykov, Prime Minister Stolypin threatened to resign and insisted "that Russia should not give her consent to the annexation of a Slavonic land by a Germanic State, whatever political advantages this might bring to Russia."[15] Tsar Nicholas II deserted Izvolsky and issued new orders to oppose the annexation. Since war was unacceptable, Izvolsky was forced to pursue a policy of "futile protest."

Aehrenthal's Strategy

Aehrenthal was not looking for trouble. He was an arch conservative and supported resurrecting the Dreikaiserbund—an alliance between Austria, Germany, and Russia. Far from setting out to humiliate Izvolsky, Aehrenthal aimed to lessen Austria's dependence on Germany by improving relations with Russia (as well as Italy).[16] However, both the Austrians and Russians were trapped in a security dilemma. Russia's efforts to secure the straits by strengthening its position in the Balkans were an objective threat to Austria's security. Russia's defensive moves meant Austria's encirclement. Vienna's efforts to check Russian moves by strengthening its position in the Balkans were a threat to the Russian position in the straits.[17]

Aehrenthal planned to create a South Slav block within the Dual Monarchy by annexing Bosnia and Herzegovina and joining them with Croatia and Dalmatia. This South Slav block would have genuine autonomy but remain under Hungarian suzerainty. In one bold stroke, Aehrenthal would resolve the internal south Slav problems, check Serbian irredentism, strengthen Austria's position in the Balkans, improve relations with Russia, and lessen Austria's dependence on Germany.[18]

---

[15] N. V. Tcharykow, "The Reminiscences of Nicholas II," *Contemporary Review* 134 (October 1928): 448; and Arthur May, *The Hapsburg Monarchy: 1867–1914* (Cambridge: Harvard University Press, 1951), pp. 415–416.

[16] Bridge, *From Sadowa to Sarajevo*, pp. 244–245, 258–260, 290–292.

[17] F. R. Bridge and Roger Bullen, *The Great Powers and the European States System, 1815–1914* (New York: Longman, 1980); Bridge, "Izvolsky, Aehrenthal, and the End," pp. 318–320. For a slightly different view, see Paul Schroeder, "World War I as Galloping Gertie: A Reply to Joachim Remak," in *The Origins of the First World War: Great Power Rivalry and German War Aims*, 2d ed., edited by H. W. Koch (London: Macmillan, 1984), p. 119.

[18] Bridge, "Izvolsky, Aehrenthal, and the End," p. 323; Edward Crankshaw, *The Fall of the House of Habsburg* (New York: Viking, 1963), p. 336.

Aehrenthal was surprised at Europe's violent reception to his announcement of annexation. For over thirty years Austria had occupied and administered Bosnia and Herzegovina; annexation changed nothing but the legal status of the territories. The Young Turks were too weak to do more than offer a formal protest. Both Italy's and Russia's approval had been secured. France was still busy in Morocco. Britain sought good relations with Austria and had earlier helped Austria occupy the territory. Germany was informed of Austria's intent, though not its method or timing, and did not object. Besides, the Algeciras Conference revealed Germany's isolation. At an August meeting to discuss the impending annexation, Aehrenthal remarked: "They could be absolutely sure of Germany . . . for she could now depend on Austria alone."[19] In short, Aehrenthal expected the annexation to go off without a hitch.

INITIAL REACTIONS TO THE ANNEXATION

Austria's announcement of its intent to annex Bosnia and Herzegovina did not please London, Paris, or Berlin. I expect these decision-makers to use dispositional attributions to explain Austria's undesirable policy. The deterrence hypothesis expects everyone to doubt German resolve because Berlin yielded in 1906, and the Germans should feel confident in future Austrian support because of Vienna's past support.

Initial British Reactions

The British objected to the annexation for three reasons. First, the annexation coupled with the Bulgarian declaration of independence was a blow against the pro-British Young Turks. Second, they had bad relations with Germany and saw in the Austrian move the hidden hand of Germany. Third, they opposed the annexation and the Bulgarian declaration because these actions violated the Berlin Treaty.[20]

---

[19] This is Gooch's paraphrase. See G. P. Gooch, *Before the War: Studies in Diplomacy*, vol. 1: *The Grouping of the Powers* (New York: Longmans, Green, 1936), p. 394. For Aehrenthal's sanguine views, see Wedel, *Austro-German Relations*, pp. 56–57; Bridge, *From Sadowa to Sarajevo*, pp. 302–303; Jelavich, *Habsburg Empire*, pp. 151–152; and Bernadotte E. Schmitt, *The Annexation of Bosnia, 1908–1909* (Cambridge: Cambridge University Press, 1937), p. 18.

[20] Dwight E. Lee, *Europe's Crucial Years: The Diplomatic Background of World War I, 1902–1914* (Hanover, N.H.: University Press of New England, 1974), pp. 192–193; May, *Hapsburg Monarchy*, p. 417; Albertini, *Origins of the War*, p. 226.

Prime Minister Edward Grey and Permanent Undersecretary of State for Foreign Affairs Charles Hardinge roundly condemned Aehrenthal and his policy. They both assumed that Austria and Bulgaria had conspired to destroy the Berlin treaty and deal a double blow to Turkey. Grey and Hardinge dismissed as lies Aehrenthal's protests that he did not coordinate his action with Bulgaria. Grey thought it "monstrous that Austria, who was always deprecating any pressure upon the Sultan ... should now arrange with Bulgaria openly to flout the Young Turkish regime which is really pure and honest."[21] And also pro-British.[22] Hardinge first reacted with equanimity; he only wished Aehrenthal had "postponed" the annexation "for at least a couple of months" until the situation in the Balkans was calm.[23] Within the next three days Hardinge decided the annexation was "a bombshell" and that there had been "a deep-laid plot on the part of several Powers" with Aehrenthal as "the chief conspirator."[24] Hardinge said he always thought the Austrians "a charming but stupid people, and this is one more indication of their want of cleverness."[25]

The Foreign Office assumed that the Austrians were acting as a German cat's paw. For example, Hardinge believed Aehrenthal's objective was to "destroy, at the instigation of Germany, the position of England at Constantinople."[26] He thought German protests of innocence were "worthy of Ananias."[27] Far from believing the Germans were irresolute because of their 1906 defeat, the Foreign Office assumed that the Ger-

---

[21] Grey to Prime Minister Herbert Asquith (October 5, 1908), quoted in F. R. Bridge, *Great Britain and Austria-Hungary, 1906–1914: A Diplomatic History* (London: London School of Economics, 1972), p. 113. See also Grey to the British ambassador to Berlin, Edward Goschen (October 5, 1908), *British Documents on the Origins of the War, 1898–1914* (henceforth cited as *BD*), vol. 5: *The Near East: The Macedonian Problem and the Annexation of Bosnia, 1903–1909*, ed. G. P. Gooch and Harold Temperley (London: HMSO, 1928), No. 299, p. 389. The king also viewed the annexation as a "breach of faith." See Alfred Francis Pribram, *Austria-Hungary and Great Britain, 1908–1914*, trans. Ian F. D. Morrow (London: Oxford, 1951), p. 101.

[22] The Young Turk revolution had more to do with saving Macedonia and the rest of European Turkey than with advancing the cause of liberty and democracy. The British gained more than any other power from the revolution and became its greatest enthusiast. See M. B. Cooper, "British Policy in the Balkans, 1908–09," *The Historical Journal* 7/2 (1964): 267.

[23] Memorandum respecting an interview between Hardinge and Albert Mensdorff (October 3, 1908), *BD*, vol. 5, No. 287, p. 378.

[24] Quoted in Bridge, *Great Britain and Austria*, p. 112.

[25] Ibid.

[26] Hardinge to Goschen (October 20, 1908), quoted in Cooper, "British Policy," p. 270.

[27] See Hardinge's minute in Lascelles to Grey (October 7, 1908), quoted in Bridge, *Great Britain and Austria*, p. 112.

mans, Austrians, and Bulgarians were united to overthrow the Berlin treaty and to harm British interests. This response supports my argument and contradicts the deterrence argument. Also, note that in this case the British were wrong. The Germans were not complicitous and the Austrians neither anticipated nor wanted the Bulgarian declaration to precede their annexation of Bosnia.

British explanations of Russian behavior were not charitable. The best Izvolsky could hope for was to be viewed as an incompetent foreign minister rather than a treacherous schemer. None of the British actors believed Izvolsky was innocent. "From my interview with M. Izvolsky," reported the British ambassador to France, "I have the impression, I may say the conviction, that he did not quite tell me the truth, the whole truth, and nothing but the truth."[28] Hardinge believed Izvolsky had been "duped by Aehrenthal" and held him "greatly responsible" for the Balkan mess, "yet it is evident that we must do our best to support him, such as he is."[29] Although Grey had little sympathy for the "clamor of Serbia," like his colleagues he felt that Russia had to be supported.[30] The British ambassador to Russia, Arthur Nicolson, also held Izvolsky partly responsible: "I know Izvolsky very well . . . He is often not firm in personal conversation—and is unwilling to say anything which might appear to be displeasing to his interlocutors, especially when he is their guest—this is a weak trait in his character."[31] In short, the British leadership thought Izvolsky either was a liar or a fool, or had a weak character. No one offered a situational explanation for the undesirable behavior.

Perhaps the most interesting aspect of the British reaction to the annexation was their outrage that Austria and Bulgaria had violated the Berlin treaty of 1878. Grey complained to Paul Metternich, the German ambassador to England, that Austria's arbitrary violation of the Treaty of Berlin "was a great shock. It was no good having any Treaties at all, if they were to be altered in this way."[32] He has a similar view of the affair in his memoirs. The annexation was not only a "cruel blow" to Turkey but, equally important, it violated the Berlin treaty. Grey did not care about mere territorial changes; what upset him was the "arbitrary alteration of a European Treaty by one Power

[28] Bertie to Grey (October 4, 1908), *BD*, vol. 5, No. 293, p. 386.

[29] Hardinge to Nicolson (October 13, 1908), *BD*, vol. 5, No. 372, p. 434.

[30] See Grey to Nicolson (October 27, 1908), *BD*, vol. 5, No. 412, p. 470.

[31] Nicolson to Grey (October 8, 1908), *BD*, vol. 5, No. 334, p. 411.

[32] Grey to Lascelles (October 9, 1908), *BD*, vol 5, No. 350, p. 419.

without the consent of the other Powers" for this "struck at the root of all good international order."[33]

Grey's explanation was self-serving, but it appears to have been genuine. Many historians accept Grey's explanation without qualification. A. J. P. Taylor argues that the British sided with Russia not out of concern for the balance of power, but because "they were outraged by Aehrenthal's offense against the sanctity of treaties."[34]

Grey's reaction illustrates a common tendency to notice broken promises that harm one's interest, but ignore broken promises that are beneficial. This tendency ties into the more general finding that our perceptions are shaped by the desirability of another's behavior. For example, the Austrian violation of the Berlin treaty did not trouble the Germans nearly as much as earlier British violations of treaties concerning Morocco. When King Edward expressed his view in a letter to Kaiser Wilhelm that the annexation was a violation of the Berlin treaty, the kaiser responded: "Pharisee! Look at the Morocco Agreement of 1904 with France in which England threw over the Treaty of Madrid."[35]

When the Germans violated Moroccan treaties, they had no pangs of guilt. Nor did the British worry much about treaty violations that were in their own interest. In a Franco-German agreement over Morocco in February 1909, the British supported the treaty even though it violated the 1906 Algeciras Agreement.[36] Hardinge was thrilled with the agreement which increased French political control and German economic control. Although the rights of others were trampled on, Grey was not too concerned: "It will need tact and a liberal interpretation to work this agreement and the pledge for French and German co-operation in concessions is ominous for the chances of others, but politically the effect should be excellent."[37] As for the Open Door, well, it need only be "preserved on paper."[38] Nonetheless, the British *were* outraged at Aehrenthal's violation

---

[33] Edward Grey, *Twenty-Five Years, 1892–1916*, vol. 1 (New York: Frederick A. Stokes, 1925), p. 169.

[34] A. J. P. Taylor, *The Struggle for Mastery in Europe, 1848–1918* (New York: Oxford University Press, 1971), p. 454. See also Gooch, *Before the War*, pp. 46–47.

[35] Quoted in Pribram, *Austria Hungary and Great Britain*, p. 264.

[36] E. W. Edwards, "The Franco-German Agreement on Morocco, 1909," *English Historical Review* 78 (July 1963): 507; Herbert Feis, *Europe the World's Banker: 1870–1914* (New Haven: Yale University Press, 1930), p. 415; Schroeder, "World War I as Galloping Gertie," p. 121.

[37] Grey to Bertie (February 11, 1909), *BD*, vol. 7: *The Agadir Crisis*, No. 157, pp. 140–141 (this dispatch was based on a Hardinge and Grey minute; see their minutes to this document).

[38] See Grey's minute, Bertie to Grey (February 6, 1909), *BD*, vol. 7, No. 149, p. 135.

of the Berlin treaty. It threatened their interests in Turkey and upset their Russian ally. They invoked the high principle of the sanctity of treaties because the annexation had an undesirable effect on British interests.

One reason that the British reacted so self-righteously may stem from a general tendency to remember those who transgress against us, but to belittle our transgressions against others. We also tend to remember promises that help us and often have difficulty recalling those promises we wish had never been made. It appears that neither Izvolsky nor the tsar realized until after the crisis began that, in the 1870s and 1880s, Russia had three times promised the Austrians the right to annex Bosnia and Herzegovina. In a letter to his mother at the end of October, the tsar wrote: "You will understand what an unpleasant surprise this is, and what an embarrassing position we are in."[39]

Just as we are likely to forget undesirable promises, we are likely to remember desirable ones. For example, the Austrians never forgot the British support for Austrian annexation of Bosnia at the 1878 Berlin Conference. The British did forget. In a note to Nicolson, Hardinge said it was "quite possible" that they supported annexation in 1878, but they were only committed to that which they signed.[40]

The initial British reaction to the Austrian annexation of Bosnia is not surprising. As expected, British policy-makers used dispositional attributions to explain undesirable Austrian and Russian behavior. The Foreign Office held Aehrenthal primarily responsible for a policy that harmed British interests and viewed Izvolsky as a dimwitted accomplice. Also, and in contrast to deterrence's expectations, British decision-makers did not believe the German leaders were irresolute despite Berlin's 1906 retreat. The way we tend to remember and forget promises may help explain why the British were indignant at the Austrian violation of the Berlin treaty, even though they lost their moral compass when broken promises advanced their interests.

Initial French Reactions

In contrast to the thunderous British denunciation of the Austrian gambit, French leaders responded ambiguously. In a fashion similar to the Austrian view of their German ally's adventure in Morocco in 1905, the French fell in line with their Russian and British counterparts but

[39] Quoted in Lee, *Europe's Crucial Years*, p. 193; Wedel, *Austro-German Relations*, p. 56.
[40] Hardinge to Nicolson (November 25, 1908), *BD*, vol. 5, No. 464, p. 511; also quoted in Wedel, *Austro-German Relations*, pp. 56–57.

did not initially view the matter as serious. The French were uninterested in a Balkan conflict and feared either an Anglo-German war or an Austro-Russian war that might pull them into conflict with Germany. Their continuing squabble with Berlin over Morocco made them all the more reluctant to enter the fray over Bosnia.

French policy-makers worried about England's ability to make a continental commitment and were wary of German intentions.[41] Even good-faith German efforts to improve relations with France were met with suspicion. For example, after a mob attacked and killed nine Europeans near Casablanca in July 1907, the French mercilessly bombed the city and then occupied it and two other cities. Although the French had earlier occupied a Moroccan village and used other strong-arm tactics to enforce "order," the Germans remained sympathetic.[42] German interests were harmed and France stretched its rights under the Algeciras Agreement, but when the French presented their view of the incident to the Germans, they responded: "France had all our sympathies in her work of chastisement in order to safeguard the interests and guarantee the security of all the Europeans."[43] This prompted French prime minister Georges Clemenceau to remark: "As for Germany, I continue to be wary of her 'Well Done!' for if we give the least pretext, and if Bülow can pretend to believe that we have gone beyond the Algeciras Agreement, we will have a sudden about-turn, in which they seek revenge."[44]

The German defeat in the first Moroccan Crisis appears to have made Clemenceau wary of German revenge, not confident in German irresolution. His remark illustrates how observers may expect states that yield in a crisis to be more resolute in the future because they vow "Never again!" It also supports one of my propositions on when reputations form: adversaries rarely get reputations for lacking resolve.

By August 1908, the Germans had become less cooperative and Franco-German tension rose. In September, another crisis nearly as severe as the crises of 1905 and 1911 rocked Franco-German relations.[45]

---

[41] See Edwards, "Franco-German Agreement," p. 498. See also an interview between Clemenceau and Grey (April 28, 1908), in Grey, *Twenty-Five Years*, vol. 2, appendix C.

[42] Ima Christina Barlow, *The Agadir Crisis* (Chapel Hill: University of North Carolina, 1940), pp. 47–52; Geoffrey Barraclough, *From Agadir to Armageddon: Anatomy of a Crisis* (London: Weidenfeld and Nicolson, 1982), pp. 83–85.

[43] Tschirschky to Cambon (August 7, 1907), quoted in Barlow, *Agadir Crisis*, p. 52.

[44] Clemenceau to Pichon (August 10, 1907), quoted in David Robin Watson, *Georges Clemenceau: A Political Biography* (Great Britain: Eyre Methuen, 1974), p. 228.

[45] Barlow, *Agadir Crisis*, p. 62; Sidney Fay, *The Origins of the World War*, 2d ed. (New York: Macmillan, 1930), pp. 246–250.

The German consul at Casablanca assisted six deserters from the French Foreign Legion, but a French representative forcibly seized the deserters from the Germans. This trivial issue sparked a crisis that lasted until an agreement was reached in early November 1909. While the British prepared their fleet for war in defense of France, the Austrians pushed the Germans to settle with France and turn their attention to the crisis in the Balkans.[46]

Needless to say, the French were initially inattentive to the Bosnian Crisis, which began in early October. They could not have been eager to aggravate their relations with Austria, who they rightly hoped would moderate German behavior in Morocco. Yet they could not abandon their Russian ally, especially when England was taking a strong pro-Russian line. Morocco was important, but presumably not as important as maintenance of the Triple Entente.

There is a consensus among historians that among the Entente Powers, France gave the warmest response to the Austrian annexation and played a passive role in the crisis.[47] Seeking to antagonize neither its allies nor the Central Powers, the French were eager to mediate. Indeed, the French ambassador to Germany intimated to the Germans on October 3, 1908, that France would be willing to play the role of disinterested intermediary in the Near Eastern conflict.[48] Instead of believing that the Germans were irresolute for backing down at Algeciras, the French were suspicious that the Germans would seek revenge. They feared the consequences of a Balkan war and took a passive role in the crisis.

Initial German Reactions

"This much is certain," said Chancellor Bülow to the kaiser, "the circumstances attending the Austrian action, as well as its consequences, are highly undesirable for us." "Yes, very," noted the kaiser.[49] The Germans were displeased for three reasons: they had not been sufficiently consulted beforehand; they feared being dragged by Austria into a

[46] Paul M. Kennedy, *The Rise of the Anglo-German Antagonism, 1860–1914* (Boston: George Allen and Unwin, 1980), p. 444; Barlow, *Agadir Crisis*, p. 66.

[47] Gooch, *Before the War*, p. 403; Lee, *Europe's Crucial Years*, p. 192; Wedel, *Austro-German Relations*, p. 67; Cooper, "British Policy," p. 278. Albertini believes the French were first indignant but then favored Austria (*Origins of the War*, pp. 225, 227).

[48] Edwards, "Franco-German Agreement," p. 500.

[49] Quoted in Sir Sidney Lee, *King Edward VII: A Biography*, vol. 2: *The Reign: 22nd January to 6th May 1910* (New York: Macmillan, 1927), p. 638.

Balkan conflict; the Austrian action damaged further the German position in Turkey.

German foreign policy was run by Chancellor Bernard Bülow, Secretary of Foreign Affairs Wilhelm Schoen (until he became ill in November 1908 and was replaced by Alfred von Kiderlen-Wächter until March 1909), Kaiser Wilhelm, and Friedrich von Holstein. Although Holstein had resigned from his post after the Algeciras Conference, he remained influential.[50]

Although the Algeciras defeat influenced German policy-makers in many ways, it did not lead them to put more faith in their Austrian ally. Because they made situational explanations for Austrian support in 1906, they should not—and did not—credit the Austrians as reliable allies in 1908. This reaction contradicts the deterrence argument and supports my argument. It also illustrates one of my four propositions: allies rarely get reputations for having resolve.

Both Bülow and Holstein feared that Austria might defect to the Entente if not given sufficient support or if Vienna believed that Germany and Russia were becoming too close. In a note to the kaiser, Bülow warns of Austrian unreliability: "We must be exceedingly careful with all *démarches* and soundings in Petersburg. If the Russians allow the least bit to reach Vienna, the Austrians will promptly desert us and will join the Anglo-French camp with banners flying."[51] Holstein also reasoned that if Austria felt it could not count on Germany, Vienna would turn elsewhere.[52] Nor did Holstein feel that they could count on Austria to support Germany in the continuing difficulties with France in Morocco. Fearing that the French were angling for another international conference in the summer of 1908 to settle Moroccan affairs, Holstein warned: "Such a Conference would be a certain second defeat for Ger-

---

[50] In a note to Holstein, Bülow remarked: "I find that we three—you, Kiderlen, and I—work very well together." According to Norman Rich, when Kiderlen replaced Schoen in early November, Holstein's influence "had never been greater" and "all the tactics recommended by Holstein were adopted by the German government." See Bülow to Holstein (January 13, 1909), *The Holstein Papers: The Memoirs, Diaries and Correspondence of Friedrich von Holstein, 1837–1909*, ed. Norman Rich and M. H. Fisher, vol. 4: *Correspondence, 1897–1909* (Cambridge: Cambridge University Press, 1963), No. 1178, pp. 614–615 (henceforth cited as *Holstein Papers*); Norman Rich, *Friedrich von Holstein: Politics and Diplomacy in the Era of Bismarck and Wilhelm II*, vol. 2 (Cambridge: Cambridge University Press, 1965), pp. 808–809, 827, 828.

[51] Bülow to the kaiser (July 15, 1908), quoted in Ralph Menning, "The Collapse of 'Global Diplomacy': Germany's Descent into Isolation, 1906–1909" (Ph.D. diss., Brown University, 1986), p. 146.

[52] Memorandum by Holstein (June 15, 1908), *Holstein Papers*, No. 1097, pp. 535–536.

many. For, with the way the fleet question stands at present, England would adhere to France more than ever. Russia needs a French loan of a billion. We know how Italy and Spain behave. And Austria is still angry with us about the 'Seconding' telegram."[53] They could not count on Austrian support.

Holstein did not credit the Austrians with showing loyalty or resolve at Algeciras, but he did accuse Germany of showing irresolution. Algeciras was lost because the Germans yielded unnecessarily: "When the time came when Russia and others would obviously have *had* to mediate [in the Moroccan Crisis] H. M. suddenly said: 'We surrender'."[54] Holstein feared not the ambitions of Germany's enemies, but Germany's own irresolution.[55] More specifically, he believed the kaiser irresolute and assumed everyone else had a similar view: "He likes to begin his foreign policy with an attempt at intimidation, but retreats if the opposition does not at once give in. (Kruger Telegram, speech at Tangier.) This characteristic, which at first was recognized only by Uncle Edward [the king of England], is by now common knowledge. For that reason it will be difficult to find anyone stupid enough to give in to us before H. M. has time to do it himself."[56] This meant other states were likely to try and bluff Germany.

Bülow and Holstein felt they had no choice but to support Austria in its bid to annex Bosnia and Herzegovina. Shortly before the annexation, Bülow stated that the "needs, interest and desires of Austria-Hungary" governed German foreign policy in the Balkans.[57] Bülow instructed the Foreign Office to support the annexation without grumbling or hesitation.[58] Later in the crisis, Bülow argued that German security depended on supporting Austria "unconditionally" or Vienna would suffer certain defeat: "An Austrian retreat . . . would be our retreat; her humiliation would be our humiliation."[59]

Like Bülow, Holstein felt German self-interest required backing Austria. At the start of the crisis, Holstein observed that "Austria is fighting our fight."[60] The fight was to prevent a regrouping of the Algeciras powers: "Austria is fighting today—for egotistical reasons—*our* battle

[53] Holstein to Bülow (August 25, 1908), *Holstein Papers*, No. 1121, p. 556.
[54] Holstein to Monts (April 22, 1906), quoted in Rich, *Friedrich von Holstein*, p. 757.
[55] Holstein to Harden (May 4, 1907), *Holstein Papers*, No. 1026, p. 467.
[56] Holstein to Bülow (August 29, 1907), *Holstein Papers*, No. 1047, p. 488.
[57] Bülow to the kaiser (June 23, 1908), quoted in Menning, "The Collapse," p. 139.
[58] Wedel, *Austro-German Relations*, p. 69.
[59] Bülow to Monts (December 24, 1908), quoted in Wedel, *Austro-German Relations*, p. 83.
[60] Holstein to Bülow (October 11, 1909), *Holstein Papers*, No. 1141, p. 581.

against the *concert européen*, alias English hegemony, alias encirclement. . . . Once they have us at the Congress conference table, the old grouping of Algeciras will once again take shape."[61] The memory of the German defeat at Algeciras shaped Berlin's response to the Bosnian Crisis. Support for Austria ensured that Germany's only ally would not defect and England's bid for hegemony would be checked. As clear as this was to Bülow and Holstein, the kaiser had to be convinced.

The kaiser was furious with Aehrenthal for not giving prior notice of the annexation and for its effect on the German position in Turkey. He complained to Bülow: "Of course we shall do nothing against the annexation! But I am deeply offended in my feelings as an ally not to have been admitted into His Majesty's secret! . . . I keenly deplore the form the affair has taken. The lying hypocrite Ferdinand [King of Bulgaria], and the aged and venerable Emperor [of Austria] appear together on the stage amid Bengal lights as despoilers of Turkey."[62]

Bülow reports in his memoirs that a week later the kaiser had decided to oppose the annexation. After a long discussion, the kaiser accepted the Bülow-Holstein policy of unconditional support for Austria.[63] The kaiser still viewed the annexation as undesirable and regretted Aehrenthal's "fearful stupidity."[64]

Initial British, French, and German reactions to the annexation of Bosnia and Herzegovina show that undesirable behavior generally elicits dispositional attributions. This section also illustrates the various ways the Algeciras Conference influenced decision-makers' strategies. In spite of—and sometimes because of—Germany's retreat at Algeciras, the British and French saw Berlin's menacing influence everywhere. The Germans were not going to allow themselves to become trapped at another international conference where they would be in the minority and on the defensive. Their adversaries—as well as their ally—would have to be shown that Germany's irresolution was a thing of the past.

---

[61] Holstein to Bülow (October 8, 1908), *Holstein Papers*, No. 1138, pp. 577–578. Also note in this document Holstein's situational explanation for undesirable Italian behavior. He believed Italy would side with the Entente, "even if she does not want to." This opinion contradicts the desires hypothesis.

[62] Kaiser Wilhelm to Bülow (received October 6, 1908), quoted in Albertini, *Origins of the War*, p. 228.

[63] Albertini, *Origins of the War*, pp. 229–230.

[64] See the kaiser's note in Bülow to Jenisch (October 7, 1908), *German Diplomatic Documents, 1871–1914* (henceforth cited as *GDD*); vol. 3: *The Growing Antagonism, 1898–1910*, trans. and ed. E. T. S. Dugdale (New York: Harper and Brothers, 1930), No. 110, p. 306.

As Holstein put it: "It is important to show Austria that, despite the attitude of His Majesty, she *can* count on us. Later she will also have to reckon *with* us."[65]

PERCEPTIONS DURING THE CRISIS

Because the Germans yielded at Algeciras, the deterrence argument expects everyone to view the Germans as irresolute and likely to yield again. In contrast, I argue that observers can only use past behavior which elicited dispositional attributions to predict behavior. Once the Entente Powers have explained the German's defeat at Algeciras in situational terms, they should not then view the Germans as irresolute. In this section I concentrate on German, French, British, Austrian, and Russian perceptions up to the Russian capitulation at the end of March 1909.

German Perceptions and the Algeciras Conference

As if following the prescripts of deterrence—or more accurately, helping to provide those prescripts—Holstein assumed that other states inferred future German resolve from past German behavior. Stand firm! implored Holstein, for then the others will have to yield: "If we had held firm another few weeks three years ago, the Russians would have been compelled—for the sake of their loan—to advise France to give in. Now the opposite will probably occur, because France does not want a war in the east. But first they are trying their luck in Berlin."[66] Holstein thought the situation would compel the French to urge moderation on its Russian ally. By standing firm, "France will at last be forced to urge Russia to adopt a calm attitude."[67]

To the end, Holstein remained confident that German adversaries were driven by a perception of German irresolution. Just as Eyre Crowe, who was senior clerk to the British Foreign Office, earlier believed German aggression was driven by England's reputation for irresolution, Holstein believed that unblinking German support for their Austrian ally would shake the Entente from its belief in German

[65] Holstein to Bülow (October 13, 1908), *Holstein Papers*, No. 1142, p. 583.
[66] Holstein to Bülow (January 27, 1909), *Holstein Papers*, No. 1181, pp. 617–618.
[67] Ibid.

irresolution. After urging Bülow to inform the Austrians (and the world) of total German support, Holstein added: "This cold bucket of water should put a quick end to the most recent concentric bluff probably inspired by King Edward, because no one wants war." Holstein dated this letter, "12 March, Anniversary of the retreat over Morocco."[68]

During the Bosnian Crisis, as in the Moroccan Crisis, Holstein tended to explain desirable behavior in situational terms and undesirable behavior in dispositional terms. When states bowed before the German threat it was because they had no other choice; when states stood firm, it was because of Germany's reputation for irresolution. For example, when events went well in the Balkans, Holstein made situational attributions:

> The international situation has changed to our advantage because the Balkan question, which has been pending since September, has led to a defeat of the encirclement powers by Austria (who was backed by Germany). Neither England nor Russia have been able to assert their will. I am pleased, for I advised this policy and thereby brought about a change of course.[69]

He did not view the English and the Russians as irresolute; they wanted but were unable to assert their will. When events went against German interests, Holstein replaced situational attributions with dispositional ones. As the situation in the Balkans turned against German interests, Holstein found the explanation in Germany's reputation for lacking resolve:

> The Russians were ready to give in, but the English Ambassador in St. Petersburg [Sir Arthur Nicolson] advised them to remain firm because if things came to a crisis Germany would certainly retreat and leave Austria to her fate. Thereupon the Russians once again stood firm. I would like to bet that King Edward, who is in Paris at the moment, is advising there in similar fashion: "Stand firm, my nephew will give in in the end. I know him exactly, he will behave just as he did at Algeciras." There is absolutely

---

[68] Holstein to Bülow (March 12, 1909), *Holstein Papers*, No. 1185, p. 621. Holstein died May 8, 1909.

[69] Holstein in a letter to his cousin (February 12, 1909), quoted in Rich, *Friedrich von Holstein*, p. 830. Note that Holstein does not refer to France. Probably because the French had days earlier signed an agreement with Germany over Morocco, he did not view them as a hindrance to German policy.

no one who credits the Kaiser with any courage, neither foreign politicians nor the German army. Therein lies the real danger for Germany.[70]

The conniving British aimed to exploit the kaiser's irresolution. Everywhere Holstein saw indications that "Germany's reliability is being questioned."[71]

Bülow and Holstein were confident that they needed only to stand firm to "win." Bülow believed the French were uninterested in war, especially after the Franco-German agreement over Morocco: "That France wants no war in the *east* can be seen not only in the French Press but in *every* word of [French ambassador to Germany Jules] Cambon."[72] It was not that the French were bad allies or that they were afraid of war, but that their economic interests in the Balkans and in Russia made it too costly for them: "The French do not want a catastrophe on the Balkan peninsula, not only because they hold between 11 and 13 billion [francs] in Russian loans but also because they have several billion [invested] in Turkish obligations."[73] The situation, thought the Germans, called for French caution.

Bülow also felt confident that the Russians would not fight for the sensible reason that they could not win. Before Aehrenthal announced his bid for Bosnia, Bülow confided to Aehrenthal: "Concerning Russia, I am in agreement with you that she is at present hardly in a position to inaugurate an active policy."[74] Bülow remained confident that Russia would not fight: "The whole crisis can be brought to a good end by firmness towards Russia . . . Neither Izvolsky nor any other serious Russian statesman was thinking of war" and France "was firmly determined to keep the peace."[75] By the end of February, Bülow confidently wrote to the kaiser that "After all, Russia could not fight; France obviously did not wish to fight; these two Powers, therefore, would remain quiet."[76]

---

[70] Holstein letter to his cousin (March 3, 1909), quoted in Rich, *Friedrich von Holstein*, p. 830.

[71] Memorandum by Holstein (March 8, 1909), *Holstein Papers*, No. 1184, p. 620.

[72] Bülow to Holstein (January 28, 1909), *Holstein Papers*, No. 1182, p. 618.

[73] Bülow to Holstein (January 1909), quoted in Menning, "The Collapse," p. 195.

[74] Bülow to Aehrenthal (July 23, 1908), quoted in William C. Wohlforth, "The Perception of Power: Russia in the Pre–1914 Balance," *World Politics* 39 (April 1987): 361.

[75] Bülow to Aehrenthal (January 8, 1909), quoted in Schmitt, *Annexation of Bosnia*, pp. 94–95.

[76] Wedel's paraphrase of a memorandum from Bülow to the kaiser (February 22, 1909), in Wedel, *Austro-German Relations*, p. 87.

From Berlin it appeared that French and Russian disinterest in war was caused by their situation. The Germans believed that British support for Russia was a consequence of London's belief that Berlin was irresolute. These examples support the desires hypothesis.

German policy-makers continued to doubt Austrian resolve: "I hope the old Kaiser [Franz Joseph] will not lose his nerve," said Bülow. "He tends to become impatient if difficulties are not solved overnight, because in the twilight of an unhappy life he above all wants peace and quiet."[77] Holstein urged total German support for Vienna to prevent the Austrians from being frightened into submission by the Entente Powers. While Bülow and Holstein doubted Vienna's resolve in the crisis, they never doubted their adversaries' resolve.

The Germans left their Algeciras defeat with three lessons: Germany had a reputation for lacking resolve and other states would seek to exploit it; Germany was alone in the world except for Austria and so Vienna must be supported; Germany should avoid conferences when in the minority. They did not learn that Austria could be counted on in the future. Only Austria supported them at Algeciras, and it was only Austria whose resolve they doubted. German views of Vienna illustrate the proposition that while allies rarely get reputations for having resolve, they can get reputations for lacking resolve.

French Perceptions and Algeciras

The French view of Germany is ambiguous. As noted earlier, I found little evidence bearing on French explanations of German behavior after the French victory at Algeciras. In the last chapter I suggested that Paris viewed the German defeat at Algeciras in situational terms. Yet in early December 1908, when Clemenceau was asked his view of German fidelity to Austria, a British ambassador in Paris reported that Clemenceau thought the kaiser "had a physical dread of war and he thought he would hesitate if he saw himself face to face with a possible war with Russia, France and England."[78] If we assume Clemenceau's comments were genuine (rather than strategic), this evidence contradicts my argument. It also contradicts his fear stated earlier that the Germans would seek revenge. Nonetheless, it shows that an adversary can get a reputation for lacking resolve.

---

[77] Bülow to Holstein (December 7, 1909), *Holstein Papers*, No. 1163, p. 601.
[78] Memorandum by Fairfax Cartwright (December 4, 1908), *BD*, vol. 5, No. 475, p. 518.

Clemenceau's attribution is also at variance with the policy pursued by the French government in the Bosnian Crisis. If the French believed the kaiser was bluffing, they should have pursued a course that would test German resolve. Yet the French pursued a policy of moderation and conciliation. Just as the French cabinet disagreed with Delcassé's belief that the kaiser was bluffing in 1905, perhaps Clemenceau's colleagues doubted his belief that the kaiser was bluffing in 1908.[79]

The French did not press the Germans or the Austrians in the Bosnian Crisis. Instead, in January they cut a deal with the Germans over Morocco and signed the agreement on February 9, 1909. The Germans proposed this accord in early January to reduce the probability of French intervention in the Balkans should conflict occur. To obtain French pressure for Russian moderation, they needed to create a divergence of interests between the two allies. Schoen, the German foreign minister, summed up the German strategy: "Only what Russia is told by France, its ally and creditor, creates an impression there. France must exert pressure so that Russia in turn pressures Serbia and Montenegro and so that Russia will not escalate [the crisis] to [the point of] war with Austria-Hungary."[80] France would not want to pressure Russia, continued Schoen; it would do so only to prevent war. This reasoning explains why the Germans would concede to the French in February 1909 the very terms they rejected in 1907.[81]

The Germans proposed the Moroccan deal on January 6, 1909. The French responded eagerly three days later. French foreign minister Stephen Pichon insisted that the talks be viewed as a continuation of negotiations begun in 1907 so that a settlement "would have no apparent link with events in the East."[82] On the same day, the German ambassador to France reported to Bülow that Pichon told him that France would remain neutral in case of war over Bosnia.[83] Fearing war in the Balkans and aiming to remove any French temptation to intervene, and with the French seeking peaceful relations and expressing a desire to remain neutral if war occurred, Bülow believed that his Moroccan con-

---

[79] D. R. Watson argues that Stephen Pichon and Georges Clemenceau shared similar views on all major issues. See Watson, "The Making of French Foreign Policy during the First Clemenceau Ministry, 1906–1909," *English Historical Review* 86 (October 1971): 774–782.

[80] Schoen (February 22, 1909), quoted in Menning, "The Collapse," p. 193.

[81] See Watson, *Georges Clemenceau*, p. 230.

[82] Ibid.

[83] Ibid.

cession would have a considerable political pay-off in the Balkans.[84] He was right.

The French agreed to the deal because it advanced their position in Morocco and, by reducing Franco-German tension, insured against a possible war with Germany over the Balkans. The French now made clear to the Russians that if they chose war in the Balkans, they would fight alone. Shortly after signing the Franco-German agreement, the French ambassador to Russia informed Izvolsky with Pichon's authority that French public opinion would not support a Balkan war that did not involve vital Russian interests.[85] On February 26, the French ambassador in Berlin, Jules Cambon, and Kiderlen drafted an identic note to present to Belgrade with the acceptance of the other powers. Pichon then sent a note to the Russians pressuring them to accept the *démarche* to Serbia.[86] The French were now working with Germany to settle the crisis. The French proposal was quickly denounced by the Russians and rejected by the British.

French policy was at variance with a view that the Germans were bluffing. Clemenceau may have described the kaiser as irresolute, but he also feared that France would play the role of hostage in an Anglo-German war or be sucked into a Balkan war. It was fear of war in the Balkans that jump-started the stalled Paris-Berlin negotiations over Morocco. The Germans sought a free hand in the East, which the French sold to them for concessions in the West. Clemenceau may have thought the kaiser was bluffing, but this judgment is not reflected in French policy during the Bosnian Crisis. Clemenceau's view of the kaiser confirms deterrence's hypothesis on resolve. However, it appears that only one French policy-maker held this view of only one German decision-maker and it did not govern French policy. Even when a reputation for irresolution forms, it may not be consequential.

British Perceptions and Algeciras

The British disagreed with Clemenceau's view that the Germans might abandon Austria and, while sympathetic to his view of the kaiser, believed the kaiser's potential irresolution unimportant. Instead, they

---

[84] For this interpretation of German policy, see Edwards, "Franco-German Agreement," pp. 483–513; Menning, "The Collapse," pp. 174–176, 191–195; Watson, *Georges Clemenceau*, pp. 229–233.

[85] Edwards, "Franco-German Agreement," pp. 510–511.

[86] Note of the French embassy to the Russian government (February 26, 1909), quoted in Schmitt, *Annexation of Bosnia*, p. 160.

stressed situational factors that could compel the Germans to war. Responding to the French views, Hardinge and Grey noted:

> It is difficult to believe in the possible infidelity of Germany towards Austria. The information in our possession is in the opposite sense, and that Germany will repay to Austria the support given by the latter at Algeciras. It is probably true that the German Emperor has a physical repugnance to war, and that Germany would help to keep the ring in the event of war between Austria on the one hand and Serbia and Montenegro on the other. But, in the almost certain event of the complete annihilation of Serbia and Montenegro, . . . it is difficult to see how it would be possible for Germany to stand on one side.[87]

Hardinge and Grey expected the Germans to pay back Austria in the Bosnian Crisis for its loyalty in the Moroccan Crisis. As for the kaiser, he might be irresolute, but, they thought, so what? If there was a Near East conflict, they expected the Germans to go to war whether the kaiser wanted to or not.

This understanding fits with Grey's earlier view of Kaiser Wilhelm: "The Emperor's assertion that the decision of peace or war rests with him personally is worth very little: he could not refuse to declare war if his country and Ministers demanded it."[88] The kaiser's own probable "repugnance to war" would be swept aside by the rush of events. Neither Grey nor Hardinge doubted that the Germans would prefer a peaceful outcome to the Bosnian Crisis. However, they noted that Germany was in the best position to urge moderation on Austria "and we have no indication of her having attempted so far to do so."[89]

Neither the British nor the French were willing to bank on German irresolution in the Bosnian Crisis. Even if one believes that a policymaker is irresolute, situational factors can still lead to war. Not only is it difficult for an adversary to get a reputation for lacking resolve, it is still more difficult for this belief to be exploited. For example, there was a consensus among European heads of state that Russia lacked the capability for a major war.[90] Yet Russian leaders' need and preference for

---

[87] Hardinge and Grey minute to a memorandum by Cartwright (December 4, 1908), *BD*, vol. 5, No. 475, p. 519.

[88] See Grey's minute in Lascelles to Grey (August 14, 1908), *BD*, vol. 6: *Anglo-German Tension: Armaments and Negotiation, 1907–1912*, No. 115, p. 183.

[89] Hardinge and Grey minute to a memorandum by Cartwright (December 4, 1908), *BD*, vol. 5, No. 475, p. 519.

[90] See for example, Wohlforth, "Perception of Power."

peace might nonetheless be overwhelmed by events beyond their control. In dispatches from St. Petersburg, Nicolson warned that "in moments of national excitement financial considerations are lost sight of, and the torrent would break lose." Nicolson was almost certain that "the Russian government will be compelled to take up arms" if Austria attacked Serbia.[91] Holstein was certain Russia could not fight, but observed that Izvolsky might "bluff until sometime he will not be able to back down."[92] Similarly, the chief of the German General Staff, Helmuth von Moltke, believed that although France did not want war, it could not remain idle if Germany were to defeat Russia.[93] In these cases, as in the British view of Clemenceau's opinion of the kaiser, situational factors for war could overwhelm statesmen who preferred peace.

British decision-makers did not think the Germans irresolute after their defeat at Algeciras; instead, they thought them likely to seek revenge. The responsibility for most of the difficulties confronting the British Empire were found at the doorstep of Austro-German intrigue.[94] When the Austrians sought to strengthen their position in the Balkans in January 1908, the British ambassador to Austria warned that the Germans were behind that move and aimed to test the Entente in another Morocco-like challenge.[95] The Entente's victory in Morocco gave London little confidence that Berlin would not repeat the challenge. For example, in Crowe's well-known January 1907 report, he argued that German challenges were largely a function of a British reputation for lacking resolve. Their smashing victory over the Germans in Morocco meant "that Germany will think twice before she now gives rise to any fresh disagreement."[96] Crowe's optimism faded with time.

When the Germans began in September 1908 to resist the gradual French takeover of Morocco, the first Moroccan Crisis flashed before Crowe's eyes: "We are face to face with a situation resembling that which preceded the fall of M. Delcassé, and we may expect the beginning of another dose of bullying administered to the French gov[ernmen]t."[97] It seemed likely to

[91] Nicolson to Grey (February 24, 1909), *BD*, vol. 5, No. 605, p. 623; Nicolson to Grey (February 18, 1909), quoted in Schmitt, *Annexation of Bosnia*, p. 161.

[92] Holstein to Bülow (November 26, 1908), *Holstein Papers*, No. 1158, p. 598.

[93] Norman Stone, "Moltke and Conrad: Relations between the Austro-Hungarian and German General Staffs, 1909–1914," in *The War Plans of the Great Powers, 1880–1914*, ed. Paul Kennedy (London: George Allen and Unwin, 1979), p. 227.

[94] See May, *Hapsburg Monarchy*, p. 417.

[95] See Cooper, "British Policy," pp. 260–263.

[96] Crowe Memorandum (January 1, 1907), *BD*, vol. 3: *The Testing of the Entente, 1904–1906*, appendix A, p. 419.

[97] See Crowe's minute in Bertie to Grey (September 2, 1908), *BD*, vol. 7, No. 96, p. 84.

Crowe that Bülow would launch "another bullying campaign intended to frighten and cow France into a yielding mood."[98] Turning Holstein's fears on their head, Crowe reasoned that Germany was more resolved because of its Algeciras defeat: "We know of the existence of a strong and pent-up feeling of rage in Germany at the want of success she has lately had in the domain of foreign policy . . . If an 'untoward event' were to occur anywhere, it should be remembered that the present is the very time when Germany is most ready for an armed adventure."[99] The problem was not, as Holstein feared, that the British thought the Germans were irresolute, but that British decision-makers believed the Germans were resolved to avenge their earlier diplomatic defeats. Crowe viewed the Germans as resolute and willing to challenge the Entente Powers even in the same geographical area, over a similar issue, and in the same way.

Nor did the French have reason to fear for their reputation. Recalling the French ouster of Delcassé, Crowe expected that this time the French would stand firm: "It is at least possible that France will not this time be as conciliatory as was M. Rouvier's government when they dismissed M. Delcassé." And later he noted: "The French are clearly not in a temper to allow themselves to be bullied."[100] Crowe saw no reason why the earlier French "concession" meant the French would yield again. Even if Crowe viewed former French prime minister Maurice Rouvier's government as irresolute—and it appears he did not—a new government in a different situation might behave differently.

Holstein's fear and deterrence's expectation that the earlier German retreat would result in a British perception of German irresolution were wrong. British decision-makers "learned" only one lesson from the Algeciras Conference: beware the Germans for they are aggressive. Indeed, they may be more aggressive because of their earlier defeats. While Holstein was certain that the British thought Germany was irresolute and viewed this reputation as a principle source of German difficulties, the British thought the Germans resolute, aggressive, and everywhere testing the Triple Entente. This British view of the German leadership illustrates the more general proposition that while adversaries rarely get reputations for lacking resolve, they can get reputations for having resolve.

[98] See Crowe's minute in de Bunsen to Grey (September 7, 1908), *BD*, vol. 7, No. 101, p. 90.

[99] Ibid.

[100] See Crowe's minutes in de Bunsen to Grey (September 7, 1908), *BD*, vol. 7, No. 101, p. 90; Bertie to Grey (September 13, 1908), *BD*, vol. 7, No. 104, p. 93.

Austrian and Russian Perceptions during the Crisis

Unlike the Germans, French, and English, the Austrians and Russians were bit players in the first Moroccan Crisis. They stood by their respective allies at Algeciras, but were more concerned with fending off domestic turmoil than with determining who obtained what in North Africa. This disinterest may explain why the earlier crisis did not play a prominent role in their thinking during the Bosnian Crisis.

As discussed earlier, the Austrians sought to annex Bosnia to resolve their South Slav problem, not to help the Germans or avenge the German defeat at Algeciras. Aehrenthal aimed to strengthen Austria's position domestically, as well as internationally by reducing its dependence on Germany. Much to Aehrenthal's chagrin, his little annexation turned into a major crisis and, by worsening relations with the Entente Powers, increased Austria's dependence on Germany.

British denunciations of the annexation puzzled, then infuriated, Aehrenthal. He found incredible the principled British stand on the sanctity of treaties and commented sarcastically: "As far as the inviability of treaties is concerned, I suppose that this principle is about as important to England as the rights of neutral states at sea." He could not believe that "a responsible British policy-maker finds that principle so essential that he would even take the risk of war to safeguard it."[101] He thought British policy was either "an inexplicable, evil frenzy" or a "hostile policy" whose real target was Germany.[102] Seeking a rational explanation for Britain's undesirable behavior, which contrasted sharply with amenable French behavior, Aehrenthal concluded that British policy was motivated by the fight against Germany.[103] This is neither clearly situational nor dispositional. British policy sprung from London's anti-German feelings, but the cause of these feelings is unclear.

Aehrenthal stuck to his beliefs in spite of Mensdorff's best efforts to persuade him otherwise. As the Austrian ambassador to England, Albert Mensdorff felt duty-bound to report that the undesirable British behavior did indeed arise from a genuine British concern over both the sanctity of treaties and the continuing viability of the Young Turks.[104]

---

[101] Aehrenthal to Mensdorff (December 17, 1908), *Österreich-Ungarns Aussenpolitik von der Bosnischen Krise 1908 bis zum Kriegsausbruch 1914*, ed. L. Bittner and H. Uebersberger (Vienna, 1930), Nr. 768, pp. 627–630. This translation by Michael Jochum.

[102] Ibid.

[103] Bridge, *Great Britain and Austria-Hungary*, pp. 118–119.

[104] Ibid., p. 119. The situation was viewed similarly by the German ambassador to London. See Metternich to the German Foreign Office (January 7, 1909), *GDD*, No. 393, p. 319.

Mensdorff's beliefs again illustrate earlier findings that ambassadors may be better able to assess undesirable behavior and be more likely to view it in situational terms than policy-makers who remain in their own country.

Like their Austrian adversaries, the Russians do not appear to have been influenced by the Austro-German defeat at Algeciras. Far from doubting Austro-German resolve, Russian decision-makers assumed that Austria would fight and that Germany would support Vienna. Knowing that Russia could not fight, Izvolsky had originally sought to avoid the very policy of "futile protest" that he had been forced to adopt.

Izvolsky warned Serbia in October 1908 that Russia could not go to war: "Russia is not yet ready with her armaments and cannot now make war, and she is not willing to do so now on account of Bosnia and Herzegovina, come what may."[105] At the height of the Bosnian Crisis, Russian minister of war A. F. Rediger reportedly said that Russia's forces "were completely unfit for battle."[106] Rediger later informed the civilian leadership that Russia could not repel even an Austrian attack, let alone wage an offensive war.[107] Additionally, the revolutionary disturbances of 1905–1907 were a continuing concern and offered a compelling reason to avoid war. From beginning to end, Izvolsky never considered fighting Austria over Bosnia and never doubted Austrian or German resolve. The Russians did doubt French resolve and, as I discuss in the final part of this chapter, held the French partially responsible for their defeat.

German decision-makers thought that they themselves were irresolute, not that their adversaries were resolute. They doubted only their ally's resolve, fearing that Austria might either split to the Entente or yield to the enemy bloc. Whereas British opposition was driven by German irresolution, French moderation was driven by economic interests; the Germans attributed to neither power a reputation for resolve. British decision-makers learned from the Algeciras Conference that the Germans were aggressive and eager to avenge their earlier defeat. Their

---

[105] Memorandum by Nikola Pašić (October 29, 1908), quoted in Schmitt, *Annexation of Bosnia*, p. 71.

[106] Quoted in Wohlforth, "Perception of Power," p. 365.

[107] William C. Fuller, Jr., "The Russian Empire," in *Knowing One's Enemies: Intelligence Assessment before the Two World Wars*, ed. Ernest May (Princeton: Princeton University Press, 1984), p. 99.

opposition to Germany sprang from fear of Berlin's resolution, not ir-resolution. Aehrenthal found British explanations incredible and settled on the belief that London aimed to harm Germany through Vienna. The Russians never doubted either German or Austrian resolve. Not only did Russia lack the capability to defeat even Austria alone, but since 1905 Russian policy-makers had accepted as bound together the twin evils of war and revolution. From start to finish, Russian leaders never considered going to war.

The French case illustrates a difficulty in testing interdependence. Clemenceau may have thought the kaiser would yield before the Triple Entente, but where did this belief come from? Clemenceau repeatedly expressed alarm at the inadequate state of the British army and the overly adequate state of the German army. He had assumed since 1906 that the Germans would seek revenge for their Algeciras defeat and oversaw a policy of conciliation toward Germany and Austria during the Bosnian Crisis. Clemenceau's belief that the kaiser was a bluffer may stem from Algeciras, though it appears that French decision-makers explained Berlin's defeat in situational terms. It may have resulted from continuing Franco-German interaction over Morocco. Regardless, two points are clear: Clemenceau may have viewed the kaiser as irresolute; this view did not govern French behavior in the crisis.

EXPLAINING THE RUSSIAN CAPITULATION

The acting German secretary of state for foreign affairs instructed his ambassador in St. Petersburg to speak firmly:

> Tell Izvolsky we are ready to propose to Austria to invite the Powers to accept the abrogation of Article 25 of the Berlin Treaty. Before, however, we approach Austria, we must know definitely that Russia will unconditionally accept. You will inform him that we expect a precise answer—yes or no. We should regard an evasive, conditional or ambiguous reply as a refusal. We should then withdraw and let things take their course.[108]

Izvolsky said "yes" to this German note and the Bosnian Crisis ended soon afterward. How did the various powers explain this Russian capitulation? According to the deterrence argument, the Russians should

---

[108] Kiderlen's note read to Izvolsky by the German ambassador (March 21, 1909), quoted in Gooch, *Before the War*, pp. 281–282.

get a reputation for irresolution with adversary and ally alike. In contrast, I expect actors who viewed the defeat as undesirable to make dispositional attributions and those who desired a Russian retreat to make situational explanations. Most of the evidence supports my argument.

Russian Explanations

Because the Russians viewed Austrian, German, and French behavior as undesirable, I expect them to offer dispositional explanations for this behavior. The deterrence argument expects the Russians to view the French as irresolute and the Germans, Austrians, and British as resolute. My hypothesis comes closest to capturing Russian explanations.

Izvolsky could hardly be pleased that his French ally made a pact with Germany over Morocco at the height of the Bosnian Crisis, then pressured Russia to accept a Franco-German note to Serbia. The British ambassador to Russia, Arthur Nicolson, reported that Izvolsky "does not feel that he is justified in relying with any certainty on Russia obtaining any effective aid from France."[109] After the French urged Russian acceptance of the Franco-German proposal, Izvolsky reportedly said that "France had gone over bag and baggage to Austria."[110] According to Nicolson, Izvolsky was disappointed to discover that the French could not be counted on as the Austrians could depend on the Germans.[111] Izvolsky thought French support had been "très mollement" or halfhearted and weak.[112] Although these attributions are not rich with colorful invective, they are more dispositional than situational.

Izvolsky was satisfied with British diplomatic support. He was quick to contrast the vigorous and loyal support Russia received from London to the grudging, half-hearted behavior of Paris.[113] It seems likely that Izvolsky viewed the British as overly willing to risk a Russian-Austrian confrontation. When the British refused to accept the same German demands accepted by Russia, Izvolsky quickly disclaimed any responsibility for the truculent British.[114]

In a memo written April 1 to Izvolsky, the Russian ambassador to France, Alexander Nelidov, blamed the Russian defeat on Russian ca-

[109] Nicolson to Grey (March 15, 1909), *BD*, vol. 5, No. 690, p. 686.
[110] Nicolson to Grey (February 26, 1909), *BD*, vol. 5, No. 612, p. 628.
[111] Nicolson to Grey (March 23, 1909), *BD*, vol. 5, No. 752, p. 727.
[112] Quoted in Schmitt, *Annexation of Bosnia*, p. 200.
[113] Nicolson to Grey (February 27, 1909), *BD*, vol. 5, No. 617, p. 635.
[114] Schmitt, *Annexation of Bosnia*, p. 205.

pability and inadequate support from France and Britain. Drawing on the Moroccan Crisis, Nelidov noted that the "close unity of the Dual Alliance in conjunction with England brought the German attempts to a standstill."[115] To repeat the French Algeciras victory, and to resist continued Austro-German penetration of the Balkans, Russia needed to bind itself more closely to the Triple Entente. Austria demonstrated that Europe's legitimate protests could be ignored, "so we, too, once we had recovered our military power, could, in concert with France and England, at the opportune moment compel Austria-Hungary to renounce her Balkan schemes and restore freedom of action to the now subjected Serbia." The lesson of the Bosnian Crisis was simple: "diplomatic questions may be solved by threats and the exercise of strong pressure."[116] The issue was one of brute force, not resolve.

In his memoirs, former Russian foreign minister Serge Sazonov offers situational explanations for British support (which supports my hypothesis) and situational explanations for French behavior (which contradicts my hypothesis). Sazonov explains Austrian and German behavior in dispositional terms, yet at one point he does recognize that Serbia posed a serious threat to the Dual Monarchy's security. Sazonov explained Russian behavior in strict situational terms; Russia had yet to recover economically from its Far East war, the military was weak, and revolution continued to threaten: "These facts serve to explain why Russia did not take up the challenge hurled at her by the Austro-German alliance."[117]

Like Nelidov and Sazonov, Izvolsky explained the Russian defeat as a function of capability, not of resolve. Reporting Izvolsky's view, Nicolson wrote: "Russia was compelled to submit to the humiliation."[118] Izvolsky viewed the German note as an ultimatum which could not be refused without dire consequences. As an aide to Izvolsky put it: Izvolsky "capitulated in March 1909 not to a German ultimatum, but to the practical impossibility—this must be admitted and recognized openly—of making war on Austria."[119] Six months later, Izvolsky began portraying Russia's retreat as a compromise rather than a humiliation.

---

[115] Quoted in Albertini, *Origins of the War*, p. 294.

[116] Ibid., p. 293.

[117] Serge Sazonov, *Fateful Years, 1909–1916: The Reminiscences of Serge Sazanov* (London: Jonathan Cape, 1928), pp. 20, 14–20.

[118] Nicolson to Grey (March 23, 1909), *BD*, vol. 5, No. 753, p. 729. See also Nicolson to Grey (March 24, 1909), *BD*, vol. 5, No. 761, pp. 732–733.

[119] Quoted in Schmitt, *Annexation of Bosnia*, p. 199.

The Germans had acted as friends and approached the Russians "like a cooing dove bearing a message of peace."[120] It is hard to know what to make of Izvolsky's shift, except that the latter explanation puts him in a better light and might allow for improved Russian-German relations.

Russian decision-makers credited the Austrians and the Germans with being both militarily strong and aggressive. They resented the Austro-German power play and reasoned it was better to accept humiliation now in order to savor victory later. As the tsar noted to his mother: "The form and the method of Germany's action—I mean towards us—has simply been rude and we won't forget it."[121]

While I found little evidence bearing on Russian explanations of the strong British support, it appears that Russian decision-makers used dispositional attributions to explain undesirable French behavior. This response confirms both sets of hypotheses. Both the deterrence argument and my argument also expect the Russians to use dispositional attributions to explain their adversaries' undesirable behavior. In this case, it appears the Russians both stressed superior Austro-German capability (a situational attribution) and viewed the Central Powers as aggressive, menacing, and "rude."

French Explanations for the Russian Defeat

Like the Austrians after Germany's defeat at Algeciras, the French were relieved with the peaceful outcome of the Bosnian Crisis, but distressed that the crisis had come so close to war. The outcome was neither clearly desirable nor undesirable to the French. Because French policy-makers wanted the Russians to concede, they should not view the Russians as lacking resolve. The deterrence argument expects the French to view Izvolsky and his government as irresolute.

It appears that French decision-makers were speaking out of both sides of their mouth. To the Germans, Pichon said he was "very pleased" with the result of the German *démarche* to St. Petersburg.[122] To the British, Pichon assumed a slightly different position and said he was "very much disgusted at [the] result of M. Izvolsky's policy of bluff."[123]

---

[120] This is Cartwright's view of Izvolsky's position, Cartwright to Hardinge (September 20, 1909), *BD*, vol. 5, No. 870, p. 809. See also Langer, *Explorations in Crisis*, p. 89.

[121] Quoted in Lee, *Europe's Crucial Years*, pp. 203–204.

[122] Radolin to the Foreign Office (March 24, 1909), quoted in Schmitt, *Annexation of Bosnia*, p. 203.

[123] This is Bertie's paraphrase, Bertie to Grey (March 24, 1909), *BD*, vol. 5, No. 759, p. 732.

Even in this case, the onus fell on Izvolsky rather than on the Germans or Austrians. The French portrayed the German *démarche* to St. Petersburg as a reasonable and friendly offer—this portrayal elicited commentary from London: "This is a milk and water version of what actually happened."[124]

After Bülow's success in St. Petersburg, he sent identical notes to London, Paris, and Rome. Luigi Albertini observes that while the French "had been pleased with the result of the German step," they fell in line with their British ally and politely declined to accept the ultimatum.[125] London was quick to take credit for the changed attitude in Paris. Hardinge noted that stout British resistance "had the admirable effect of stiffening France, who was rather 'wobbly' in her attitude."[126] London viewed the warm French acceptance of the *démarche* with distaste, interpreted it as indicating a lack of resolve, and was pleased when the French assumed a tougher position. Berlin viewed it differently. After reading a report from Metternich that neither England nor France would accept the German note, the kaiser remarked: "This for all our politeness to Paris. That unreliable rabble follow absolutely in London's train!"[127] As expected, the desirability of French behavior determined the type of attribution.

In part because the French hid in the shadows for most of the crisis, evidence for their explanations remain sketchy. Pichon was "disgusted" with the results of Izvolsky's policies, presumably because the Russians should have accepted earlier compromises sponsored by France and Germany rather than pursue a policy which risked war but had little chance of success. In this case, Russian resolution was undesirable and therefore disparaged.

British Explanations for the Russian Defeat

Unlike their French colleagues, British decision-makers unanimously condemned Izvolsky's capitulation. As a result, I expect them to use Russian character rather than situation to explain the Bosnian defeat. Because the British were dissatisfied with the behavior of both their ally

---

[124] See Mallet, Hardinge, and Grey minute, Bertie to Grey (March 24, 1909), *BD*, vol. 5, No. 759, p. 732.

[125] Albertini, *Origins of the War*, p. 289.

[126] Hardinge to Nicolson (March 30, 1909), private letter, *BD*, vol. 5, No. 807, p. 764.

[127] Metternich to the German Foreign Office (March 26, 1909), *GDD*, No. 714, pp. 324–325.

and their adversaries, they should use dispositional attributions to explain this behavior. Since I cannot specify the content of a dispositional attribution, I assume that the attribution will bear on the other's resolve. In this case, the desires and deterrence hypotheses expect the same type of attribution. London should view St. Petersburg as irresolute, and should view Berlin and Vienna as resolute. Note that an attribution is not the same as a reputation. Only if the British use these attributions to predict or explain future behavior can we say that a reputation has formed.

Hardinge thought "Izvolsky's capitulation . . . is really too deplorable!" To prevent another such rebuff, Hardinge thought it "absolutely necessary to find a new Minister for Foreign Affairs, who shall be endowed with such character and qualities as Monsieur Stolypin possesses. This is, however, not an easy thing to find in Russia."[128] Apparently, not only was Izvolsky irresolute and "not a statesman," but so were most of the decision-makers in Russia.[129] Like Hardinge, Nicolson was "astonished that the Russian Gov[ernmen]t had capitulated with such promptitude and so completely" and regretted Stolypin's absence. "I wish," Nicolson continued, "that Izvolsky and his colleagues had stiffened their backs."[130] He thought they had exaggerated the danger.

Grey also viewed the retreat as highly undesirable and blamed Izvolsky for a needless capitulation: "The result would not be so bad, if only Izvolsky had withstood German hustling for forty-eight hours."[131] In the same dispatch, Grey pondered the consequences of Russia's retreat: "Germany will not make war upon [Russia] if not provoked, but Russia may have to withstand some provocation and bluff now and then: which however will cease if she makes her internal administration efficient and strong." This opinion is similar to Holstein's earlier belief that other states were more likely to try to bluff Germany due to Berlin's reputation for lacking resolve. When the St. Petersburg "internal administration" becomes "efficient and strong" the bluffs will cease. This prescription has more to do with organization and leadership than with military capability. In other words, the Russians yielded due to weak leadership.

In addition to their dispositional attributions, Hardinge, Nicolson, and Grey also explained Russia's defeat in situational terms. Each man

[128] Hardinge to Nicolson (March 30, 1909), *BD*, vol. 5, No. 807, p. 764.
[129] Hardinge to Nicolson (May 10, 1909), *BD*, vol. 5, No. 860, p. 799.
[130] Nicolson to Grey (March 24, 1909), *BD*, vol. 5, No. 764, p. 737.
[131] Grey to Nicolson (April 2, 1909), *BD*, vol. 5, No. 823, p. 772.

viewed the situation as difficult, but, as shown above, not difficult enough to justify the Russian surrender. For example, during the crisis Hardinge observed that Aehrenthal knew Izvolsky was in a "critical situation" and held the "trump cards" in his negotiations with the Russians.[132] After the crisis, Hardinge observed: "Izvolsky should realize the great advantage of war in the Balkans having been postponed to a later date when Russia may be in a better state of preparation, and I only hope that Russian statesmen will take the recent lesson to heart."[133] Hardinge hoped that the Russians would be better prepared next time; in a different situation, one in which the Russians had greater capability, he hoped for a different outcome.

Nicolson also looked to the situation to help explain the Russian defeat: "We should not forget that in a very few years Russia will have regained her strength, and will again be a most important factor."[134] Like Hardinge, Nicolson felt Russian policy-makers would better defend their interests when Russia was stronger. On the day of the capitulation (though perhaps before hearing about Izvolsky's retreat), Nicolson reported his view that there was little the Russians could do: Russia "sees before her, and M. Izvolsky has more than once recognized the fact in conversation with me, two powerful adversaries acting in close harmony towards a common object, which is to establish Austrian and indirectly German influence firmly in the Balkan Peninsula."[135] It seems that Nicolson believed situational and dispositional factors worked hand in hand to produce the distasteful outcome of the Bosnian Crisis: "Russia is temporarily weak, with a timorous Foreign Minister."[136] Izvolsky's personal failings were compounded by the situation.

Grey also realized that the Russians were still "unprepared for war."[137] The British rejected the argument that the Austro-German victory revealed the Triple Entente too weak to resist the Austro-German combination. "It is not the right deduction," minuted Louis Mallet, "to say that the Triple Entente was too weak to resist the Central Powers in this matter. It was not worth their while to do so." "This is true," added Grey, "and it is also true that M. Izvolsky did not give either us or

---

[132] Hardinge to Nicolson (November 25, 1908), *BD*, vol. 5, No. 464, p. 511.

[133] Hardinge to Nicolson (April 12, 1909), *BD*, vol. 5, No. 834, private letter, p. 781. See also Hardinge's April 1909 memorandum, *BD*, vol. 5, appendix 3, p. 824.

[134] Nicolson to Grey (March 24, 1909), *BD*, vol. 5, No. 764, p. 737.

[135] Nicolson to Grey (March 23, 1909), *BD*, vol. 5, No. 752, p. 726.

[136] Nicolson to Grey (March 24, 1909), *BD*, vol. 5, No. 764, p. 736.

[137] Grey to Bertie (April 30, 1909), quoted in C. J. Lowe and M. L. Dockrill, *The Mirage of Power*, vol. 3: *The Documents* (Boston: Routledge and Kegan Paul, 1972), p. 467.

France the chance of saying whether we should help him to make better terms."[138] In these quotes we see both situational and dispositional attributions. The Triple Entente did not fail. Had the interests been greater, and had Izvolsky consulted his allies before yielding, the outcome would have been different.

In the above examples, British decision-makers offered both dispositional and situational explanations for undesirable behavior. They understood that Izvolsky's situation was difficult, but nonetheless believed the capitulation unnecessary. A different actor, such as Stolypin, would have held out for better terms. Situation did not govern the outcome; the irresolution of Izvolsky and his colleagues did. The deterrence hypothesis on resolve also expected the British to view the Russians as irresolute.

The British view of the French is ambiguous. London was on the whole pleased with the improvement of Franco-German relations, but doubted French fidelity to the Triple Entente. As earlier noted, Hardinge thought the French irresolute. It took British resolve to stiffen the backs of the "wobbly" French. The French kept secret their Moroccan negotiations with the Germans and consulted neither the British nor the Russians; both were informed of the agreement on the eve of its signing. Before the agreement was signed, Hardinge speculated that the French were "secretly coquetting" with the Austrians to obtain German concessions in Morocco. He then contrasted British and French support for the Russians: "[Britain] has been perfectly loyal which is more than can be said of the attitude of the French which has been incomprehensible to me."[139] This opinion fits with Hardinge's later view of the "wobbly" French.

Nicolson also believed the French "were anxious to give Austria a lift" in exchange for Austrian help in Morocco.[140] The unreliability of the French, thought Nicolson, contributed to Russia's difficulties: "Had Russia been stronger at this moment, and had she been able to rely with more confidence than is actually the case on material support from her ally France, she would, I am disposed to believe, have adopted a firmer attitude and employed sterner language."[141] Nicolson thought the

---

[138] Nicolson to Grey (March 29, 1909), *BD*, vol. 5, No. 801, p. 758.

[139] Hardinge to Cartwright (January 26, 1908), quoted in Cooper, "British Policy," p. 278.

[140] Nicolson to Grey (January 20, 1909), quoted in Bridge, *Great Britain and Austria-Hungary*, p. 279.

[141] Nicolson to Grey (March 23, 1909), *BD*, vol. 5, No. 752, p. 727. This note may have been written before Nicolson heard of Izvolsky's retreat.

Franco-German agreement was the beginning of the end of the Triple Entente, for France was now "a quarter of the way towards a fuller understanding with Germany."[142]

While British policy-makers were pleased that a trouble spot in Franco-German relations had been settled, they were disappointed with the tepid French support for Russia. Hardinge believed the source of French behavior, which he viewed as disloyal, sprung from French interests in Morocco. Both Hardinge and Nicolson feared Paris might defect from the Entente if France lost its Russian ally. They deduced this possibility from the logic of the situation rather than from the personal qualities of Parisian policy-makers. Whereas they viewed disposition as governing the Russians in an admittedly difficult situation, they used situation to explain the disloyal French behavior. In his memoirs, Grey also offers a situational explanation for French behavior in the Bosnian Crisis.[143] Because London viewed French behavior as partly desirable and partly undesirable, my hypothesis cannot determine which type of perception will govern. Had the British opposed the Franco-German deal over Morocco, their explanation would probably have become more dispositional.

Both my argument and the deterrence argument expect the British to view the Germans as resolute. For example, Nicolson was certain that their adversaries' policy arose from a desire to avenge Algeciras and destroy the Triple Entente: "My firm opinion is that both Germany and Austria are carrying out a line of policy and action carefully prepared and thought out. Algeciras had to be revenged; the ring broken through; and the Triple Entente dissipated.... [Russia] had to be frightened out of the entente, and the first step towards this has been eminently successful."[144] Nicolson then argued that London should not be surprised if both France and Russia moved into the German orbit, since neither trusted the other nor could stand alone against the Central Powers.

Hardinge also feared that Russia "would be compelled by her military weakness to come to terms with Germany."[145] France, continued Hardinge, would prefer allying with Germany to standing alone. Both Hardinge and Nicolson viewed the Germans as a continuing threat and Fairfax Cartwright (the British ambassador in Vienna) thought the Germans were extortionists.[146] To summarize their view: the Germans and

---

[142] Nicolson to Grey (March 24, 1909), *BD*, vol 5, No. 764, p. 736.

[143] Grey, *Twenty-Five Years*, p. 167.

[144] Nicolson to Grey (March 24, 1909), *BD*, vol. 5, No. 764, p. 736.

[145] Memorandum by Hardinge on the possibility of war, *BD*, vol. 5, appendix 3, p. 825.

[146] Cartwright to Grey (March 29, 1909), *BD*, vol. 5, p. 759.

their Austrian second were driven by their twin ambitions to revenge Algeciras and to deal a death blow to the Triple Entente; the Central Powers exploited Russian military weakness and Izvolsky's irresolution to accomplish these aims. As at Algeciras, British policy-makers found German behavior frightening because they did not believe it was governed by the situation.

Further insight into London's views may be found in Cartwright's explanation of Aehrenthal's behavior. Why did the Austrians choose peace rather than war, especially when they could finally be rid of troublesome Serbia? Rather than credit Aehrenthal for his choice, Cartwright explained it away: "I believe that [Aehrenthal] felt that it was in his own personal interest to solve the crisis peacefully for should war have ensued from it, he would have had to encounter the displeasure of the Emperor and of public opinion to which the idea of a war for such issues was highly unattractive and even repugnant."[147] Aehrenthal's desirable behavior elicited from Cartwright a situational explanation.

British perceptions of the Russians, Germans, and Austrians support my hypothesis. British decision-makers viewed the undesirable Russian behavior in sharply dispositional terms even while recognizing situational constraints. They viewed French behavior as mixed and tended to use situation more than disposition to explain this behavior. There were no redeeming qualities to Austrian or German behavior.

After Algeciras, the Germans worried that others viewed them as irresolute. They should have had the opposite worry; the British viewed them as aggressive and bent on revenge. British policy-makers could have explained Austro-German behavior in the Bosnian Crisis in situational terms—the Austrians aimed to resolve their South Slav dilemma with a simple juridical change which had Russian support; the Germans felt compelled to assist their ally to prevent an Austrian defection to the Entente. Instead, British policy-makers preferred a more devious explanation. They assumed that the Dual Powers conspired to revenge Algeciras, break the Entente, and dominate the Balkans. Although the British felt compelled to assist the Russians to preserve the Entente, they did not assume that the Germans felt similarly constrained to assist Austria. They explained undesirable Austro-German behavior in dispositional terms.

[147] Cartwright to Grey (March 29, 1909), *BD*, vol. 5, No. 802, p. 760.

German Explanations for the Russian Defeat

Because the Germans were pleased with their solution to the Bosnian Crisis they should explain the Russian defeat in situational terms. The deterrence argument predicts the opposite: the Germans should view the Russians and the French as irresolute and the Austrians as resolute. The evidence supports my hypothesis. Acting Secretary of State for Foreign Affairs Kiderlen, Chief of the General Staff Moltke, and Chancellor Bülow all offered situational interpretations of the Russian capitulation.

Kiderlen took great pride in the *démarche* he drafted and sent to St. Petersburg which resulted in their retreat: "I knew that the Russians were not ready for war, that they could not go to war in any case, and I wanted to make what capital I could out of this knowledge."[148] Kiderlen reported to the Austrians that he intended with the *démarche* "to press Izvolsky to the wall and expedite a clear and precise answer."[149] This was also Moltke's view. Moltke reported to Franz Conrad, his Austrian counterpart: "Your Excellency, let us look into the future with confidence. As long as Austria and Germany stand shoulder to shoulder . . . we shall be strong enough to blast any ring [around us]. Many will break their teeth [trying to crack] this Central European bloc."[150] Their adversaries were not irresolute. They would try again to break Austro-German power. But the chance for war had been missed; the Entente was growing stronger by the day. The Bosnian Crisis, continued Moltke, had offered an opportunity for war "which will not come so soon again under such propitious circumstances." The Triple Entente lacked capability, not resolve. The favorable situation of 1909 might not again appear.

Bülow appears to have viewed the event in similarly situational terms. In his farewell address to the kaiser, Bülow claims to have offered the following advice: " 'Don't repeat the Bosnian business.' His Majesty (mistrustful): 'That was a triumph for you.' Myself: 'Situations in foreign policy seldom repeat themselves. Last winter we had a set of circumstances which will probably never be so favourable to us

---

[148] Kiderlen made this boast to a Romanian politician, Take Jonescu, as reported in Jonescu, *Some Personal Impressions* (New York: 1922), p. 53, quoted in Schmitt, *Annexation of Bosnia*, p. 195. Schmitt observes in a note that one historian doubts the authenticity of the language.

[149] Austria-Hungary's ambassador in Berlin, Ladislaus von Szögyény to Aehrenthal (March 21, 1909), quoted in Schmitt, *Annexation of Bosnia*, p. 195.

[150] Moltke to Conrad (March 19, 1909), quoted in V. R. Berghahn, *Germany and the Approach of War in 1914* (London: Macmillan, 1973), p. 80.

again.'"[151] Bülow's memory may have been "helped" by later events. Nonetheless, it does fit with the contemporary view held by his chief of staff. Bülow probably believed that his Bosnian victory was a vindication of his tactics and the military build-up he oversaw. Elsewhere in his memoirs and in spite of 1914, he thought that "by means of our strength as a Continental Power, we tore the web which encompassed us."[152] Again, he used German capability, rather than Russian resolve, to explain the Austro-German victory. These explanations support the desires hypothesis and contradict the deterrence hypothesis.

I found no evidence immediately after the Russian capitulation bearing on German perceptions of France or Britain. By standing firm even after the Russian capitulation, the British were practically more Russian than the Russians. I would expect Berlin to use dispositional attributions to explain London's undesirable behavior. The preceding section shows that German decision-makers did not view the French as irresolute, but rather as compelled by their financial and Moroccan interests to support a peaceful settlement. The German emphasis on capability also suggests that the Austrians were not credited for being resolved.

Austrian Explanations for the Russian Defeat

As in the above case, the desires hypothesis expects the Austrians to use situational attributions to explain the desirable outcome of the crisis; the deterrence hypothesis expects Vienna to view the Russians as irresolute. It appears that the Austrians preferred situational to dispositional explanations.

Aehrenthal thought his Bosnian adventure would increase Austria's independence from Germany; instead, the Austrians felt ever more dependent on their German neighbor. The British ambassador to Austria noted Austrian discomfort with the German role in resolving the crisis: "There is not much rejoicing here over the idea that Austria-Hungary is under a debt of obligation to Germany. Germany has a way of making Austria-Hungary feel how dependent she is upon Berlin and all the love she is now showering upon this country is little appreciated for the embraces of Germany rather resemble a strangle."[153] The Austrians did

---

[151] Quoted in Albertini, *Origins of the War*, p. 287. Bülow offered similar advice to his successor, Bethmann Hollweg; see *Memoirs of Prince von Bülow*, trans. Geoffrey Dunlop, vol. 3 (Boston: Little, Brown, 1932), p. 15.
[152] Quoted in Schmitt, *Annexation of Bosnia*, p. 252.
[153] Cartwright to Tyrrell (April 7, 1909), *BD*, vol. 5, No. 829, p. 777.

not wish to credit the Germans for causing Izvolsky's retreat. Instead, they advanced the theory that Izvolsky yielded to prevent publication of compromising documents held by Austria. Izvolsky's story of the terrible German ultimatum was merely a cover to justify his retreat before his colleagues.[154]

The Austrians not only passed this interpretation on to foreigners, but accepted it as the correct interpretation of the event. For example, the Austrian ambassador to Russia, Leopold Berchtold, attributed the victory to Aehrenthal's forcefulness: "The hint I dropped, after receiving the instructions of 7 March, of the possibility of the publication of the documents seems to have brought him to his senses. There is no doubt that without that step we should today be exactly where we were."[155] Berchtold's explanation is more situational than dispositional. Rather than viewing Izvolsky as irresolute, Berchtold thought Izvolsky behaved as would any sensible person.

Aehrenthal also believed Izvolsky's surrender a product of the situation. According to G. P. Gooch, Aehrenthal offered situational explanations for the Austrian victory in a dispatch to Berchtold: "The failure of Russian policy, first in the Far East, then in the Near East, was due to a misreading of the real situation by her rulers. Perhaps a more realistic course might now be adopted, virtually involving a return to the policy of the Three Emperors' League."[156] The Russians were not irresolute, they simply misread the situation. The Russian defeat should awaken the Russians to pursue the "more realistic" course which Aehrenthal had advocated for years: a return to the conservative triumvirate of the Dreikaiserbund.

The Austrian chief of staff, Franz Conrad, believed a great opportunity had been missed. Sooner or later, war would erupt in the Balkans. He reasoned better war now, when Russia was weak, "before she regained her strength."[157] The Austrian emperor consoled the dispirited Conrad by pointing out that Austria could not rely upon German promises of support; "one must not presume too much of her," warned Franz Joseph.[158]

---

[154] Ibid., pp. 776–777.

[155] Berchtold to Vienna (April 4, 1909), quoted in Albertini, *Origins of the War*, p. 292.

[156] This is Gooch's paraphrase of a dispatch from Aehrenthal to Berchtold (*Before the War*, p. 416).

[157] This is Gooch's paraphrase of a July 2, 1909 memo to Aehrenthal (*Before the War*, p. 417).

[158] Quoted in Bridge, *From Sadowa to Sarajevo*, p. 316.

As noted earlier, the British refused to accept the "yes" or "no" *démarche* when it was delivered to London, though they eventually accepted nearly identical terms. Hardinge thought this "might be a climb-down" but it had "the advantage of showing to the whole world that we are ready to stretch a great many points to secure European peace."[159] The Russians immediately disclaimed any responsibility and the French went along only grudgingly. According to Alfred Pribram, Aehrenthal fiercely resented the British action and became convinced that London aimed to create new difficulties and further obstruct Austria's efforts to reach a peaceful settlement.[160] Aehrenthal viewed Britain as an obstinate trouble-maker, not, as Hardinge expected, as a state resolved to secure peace in the Balkans.

Aehrenthal did not consider London resolute or St. Petersburg irresolute. Paris had been reasonable (rather than irresolute) throughout the crisis. The Germans had been helpful, but it was Vienna's blackmail that had tipped the scale and forced Izvolsky to surrender. It was now hoped that Russia would pursue a sensible policy and ally with, rather than against, Austria-Hungary. In short, Vienna used situational attributions to explain the Russian capitulation rather than attribute to the Russians a lack of resolve. Austrian policy-makers also used the situation to explain desirable French behavior, and gave Berlin little credit for its help in successfully ending the crisis. Finally, it appears they explained undesirable British behavior in dispositional terms.

Russian, French, British, German, and Austrian explanations for the outcome of the Bosnian Crisis confirm the desires hypothesis. The Russians thought of the French as irresolute and unreliable and the Austrians and Germans as co-conspirators exploiting temporary Russian military weakness. The French wanted the Russians to yield earlier and were, if anything, dismayed that Izvolsky stood firm as long as he did. While French decision-makers referred to Izvolsky's "policy of bluff," they failed to mention, or failed to recall, Clemenceau's earlier belief that the kaiser was bluffing. The British were as alarmed as the French were relieved at the outcome. London thought the leadership in St. Petersburg irresolute and hoped for better leaders. With a different lead-

---

[159] Hardinge to the king (March 26, 1909), quoted in Lowe and Dockrill, *The Mirage of Power*, vol. 1: *British Foreign Policy 1902–1914*, p. 84.

[160] Pribram, *Austria-Hungary and Great Britain*, pp. 140–141.

ership, and with greater capability, Russia's behavior in a future conflict with the Dual Powers might be different.

Only the French and British criticized Izvolsky. The Germans stressed their clever diplomacy which exploited Russia's inability to wage war and France's disinterest in a Balkan conflict. The Austrians felt Izvolsky had sensibly yielded to Vienna's pressure. They hoped that a more realistic policy—meaning a turn toward Austria away from the Entente—would now take root in St. Petersburg. The deterrence hypothesis correctly predicted that the British would view the Russians as irresolute, but, contrary to its expectations, no one else thought the Russians were irresolute and only the Russians viewed the French as irresolute. As the desires and deterrence hypotheses expected, Russian, British, and probably French decision-makers viewed the Germans as aggressive and dangerous.

CONCLUSIONS

British explanations of German behavior illustrate how dispositional attributions can be interdependent. While the British explained away German retreats, they used dispositional attributions to explain the undesirable German challenges. Far from thinking the Germans were irresolute, the British thought the Germans were determined to avenge Algeciras and smash the Entente. This perception of Germany continued to influence British explanations of subsequent German behavior and was reinforced by heavy-handed German tactics in the Bosnian Crisis. While the Russians stressed Austro-German capability, and the British stressed Russian irresolution, both London and St. Petersburg continued to view the Dual Powers as aggressive and dangerous. The longer a state's behavior is viewed as undesirable, the greater the chance that a reputation will form.

We can begin to see that the four propositions made in Chapter 2 have validity. The British view of the Germans illustrates why adversaries can get reputations for having resolve. British decision-makers viewed German challenges as undesirable and made corresponding dispositional explanations, for example, the Germans are aggressive. And yet, because they made situational attributions to explain the German defeat at Algeciras, the image of the aggressive German persisted. Similarly, because the Germans and Austrians used situational attributions to explain the Russians' Bosnian capitulation, they could not give the Russians a reputation for lacking resolve.

According to the other two propositions, allies can get reputations for lacking resolve, but rarely get reputations for having resolve. For example, the British objected to the Russian capitulation and correspondingly viewed them as irresolute. If the British use this explanation to predict or explain future Russian behavior, then London has given the Russians a reputation for lacking resolve. It may be difficult, however, for allies to get reputations for being resolute. For example, neither Vienna nor Berlin credited the other for being resolute in their Bosnian victory. Similarly, neither Paris nor London gave the other credit for being resolute in their Algeciras victory. In both cases, decision-makers explained away their ally's desirable behavior.

The evidence in this chapter shows that policy-makers tend to use dispositional attributions to explain undesirable behavior and situational attributions to explain desirable behavior. This chapter afforded a better opportunity than the preceding one to test for interdependence. Whereas I concluded in Chapter 3 that commitments did not appear interdependent, I have now shown that dispositional attributions are sometimes interdependent. The next chapter examines the 1911 Agadir Crisis. Following on the heels of the Bosnian Crisis and occurring in the same region and over the same issues as the first Moroccan Crisis, the Agadir Crisis offers the best opportunity yet for testing the independence or interdependence of commitments.

[5]

The Agadir Crisis

The 1911 Agadir Crisis began in 1904. Delcassé hoped to obtain Morocco for France by compensating England, Russia, and Italy, but not Germany. The Germans would not stand for this treatment and their resistance started the first Moroccan Crisis, which ended in Germany's defeat at the conference table at Algeciras in 1906. The French continued to push for control of Morocco; the Germans continued to resist. In 1909, another crisis over Morocco resulted in a stalemate. The Germans obtained stronger guarantees of their economic rights in Morocco, while France obtained German recognition of predominant French political rights in Morocco.

The French continued to push. Slowly but surely, they stepped on German economic rights, ignored treaty commitments, and began turning Morocco into a French protectorate. The Germans wanted compensation and, to be sure they got it, in 1911 sent the gunboat *Panther* to a closed Moroccan port, Agadir. In the midst of Franco-German wrangling over German compensations, the British jumped into the fray. In Lloyd George's Mansion House speech, the British advised the Germans to take full account of British interests or else. London successfully turned a dangerous situation into an explosive one. But the crisis ended with a whimper, not a bang. The Germans accepted less than they wanted, the French gave away more than they wanted, and everyone expected war in the not-too-distant future—this was about the only thing upon which all the parties agreed.

During the Agadir Crisis, the British and French were certain that the Germans were aggressive bullies bent on continental domination. French and British decision-makers consistently portrayed undesirable

German behavior in menacing dispositional terms, while easily explaining away Berlin's defeats as produced either by unique situations or a bout of German good sense revealing moderation and prudence. They never thought the Germans were irresolute. Similarly, the Germans, and the kaiser in particular, came to believe that nothing but superior capability would stop the British encirclement; they never doubted their adversary's resolve. Berlin explained Russia's tepid (and therefore desirable) support of France in situational terms; the French made the same type of explanation for the reluctant support Austria offered Germany. No one viewed an adversary as irresolute.

The French thought London acted only to advance British interests, not out of a sense of treaty obligation, or love of France, or a resolute character. Most British decision-makers were never confident that the French would not split to the Triple Alliance and credited themselves for saving France. With few exceptions, neither ally used resolve to explain the other's behavior.

This chapter has four parts. The first one sketches the major events of the Agadir Crisis, then presents in more detail German reactions to the gradual French advances in Morocco, culminating with the French march to Fez and German calculations behind the decision to send the *Panther* to Agadir. This section then discusses German objectives and strategy up to the Mansion House speech. The second part presents British, French, and Russian explanations of one another from the *Panther*'s arrival at Agadir to Lloyd George's speech. The third part explores British, French, German, Austrian, and Russian explanations of one another's behavior from the Mansion House speech to the German retreat. The fourth part reviews the deterrence argument and the evidence. I also discuss the disconfirming attributions and consider (but do not adopt) an alternative theoretical assumption that might explain the empirical discrepancies. In spite of sometimes failing my first test, the events discussed in this chapter, as well as the previous two historical cases, provide a solid empirical base in support of my argument.

BACKGROUND TO THE AGADIR CRISIS

Compared to the Bosnian Crisis, the details of the Agadir Crisis are straightforward. There were four key events: the French march to Fez (May 21, 1911), the arrival of the German gunboat *Panther* at Agadir (July 1), Lloyd George's Mansion House speech (July 21), and the final

Franco-German agreement over Morocco and the Congo (signed on November 4, 1911). While historians agree that these were the signal events of the Agadir Crisis, they disagree over the motives behind these events. To take one example, the Mansion House speech has spawned a cottage industry for historians, who debate whether the speech was directed more at France than at Germany.[1] Because I am interested in how actors explained events at the time, I can sidestep most of these debates. One question is important: what did Germany want?

The controversy over German motives is important for two reasons. First, determining whether the German leadership was satisfied with the outcome depends in part on whether Berlin sought to split France from the Entente, or only to achieve "just" compensation in the Congo. Second and less important, by knowing what the Germans were after, we can better gauge how accurately the Entente Powers perceived the challenge. While the first reason is important to determining the desirability of the outcome to the Germans, the second reason is interesting for it may illuminate the reasons for the divergent views of the Triple Alliance and the Triple Entente.

The Agadir Crisis: What Happened

Though all the action in the Agadir Crisis took place in the West, it served as the catalyst for the three Balkan wars in the East.[2] The Italians exploited German preoccupation in Agadir to launch their war against the Turks for Tripoli, which further weakened the Ottoman Empire and thereby encouraged the Balkan states to begin their own wars. If during the struggle for Morocco both sets of alliances feared war, after the struggle they expected it. How the French stole Morocco, whose only value was supposedly enhancing the prestige of whomever obtained it, is the story of Agadir.

---

[1] As usual, A. J. P. Taylor started the debate. See Taylor, *The Struggle for Mastery in Europe, 1848–1918* (New York: Oxford University Press, 1971), p. 471. See also Richard A. Cosgrove, "A Note on Lloyd George's Speech at the Mansion House, 21 July 1911," *Historical Journal* 12/4 (1969): 698–701; Timothy Boyle, "New Light on Lloyd George's Mansion House Speech," *Historical Journal* 23/2 (1980): 431–433.

[2] For the best account of the crisis, see Ima Christina Barlow, *The Agadir Crisis* (Chapel Hill: University of North Carolina Press, 1940). Also see Luigi Albertini, *The Origins of the War of 1914*, trans. and ed. Isabella M. Massey, vol. 1: *European Relations from the Congress of Berlin to the Eve of the Sarajevo Murder* (New York: Oxford University Press, 1952), see esp. chap. 6.

Neither the 1906 Algeciras Agreement nor the 1909 Casablanca Agreement settled the Moroccan problem. The Casablanca Agreement gave France predominant political rights and Germany equivalent economic rights in Morocco. This distinction between politics and economics was vague and led to the collapse of the agreement. While the Germans were "scrupulous" in upholding their end of the 1909 bargain, the French consistently pressed for ever more control of Morocco.[3]

In keeping with the times, no one considered asking the Moroccans what they wanted. In early January 1911, the Zaers rebelled against the French and gave Paris an opportunity to "restore order" and further consolidate its control in Morocco. Citing the danger to European settlers, the French began military operations in Moroccan ports. It remains unclear whether the French manufactured the crisis or sincerely believed in it; the Germans had their doubts.[4] On April 28, Paris warned Berlin that French troops might have to be sent to Fez—in violation of its treaty commitments—and on May 15 Jules Cambon, the French ambassador to Germany, informed the Germans that the occupation had begun. Paris continued to insist, perhaps sincerely, that the occupation was both necessary and temporary; they claimed to be acting entirely in the spirit of their treaty commitments.

The other powers were not so sure. British, Russian, and German decision-makers all understood that while occupation was easy, leaving would be more difficult. The former Russian foreign minister, and now Russian ambassador to France, Alexander Izvolsky, thought French policy-makers were fooling themselves if they thought they could take Morocco without compensating Germany. Once the French occupied Fez, Izvolsky thought little could be done but wait for the German response: "the first act of the Morocco 'drama' has been happily brought to a conclusion; the second, and much more dangerous, phase begins now."[5]

The Germans had watched French moves warily. Although always remaining diplomatically correct, they warned Paris from the start that

---

[3] Barlow, *Agadir Crisis*, pp. 86–87; G. Lowes Dickinson, *The International Anarchy, 1904–1914* (New York: Century, 1926), p. 200.

[4] Joanne Stafford Mortimer, "The Moroccan Policy of Bethmann-Hollweg, 1909–1912" (Ph.D. diss., University of Pennsylvania, 1960), pp. 90–94; Samuel R. Williamson, Jr., *The Politics of Grand Strategy: Britain and France Prepare for War, 1904–1914* (London: Ashfield Press, 1990), p. 141; Barlow, *Agadir Crisis*, p. 187.

[5] Izvolsky to Neratov (May 11, 1911), quoted in B. De Siebert, *Entente Diplomacy and the World: Matrix of the History of Europe, 1909–14* (London: George Allen and Unwin, 1921), No. 679, p. 588.

an extended occupation of Morocco would annul the Algeciras and Casablanca Agreements. Responding in early April to Jules Cambon's insistence that the occupation was only temporary, the German foreign minister, Alfred von Kiderlen-Wächter, replied: "They will not believe you in Germany if you speak of temporary occupation. When has one seen an occupation of this nature end? Was it so in Egypt?"[6] Berlin offered increasingly stern warnings throughout April and May. Upon being told by Jules Cambon that French troops had been sent to Fez, Kiderlen warned that he would accept the occupation for a "reasonable" amount of time before declaring the Algeciras Agreement dead and resuming Germany's "liberty of action."[7]

The French thought it sensible to meet with the Germans to see if they could arrange yet another agreement over Morocco. At the end of June, Jules Cambon began negotiations with Kiderlen, who at the time was visiting a health spa to "expiate his table excesses."[8] There was vague talk of concessions outside of Morocco and the meeting ended with Kiderlen saying, "bring us something from Paris."[9]

No sooner had Cambon returned to Paris than the government collapsed on June 23. The new government was not formed until June 28; Joseph Caillaux became the new prime minister and Justin de Selves replaced Jean Cruppi as foreign minister. On July 1, the Germans politely informed the new government that they had sent the gunboat *Panther* to Agadir to protect German citizens. Because Agadir was a closed port, everyone knew there could be no German citizens there. To solve this legal difficulty, the Wilhelmstrasse ordered the nearest German to head for Agadir to be rescued. A ship's officer noted that one of the "natives" was "prancing on the beach" with his hands on his hips, suggesting that he might be a European; the *Panther* promptly rescued him.[10]

Shortly after announcing the *Panther*'s arrival, the British foreign minister gave an interview to the German ambassador to England. Sir Edward Grey expressed to Paul Metternich Britain's concern over the German move, and Metternich insisted there was nothing to be con-

---

[6] Quoted in Barlow, *Agadir Crisis*, p. 181.

[7] Quoted in Barlow, *Agadir Crisis*, pp. 194, 202; Mortimer, "Moroccan Policy," pp. 92–95.

[8] Geneviève Tabouis, *The Life of Jules Cambon*, trans. C. F. Atkinson (London: Jonathan Cape, 1938), p. 200.

[9] Cambon to Cruppi (June 22, 1911), quoted in Barlow, *Agadir Crisis*, p. 212.

[10] Recounted by Taylor, *Struggle for Mastery*, p. 467.

cerned about. The Germans never addressed the British concerns, believing they were not obliged to respond. German inaction annoyed and alarmed the Foreign Office and provided the justification for approving David Lloyd George's speech at the Mansion House.[11]

Increasingly concerned that France might concede to German demands, give away British economic interests, or damage the Entente, the Foreign Office brought out the heavy artillery: they allowed the chancellor of the Exchequer, Lloyd George, to turn the issue into one of prestige. Reading from a prepared text, Lloyd George declared that Britain's prestige would be maintained at any cost. Should anyone treat Britain "where her interests were vitally affected as if she were of no account in the Cabinet of nations, then I say emphatically that peace at that price would be a humiliation intolerable for a great country like ours to endure."[12] To be sure the Germans got the message, the Foreign Office tipped off the press to the speech's significance and target.[13] As Winston Churchill put it in a letter to his wife: the Germans "sent their *Panther* to Agadir and we sent our little *Panther* to the Mansion House."[14]

The Germans did not react well to British "big stick" tactics. Grey was so alarmed after meeting with German ambassador Metternich, that he advised Churchill: "The Fleet might be attacked at any moment. I have sent for McKenna to warn him."[15] One historian even describes the British decision-makers after the Mansion House speech as "sick with neurotic fear."[16] Fortunately, the fear of war and preparations for it led to nothing. The Germans accepted some French proposals as a basis for

[11] The Germans should have responded to British concerns, but it is not clear that they were obliged to; Grey specifically forbade Metternich from treating his oral communication as a note. See Grey to Count de Salis (July 4, 1911), *British Documents on the Origins of the War, 1898–1914* (henceforth cited as *BD*), vol. 7: *The Agadir Crisis*, ed. G. P. Gooch and Harold Temperley (London: HMSO, 1932), No. 356, p. 334.

[12] Extract from Speech of Lloyd George on July 21, 1911, at the Mansion House, *BD*, vol. 7, No. 412, p. 391.

[13] Oron James Hale, *Publicity and Diplomacy: With Special Reference to England and Germany, 1890–1914* (New York: The University of Virginia Institute for Research into the Social Sciences, 1940), pp. 388–392.

[14] Quoted in Keith M. Wilson, *Empire and Continent: Studies in British Foreign Policy from the 1880s to the First World War* (New York: Mansell Publishing Limited, 1987), p. 95.

[15] Reginald McKenna was First Lord of the Admiralty. Quoted in Winston S. Churchill, *The World Crisis*, vol. 1 (New York: Charles Scribner's Sons, 1923), p. 44.

[16] Barlow, *Agadir Crisis*, p. 311. See also Michael G. Fry, *Lloyd George and Foreign Policy*, vol. 1: *The Education of a Statesman: 1890–1916* (Montreal: McGill-Queen's University Press, 1977), pp. 141–143.

negotiation in early August and the talks ended successfully in mutual compromise on November 4, 1911: Germany guaranteed it would not object to a French protectorate in Morocco and promised its interests there were exclusively economic, while France ceded to Germany part of its holdings in the Congo.

It is difficult to say who "won." One can argue that the Germans did, for they forced the French to take account of German interests and obtained compensations from France. The French may be viewed as the victors, for they obtained their long-sought Moroccan protectorate at little cost. Both sides may be viewed as victors, for they resolved a troublesome issue that hindered better relations. In hindsight, it is evident that everyone lost. The public and press in both countries objected to the agreement, diminishing the gains and exaggerating the concessions. The German press dismissed the territory Germany gained in the Congo: "Ah! it is beautiful beyond description. And how many square miles! Its value is to be measured, not merely by square miles, but by standards of real worth—such as the export of bacilli or the prospect of a profitable traffic in sand for our breeders of canaries."[17] In contrast, the French press described the sacrificed territory as "marvelous shores frequented by all the beasts of the Garden of Eden, by all the magical beauty with which painters liked to fill their pictures of the creation of the world."[18] Both countries underwent a nationalist revival and both sides said "Never again!"[19]

Because the Entente decision-makers exaggerated German objectives—they thought the Germans aimed in the Agadir Crisis to split the Entente and get a Moroccan port—they thought the Germans suffered a defeat. The German press and elite opinion shared this view. This reaction was partly Kiderlen's fault, for it appears he purposefully excited the German nationalists so he could use domestic pressure as a lever against the French.[20] Although German decision-makers were initially satisfied with the outcome—as I discuss next, their objectives were relatively modest—they came to view it as a defeat.

---

[17] Quoted in E. Malcolm Carroll, *Germany and the Great Powers, 1866–1914: A Study in Public Opinion and Foreign Policy* (New York: Prentice-Hall, 1938), p. 683.

[18] Quoted in James Joll, *The Origins of the First World War* (New York: Longman, 1984), p. 113.

[19] For a psychological explanation of this tendency to exaggerate the value of our concessions, see the special issue of *Political Psychology* 13 (June 1992), devoted to prospect theory.

[20] Carroll, *Germany and the Great Powers*, pp. 656–657.

German Objectives and Strategy up to the
Mansion House Speech

Like Izvolsky's strategy before the Bosnian Crisis, Kiderlen's strategy before the Agadir Crisis was a limited bid to strengthen his state's security. Rather than seek to split the Entente and gain a Moroccan port (which is what some historians believe), it seems that they had a more modest agenda: save German prestige by making the French address German rights by offering Berlin compensation.[21]

Kiderlen's May 3 memo presents the German strategy. In it he argues that France will not compensate Germany unless forced to do so: "We should gain nothing by protesting and it would mean a moral defeat hard to bear."[22] Berlin would ask Paris to abide by its treaty agreements and leave Morocco, but France would be unable or unwilling to do so. As a result, Kiderlen would declare that due to the force of circumstances the Moroccan treaties were annulled and Germany regained its freedom of action. By sending the *Panther* to Agadir, Germany would have a "clenched pledge" and could then "look quietly on the further development of things in Morocco and to wait to see whether perhaps France will offer us suitable compensation in her colonial possessions."[23] Kiderlen does not discuss splitting the Entente or keeping a Moroccan port. He spends little time on Britain's probable reaction, noting only that Berlin should select a port far from the Mediterranean, which "should make it unlikely that England would raise objections."[24] It seems he wanted compensation for a German pledge renouncing Berlin's rights in Morocco.[25]

Alfred Zimmermann, the German undersecretary of state for foreign affairs, turned Kiderlen's idea into a concrete plan in his own memo written at the end of May. Were the Germans to allow France to turn Morocco into a French protectorate, it would be evident to all that the "Germans had suffered a diplomatic reversal." This outcome would

---

[21] Imanuel Geiss concludes: "Compared with Germany's ambitious aims at the beginning of the crisis, the result was nothing but a thinly disguised defeat for the Empire." See Imanuel Geiss, *German Foreign Policy, 1871–1914* (London: Routledge and Kegan Paul, 1976), p. 135; also see Fritz Fischer, *War of Illusions: German Policies from 1911 to 1914*, trans. and ed. Marian Jackson (London: Chatto and Windus, 1975), esp. chap. 5.

[22] Memorandum by Kiderlen (May 3, 1911), *German Diplomatic Documents*, vol. 4: *The Descent to the Abyss, 1911–1914* (London: Methuen, 1931), p. 3. Henceforth cited as *GDD*.

[23] Quoted in Barlow, *Agadir Crisis*, p. 221.

[24] Memorandum by Kiderlen, *GDD*, p. 3.

[25] Dwight Lee, *Europe's Crucial Years: The Diplomatic Background of World War I, 1902–1914* (Hanover, N.H.: University Press of New England, 1974), p. 250.

cause a wave of indignation in Germany and a demand for compensations in colonial areas, but France would never voluntarily offer valuable concessions. "The French press would not allow it, and the English press would support its French counterpart." For Germany to get anything, it must take firm measures.[26] Both Kiderlen and Zimmermann noted that England would need to be reassured to keep it quiet.[27]

Saying he was in complete agreement with the Zimmermann memo, Kiderlen approved it and added: "I certainly do not wish to take part if we don't now use our trump cards and let the Moroccan problem be finally decided to our disadvantage. We shall then be for a long time without political influence in the world."[28] Just as Izvolsky had hoped to turn a certain defeat into a victory, Kiderlen hoped to save Berlin's reputation by making France pay for breaking its promises to Germany. The policy was nothing more than an attempt to gain prestige and compensation.

The kaiser did not get it; he thought the more the French were tied down in Morocco, the better. Because a war over Morocco was impossible, there was nothing to be done.[29] He nonetheless approved the plan. As the talks dragged on and war seemed increasingly possible, the kaiser began objecting to Kiderlen's hard-line tactics. He would not go to war over Morocco.[30]

Twice Kiderlen offered to resign (on July 17 and 19) due to the kaiser's opposition to his policy. Kiderlen argued that to avoid "immeasurable shame" Germany must be prepared to risk war, for only then would no war be necessary.[31] The German chancellor, Theobald von Bethmann Hollweg, pleaded Kiderlen's case to the kaiser. He argued that failure to get compensations meant "our credit in the world, not only for the moment, but also for all future international actions, suffers an intolerable blow." Following Kiderlen's views, he argued that if Germany accepted only frontier rectifications, France would become "so haughty that we must, sooner or later, take her to task."[32]

---

[26] Mortimer's paraphrase of the Zimmermann memo ("Moroccan Policy," pp. 109–110).

[27] Barlow, *Agadir Crisis*, pp. 228–229.

[28] Quoted in Fischer, *War of Illusions*, p. 73.

[29] See Baron von Jensich, in the emperor's suite at Achilleion in Corfu, to Kiderlen (April 30, 1911), *GDD*, p. 2; Mortimer, "Moroccan Policy," p. 95.

[30] Barlow, *Agadir Crisis*, pp. 262–264; Sidney Fay, *The Origins of the World War*, 2d ed. (New York, Macmillan, 1930), p. 286.

[31] From Kiderlen's first offer of resignation, quoted in Mortimer, "Moroccan Policy," p. 155.

[32] Bethmann to the kaiser (July 20, 1911), quoted in Barlow, *Agadir Crisis*, p. 266.

Germany's reputation was on the line. Conceding now would cost Germany in all "future international actions" and lead the French to think that Germany was a bit actor on the international stage; such a misperception would lead to a future war with France. Both stunningly wrong and utterly predictable, Bethmann, Kiderlen, and ultimately the kaiser, continued to be hypnotized by reputation's spell.

None of the three German policy-makers—Bethmann, Kiderlen, and the kaiser—wanted war and they had no intention of fighting over Morocco; yet all three were convinced that they had to risk war to get France to concede and to save Germany's reputation. But no one else knew what the Germans wanted, let alone why they wanted it. If the British overreacted, it was in part because of the silence from Berlin and the mystery over German objectives. Kiderlen may have been able to get what he wanted without sending the *Panther*, but once it was sent, advising the British (who would tell the French) not to worry would defeat the purpose of having sent it. Even by getting what they originally wanted, compensation from France for stealing Morocco, the Germans appeared to retreat. The Kiderlen plan, which sounded so reasonable in May, ended in a German defeat as ignoble as that of the 1906 Algeciras Conference.

British, French, and Russian Explanations up to the Mansion House Speech

According to the deterrence hypothesis, the Austro-German victory over the Russians in the Bosnian Crisis should lead observers to expect the Central Powers to be resolute and the Russians to be irresolute. It may be, however, that reputations form only in a specific region or over a specific issue. For example, according to the specific deterrence hypothesis, observers will expect the Germans to be irresolute in the Agadir Crisis because they were earlier irresolute in the same region and over the same issue.

Rather than address the "specific" and "general" deterrence hypotheses on resolve for each set of attributions, I occasionally address the specific hypothesis or note when the specific and general hypotheses have identical predictions. Focusing on the specific deterrence hypothesis would not make the deterrence argument stronger; it is wrong at least as often as the general deterrence hypothesis on resolve. For example, while the general deterrence hypothesis can partially account for French and British views of Germany before its Agadir retreat, the region-specific hypothesis is completely wrong. Because the specific and general deterrence hypotheses often have opposite expectations, one of them is likely to be right in any given situation. As in the preceding two chapters, when I refer to "the deterrence hypothesis" or "the deterrence argument" the reference is to the general deterrence hypothesis on resolve. I discuss both deterrence hypotheses in the conclusion.

British Explanations

No one in the British Foreign Office doubted German resolve. From the first Moroccan Crisis to the end of the Bosnian Crisis, British decision-makers thought the Germans were aggressive "bullies" driven by their past defeats and their hope of splitting the Triple Entente. This image carried over to the beginning of the Agadir Crisis. From German negotiations with Russia at Potsdam, to German negotiations with Britain over naval limitations, British decision-makers assumed the Germans aimed to smash the Entente.[33] Charles Hardinge—permanent undersecretary of state for foreign affairs (1906–1910) and viceroy to India (1910–1916)—captures the spirit of the Foreign Office when he notes: "I fully believe in the theory of Germany's intention, if possible, to dominate Europe to which we are the only stumbling block."[34] Far from thinking the Germans irresolute because of their earlier Moroccan defeat, Eyre Crowe—senior clerk to the Foreign Office—thought the Germans aimed to try their luck again in a repeat of Algeciras with the ultimate objective of undermining the Entente.[35]

Though the Germans had yet to do anything and continued to act correctly, this behavior was only cause for suspicion. The British ambassador to Germany, Edward Goschen, observed: "The attitude of the German Government . . . is so correct that it is almost alarming."[36] Sir Edward Grey kept his balance and managed not to be alarmed by Ger-

---

[33] See for example, Goschen to Nicolson (January 7, 1911), and Nicolson to Hardinge (April 19, 1911), in Harold Nicolson, *Portrait of a Diplomatist: Being the Life of Sir Arthur Nicolson* (New York: Houghton Mifflin, 1930), pp. 245, 247–248.

[34] Hardinge to Nicolson (March 29, 1911), quoted in Zara Steiner, "Foreign Office Views, Germany and the Great Powers," in *Ideas into Politics: Aspects of European History, 1880–1950*, ed. R. J. Bullen, H. Pogge von Strandmann, and A. B. Polonsky (London: Croom and Helm, 1984), p. 39.

[35] Crowe's minute, Cartwright to Grey (April 22, 1911), *BD*, vol. 7, No. 214, pp. 197–198.

[36] Goschen to Nicolson (May 5, 1911), *BD*, vol. 7, No. 253, p. 229.

man good behavior. With the French occupation of Fez, Grey expected trouble: "We are already skating on very thin ice, in maintaining that the Act of Algeciras is not affected by all that has happened, and every week that the French remain at Fez the ice will get thinner."[37] Grey feared that if the Algeciras Agreement were abandoned, France and Spain would divide up Morocco and Germany would have to be given something for its consent. Unlike Crowe, Hardinge, and Goschen, Grey believed the Germans could be bought off with territorial compensations outside of Morocco. After the German move to Agadir, Grey's views fell more in line with his colleagues'.

That the Germans would send a gunboat to Agadir indicated to Crowe that the Germans were ready to fight for Morocco: "The fact that Germany has taken the plunge, must give rise to the supposition that she now considers herself in a position to face the danger of an armed Franco-British opposition to her." Grey minuted: "I quite agree with Sir Eyre Crowe."[38] Arthur Nicolson, the permanent undersecretary of state for foreign affairs, thought the Germans were repeating their Algeciras tactics and Grey's private secretary thought the German aim was nothing less than to split the Entente.[39] Crowe depicted the Germans as blackmailers, once again extorting France to pay off Berlin: "Nothing will stop this process except a firm resolve, and the strength to refuse, and, if necessary, to fight over it." Nicolson agreed entirely. Later, Crowe argued that in this "trial of strength" any concession, be it in Morocco or the Congo, courted disaster.[40]

"Bullying blackmailing extortionists" qualify as dispositional attributions. The British found German behavior highly undesirable and, as expected, offered dispositional rather than situational attributions to explain this behavior. The deterrence hypothesis also expected London to view Berlin as resolved. In this instance the evidence supports both hypotheses.

Both the desires and the deterrence hypotheses have common predictions (but different explanations) for how the British will interpret

[37] Grey to Bertie (June 1, 1911), *BD*, vol. 7, No. 307, p. 277.

[38] Crowe's and Grey's minutes, Count de Salis to Grey (July 2, 1911), *BD*, vol. 7, No. 343, pp. 325–326.

[39] See Nicolson to Grey (July 4, 1911), *BD*, vol. 7, No. 354, p. 333; William Tyrrell to Hardinge, (July 21, 1911), in C. J. Lowe and M. L. Dockrill, *The Mirage of Power*, vol. 3: *The Documents: British Foreign Policy 1902–1922* (Boston: Routledge and Kegan Paul, 1972), p. 434.

[40] Crowe's minute, Bertie to Grey (July 12, 1911) and Crowe's minute, Bertie to Grey (July 18, 1911), *BD*, vol. 7, Nos. 369, 392, pp. 349, 372.

French behavior. Because the British viewed French behavior in the first part of the Agadir Crisis as undesirable, I expect them to offer dispositional explanations. Since they did not credit the French for being resolved in 1906 or 1909, past behavior should have no effect. According to the deterrence argument, because the British should have viewed French behavior in the preceding crisis as revealing its ir-resolution, British expectations of the French in the next crisis will be affected.

Even before the French march to Fez, London objected to French policy. In March, Crowe described the French as pursuing a "vicious" policy which would sacrifice British economic interests on the altar of better Franco-German relations.[41] Even though they objected to French policy, the German threat gave them little choice but to support France.

As early as May, Nicolson had said that it was essential to support France against Germany. Later, he said that were Germany "to detect the slightest wavering or indifference on our side, she would no doubt press France with extreme rigor and the latter would either have to fight or surrender."[42] The British ambassador to France, Francis Bertie, also insisted on complete support of France, urging this throughout May, June, and July.[43] Like Nicolson, Bertie feared that if the French doubted British support, they would come to terms with Germany.[44] While continuing to fear that the French would sell out British interests in Morocco, Crowe urged complete support of France which was "not in a position now to refuse" German demands.[45] Because they neither trusted France, nor thought it capable of resisting Germany alone, Crowe, Nicolson, and Bertie all felt it imperative to give France unqual-ified support.

Grey intended to support France, but not to the same extent as his colleagues. As already noted, he assumed the Germans would have to be compensated. While a German port on the Mediterranean was unac-

[41] Crowe's minute, note by Paul Cambon (March 14, 1911), *BD*, vol. 7, No. 192, p. 179.
[42] Nicolson to his colleagues in early May, quoted in Keith M. Wilson, *Empire and Continent: Studies in British Foreign Policy from the 1880s to the First World War* (New York: Mansell Publishing, 1987), p. 90; Nicolson to Goschen (July 18, 1911), *BD*, vol. 7, No. 395, p. 375. See also Nicolson to Hardinge (July 5, 1911) and Nicolson minute, Bertie to Grey (July 18, 1911), *BD*, vol. 7, Nos. 359, 392, pp. 338, 373.
[43] See Wilson, *Empire and Continent*, p. 103; Steiner, "Foreign Office Views," p. 180.
[44] See Bertie to Nicolson (July 12, 1911), *BD*, vol. 7, No. 376, p. 359; Bertie to Crowe (July 21, 1911), quoted in Cosgrove, "Note on Lloyd George," p. 699.
[45] Crowe's minute, Bertie to Grey (July 12, 1911), *BD*, vol. 7, No. 369, p. 349. For Crowe's fear of a French sellout, see Crowe's minute, Goschen to Grey (July 14, 1911), *BD*, vol. 7, No. 383, p. 363.

ceptable, he would accept an unfortified port on the Atlantic.[46] In a private letter to Bertie the day before Lloyd George's speech at the Mansion House, Grey made clear the limits of British policy: "We are bound and prepared to give [France] diplomatic support, but we cannot go to war in order to set aside the Algeciras Act and put France in virtual possession of Morocco. If she can get that for herself we are bound not to stand in her way . . . but if we go to war it must be in defence of British interests."[47] Should Germany try to humiliate France, and thereby endanger the Entente, then Grey thought British interests would be at stake.

Undesirable French behavior elicited some dispositional attributions from British decision-makers; their fear that the French might jump to the Triple Alliance suggests they doubted French resolve. But they doubted French resolve at least in part because they doubted French capability. As Crowe put it, Paris was in no position to resist Berlin's demands. The British made no mention of French resolve in the first Moroccan Crisis, and no mention of the tepid support France gave Russia in 1909. The deterrence hypothesis also expects the British to view the French as irresolute, but as noted there is no evidence that this view was based on past French behavior.

There is not much evidence on British views of Russia and Austria in the period before the Mansion House speech. The British apparently did not consider Russian support of France worth discussing. Nor did they spend much time discussing Austria's tepid support of Germany. Whereas I would expect desirable Austrian behavior to elicit situational explanations from the British, the deterrence hypothesis would expect London to view Austria as irresolute because of its lukewarm support of Germany.

The British ambassador to Austria, Fairfax Cartwright, was confident that Austrian foreign minister Alois Aehrenthal would moderate German behavior if the crisis became acute, not because Aehrenthal was irresolute, but for situational reasons: "in the first place, because he does not want to help to bring about a European conflagration, and secondly, because the French Government are just beginning to be a little more

---

[46] See Grey to Bertie (July 19, 1911), quoted in Barlow, *Agadir Crisis*, pp. 279–280. The British Admiralty also had no objections to a German port on the Atlantic in Morocco; they thought it would be a German liability, not an asset. See Arthur J. Marder, *From the Dreadnought to Scapa Flow: The Royal Navy in the Fisher Era, 1904–1919*, vol. 1: *The Road to War, 1904–1914* (London: Oxford University Press, 1961), pp. 240–241.

[47] Grey to Bertie (July 20, 1911), *BD*, vol. 7, No. 405, p. 382.

amiable about the floating of Austro-Hungarian loans on the French Market."[48] Aehrenthal pursued a middle-of-the-road course, for which Nicolson gave him credit—"His position is somewhat embarrassing and he has a difficult course to steer in complicated situations like the present"—while Crowe said dismissively that "Count Aehrenthal is as usual playing a double-faced game."[49] While Cartwright and Nicolson leaned toward situational attributions to explain Austrian behavior, Crowe offered a dispositional explanation (but not one bearing on resolve). On balance, my hypothesis was supported and deterrence's expectations were contradicted.

From the beginning, London assumed the Germans were seeking a repeat of Algeciras. They believed the Germans were resolved to try the same tactics, in the same area, with the same countries, over the same issues, as they did before—even though the Germans lost before. As it appeared in 1906, it seemed even more so by July 1911: the British did not think the Germans irresolute for backing down at Algeciras. London did hope to recreate the situation that led to the German retreat: a united front willing to risk war. In spite of past demonstrations of British resolve—which decision-makers like Crowe had counted on to dispel the German perception that Britain lacked resolve—the Germans challenged again. Rather than think the Germans were responding to French bullying, or offer some other situational explanation, they preferred dispositional explanations such as the German bully, the German extortionist.

French Explanations

"The Emperor is a treacherous rogue," responded the French president, Armand Fallières, upon first hearing Berlin had sent the *Panther* to Agadir.[50] Fallières, like other French decision-makers, explained the undesirable German move in dispositional terms. For example, the French ambassador to England (Paul Cambon) commented: "It is difficult to specify immediately the reason for this German action; one could think that the German Emperor wanted to satisfy his esteem after the naval

[48] Cartwright to Nicolson (May 11, 1911), *BD*, vol. 7, No. 262, p. 235.

[49] Nicolson and Crowe minutes, Russell to Grey (July 10, 1911), quoted in F. R. Bridge, *Great Britain and Austria-Hungary, 1906–1914: A Diplomatic History* (London: London School of Economics, 1972), p. 175.

[50] Notes by Jules Cambon, *Documents diplomatiques français (1871–1914)*, second series, vol. 14 (Paris: Imprimerie Nationale, 1955), appendix, p. 751. Henceforth cited as *DDF*.

review in Portsmouth, and to show the world that he had freedom of action in the seas."[51] Because the situation did not govern the kaiser's behavior, Paul Cambon had difficulty understanding why he behaved as he did. Rather than offering the obvious situational explanation that the Germans were reacting to perceived French aggression and in defense of German treaty rights, Paul Cambon suggested the German move was inspired by the kaiser's quest to "satisfy his esteem" and demonstrate German freedom of maneuver at sea.

While Paul Cambon thought the German action sprang from the kaiser's desire to satisfy his esteem, his brother, Jules Cambon (the French ambassador to Germany), mainly blamed Kiderlen: "I attribute the act of Agadir to several causes. The first is Kiderlen's incontestable disappointment caused by the failure of his proposals on the subject of Moroccan railroads." In this example, ascribing subsequent behavior to "disappointment" could be either a situational or a dispositional attribution. Compounding Kiderlen's disappointment, continued Jules Cambon, was the kaiser's misperception: the kaiser had returned from a visit to London "with the idea that the English Government was completely disinterested in Morocco."[52] Attributing behavior to "misperception" is neither dispositional nor situational; a clear attribution would depend on what caused that misperception.

French explanations of the German move are ambiguous. Some are more dispositional than situational, some may be either type of attribution. The evidence neither clearly supports nor contradicts the desires hypothesis, which anticipated dispositional attributions. The deterrence hypothesis also expected dispositional attributions, but it expected these to be based on past behavior. The evidence in the next paragraph, which examines French explanations of British behavior, supports my argument but contradicts deterrence's argument.

French decision-makers did not count on British military support in case of conflict with Germany. In a letter to his brother early in the crisis, Paul Cambon said he expected London to back Paris diplomatically, but warned that France should not expect British military support.[53]

---

[51] Paul Cambon to Selves (July 2, 1911), *DDF*, No. 9, p. 8.

[52] Jules Cambon to Selves (July 10, 1911), *DDF*, No. 54, pp. 52–53. For background on the Moroccan railroad dispute, see John F. V. Keiger, *France and the Origins of the First World War* (London: Macmillan, 1983), p. 41; Mortimer, "Moroccan Policy," pp. 80–82.

[53] A letter to Jules Cambon (May 23, 1911), quoted in Paul Cambon, *Correspondance, 1870–1924*, vol. 2: *La Tension franco-anglaise, l'Entente Cordiale, les querelles allemandes, le coup d'Agadir* (Paris: Grasset, 1940), p. 320.

Nor did Jules Cambon put much faith in British support; referring to England, he said that "one must not count too much on the support that others could give us and work for ourselves."[54] The French ambassador to Russia explained away British support: "England has intervened in the Agadir Affair because of obligation from its agreements with France and because it signed the Act of Algeciras, but above all for the defense of its own interests."[55] British interests, not character, explained London's diplomatic support.

This evidence supports my proposition that allies rarely get reputations for being resolute or loyal allies: French decision-makers explained desirable British behavior in situational terms. They did not hark back to the glory days of the Algeciras or Bosnian victories, but explained British behavior as a function of immediate British interests.

At this point in the crisis, the French were satisfied but not thrilled with British support. They wanted a British guarantee of military support in case of conflict with Germany. Instead, Grey talked incessantly about compensations in the Congo, the acceptability of a German port on the Atlantic, and the need for a conference if negotiations failed. London's policy, guided by the twin fears of Paris defecting or dragging London into war, meant that French decision-makers gave British leaders no credit for their support, but only blame for not supporting France enough.[56]

Russian Explanations

As the Agadir Crisis began to unfold, the Russians thought their interests were not at stake. Assuming French efforts to control Morocco did not degenerate into a European war, which at the time seemed unlikely, St. Petersburg could watch events with equanimity. Because the Russians did not view events early in the crisis as either highly desirable or undesirable, my hypothesis cannot predict Russian attributions. According to the deterrence hypothesis, Izvolsky should expect the French to be irresolute in Agadir because he thought they were irresolute in the Bosnian Crisis. The evidence presented here refutes this deterrence prediction and suggests that dispositional attributions are not always interdependent.

---

[54] Cambon to Selves (July 10, 1911), *DDF*, No. 54, p. 53.
[55] Louis to Caillaux (July 7, 1911), *DDF*, No. 41, p. 38.
[56] See Geoffrey Barraclough, *From Agadir to Armageddon: Anatomy of Crisis* (London: Weidenfeld and Nicolson, 1982), p. 117.

Even before Paris took Fez, Izvolsky expected trouble. The French were "stepping beyond the bounds" of the Algeciras Agreement thus creating a new situation. "Everything depends," Izvolsky thought, "on the attitude of Berlin."[57] Although Cruppi naively thought that he controlled the situation, Izvolsky understood that "German diplomacy is in control of the situation and is able suddenly to bring the Moroccan question to a head" whenever it wants.[58] After the occupation of Fez, he doubted Paris would be able to leave and anticipated "international complications."[59]

St. Petersburg supported its ally, declaring after the Fez occupation that the "Tsar's Government regarded France's action as entirely unobjectionable."[60] Anatole Neratov—the acting Russian foreign minister— later instructed Izvolsky to inform Paris of the friendly Russian attitude and told him "to express confidence that should [the] occasion occur we should enjoy similar support from France."[61] After the crisis, the Russians tried unsuccessfully to cash in on this goodwill.

The Russians took a cautious view of the situation after news of the *Panther* reached St. Petersburg. Unlike British policy-makers, Neratov explained the German moves in situational terms: "The military side is of secondary importance; the object is a diplomatic one—the protection of Germany's political interests, since the formal terms of the Act of Algeciras have already been violated. Germany is probably desirous of conducting new negotiations with France regarding Morocco, and wishes, in this connection, to be supported by a *fait accompli*."[62] Believing that the Germans aimed only to protect their interests, Neratov advised against invoking the alliance with France in order to avoid causing Germany to bring in the Austrians and further complicate the situation.[63]

Upon French urging, the Russians delivered a *démarche* to Berlin, but it was so mild that Jules Cambon dismissed it as "extremely weak" and

[57] Izvolsky to Neratov (April 24, 1911), quoted in Friedrich Stieve, *Isvolsky and the World War: Based on the Documents Recently Published by the German Foreign Office*, trans. E. W. Dickes (London: George Allen and Unwin, 1926), pp. 30–31.

[58] Izvolsky to Neratov (May 11, 1911), ibid., p. 31.

[59] Izvolsky to Neratov (June 6, 1911), ibid., p. 32.

[60] Ibid., p. 36.

[61] Neratov to Izvolsky (May 5, 1911), quoted in Stieve, *Isvolsky*, p. 36. Sazonov replaced Izvolsky as Foreign Minister in September 1910. Sazonov became sick in March 1911 and was replaced by Neratov until he was able to resume his position in December 1911.

[62] Neratov to Benckendorff (July 2, 1911), quoted in Siebert, *Entente Diplomacy*, No. 680, pp. 588–589.

[63] See Donald R. Mathieu, "The Role of Russia in French Foreign Policy, 1908–1914" (Ph.D. diss., Stanford University, 1968), p. 56.

"pure form."[64] One historian thinks the Russian intervention may actually have encouraged the Germans.[65] The Russians adopted this cautious line because they believed their interests were not at risk and because they were still negotiating with the Germans over the Baghdad railway and Persia. They wanted to support their ally, but did not want to damage relations with Berlin.

Russian behavior in the first part of the Agadir Crisis illustrates two points. One, in spite of Izvolsky's belief that the French were irresolute in the Bosnian Crisis, it does not appear that this opinion influenced his assessments of French behavior. This example shows that dispositional attributions are not always interdependent and so contradicts the assumption of deterrence theory. Two, Neratov's situational explanation of German behavior, which he found neither desirable nor undesirable, contrasts with British and French dispositional explanations of the undesirable German behavior. This explanation illustrates the important role desires may have on policy-makers' attributions.

Although the deterrence hypothesis can account for some of the explanations, it is also sometimes contradicted. British explanations of German behavior support both arguments. Because French policy-makers used both dispositional and ambiguous attributions to explain German behavior, the evidence neither supports nor contradicts my argument. However, unlike the deterrence hypothesis, the desires hypothesis can account for how London and Paris explained each other's behavior. Whereas the deterrence argument expected each ally to give the other a reputation for resolve, the desires argument anticipated their situational explanations. Finally, only the Russians, who wanted to keep on good terms with both the French and the Germans, offered situational explanations for the German step to Agadir. And contrary to deterrence expectations, the Russians did not seem to recall their earlier view of the irresolute French.

FROM THE MANSION HOUSE TO THE GERMAN RETREAT

After the German retreat at Agadir, the deterrence hypothesis would expect everyone to view the Germans, Austrians, and perhaps the Russians as irresolute, and the French and British as resolute. In contrast,

---

[64] Jules Cambon to Selves (July 10, 1911), *DDF*, No. 54, p. 53.
[65] Barlow, *Agadir Crisis*, pp. 246–247.

the desires hypothesis expects the British to view the Germans as resolute, but to explain away with situational attributions both French resolution and Austrian irresolution.

British Explanations

British views of Germany. Most British decision-makers remained skeptical at the first signs of German retreat. While Crowe gleefully predicted the Germans were in retreat after the Mansion House speech, Nicolson and Grey disagreed, believing Berlin had only changed its tactics.[66] A week later, Nicolson wrote: "I do not consider that we are by any means out of the wood over this Moroccan question, and I should not be in the least astonished if Kiderlen gave us some surprises. . . . I should not be in the least surprised if Germany took the opportunity to put the screw suddenly on France."[67] One month later, in mid-September, Grey worried that the Franco-German negotiations could at any moment break down, which could lead the Germans "to act very quickly—even suddenly." He felt the Admiralty should be so prepared for war "that they would welcome a German attack." Grey was puzzled by the optimistic reports pouring out of Germany that an agreement was likely: "They may be and probably are intended to prepare the way for a climb down: but they may be intended to mislead and lull suspicions before a rapid coup."[68] It seems the Germans retained their credibility for action even as they retreated.

British decision-makers collectively offered four different explanations for the German retreat: miscalculation, British resolve, superior balance of capability, and German financial problems. No one even hinted that the Germans might be irresolute.

One of Nicolson's explanations for the German retreat concerned German misperceptions: "Germany evidently quite miscalculated this country after the visit of the German Emperor in May. He was convinced that he had got this country . . . comfortably in his pocket"; later he says that Germany has "committed a great blunder."[69] In this case,

[66] See Crowe, Nicolson, and Grey minutes, Goschen to Grey (August 1, 1911), *BD*, vol. 7, No. 448, p. 427.

[67] Nicolson to Hardinge (August 17, 1911), in Lowe and Dockrill, *Documents*, pp. 435–436.

[68] Grey to Nicolson (September 17, 1911), *BD*, vol. 7, No. 647, p. 639.

[69] Nicolson to Cartwright (July 24, 1911), *BD*, vol. 7, No. 418, p. 396; Nicolson to George Buchanan (August 1, 1911), *BD*, vol. 7, No. 493, pp. 465–466.

the Germans might be blunderers or foolishly doubt British resolve, but this has no bearing on German resolve. As quoted earlier, French ambassador Jules Cambon offered a similar explanation. Nicolson was confident that British resolve would "eventually render Germany more compliant and reasonable" as would a united Triple Entente.[70] Because the British were standing "manfully" by France, compared to Italy's defection and Austria's lukewarm support, the Germans would be foolhardy to go to war for it would "certainly ruin her for a generation or two."[71] In this case, British resolve and the Entente's capability worked together.

British decision-makers also thought the crash of the Berlin stock exchange in September a reason for the German retreat. Crowe noted that the German banks remained strong and were capable of financing a major war; he commented on "the pressure which the banks will inevitably exercise, at a time of prolonged crisis, to bring about—not so much a peaceful—but *any* solution, whilst they are prepared to meet the situation once war is actually decided upon."[72] Because the Germans were not bent on war, the financial crisis pushed them toward peace, but the next time, in a different situation, the outcome could be different.

Not content with these situational explanations, others in the Foreign Office claimed that the Germans conceded not because of the financial crisis, but because the Navy was not yet ready for war.[73] Even if the Navy was prepared, perhaps they retreated because they had yet to finish construction on an important canal.[74] British decision-makers unanimously chose to explain away the German retreat rather than attribute it to German irresolution.

---

[70] Nicolson to Buchanan (August 1, 1911), *BD*, vol. 7, No. 493, pp. 465–466.

[71] Nicolson to Goschen (November 7, 1911), quoted in Williamson, *Politics of Grand Strategy*, p. 164; Nicolson to Buchanan (September 12, 1911), *BD*, vol. 7, No. 546, p. 525.

[72] Crowe minute, *Appendix 1: The German Financial Crisis* (October 26, 1911), *BD*, vol. 7, p. 805; see also Assistant Undersecretary for Foreign Affairs W. Langley's minute. For background on the financial crisis, see Barlow, *Agadir Crisis*, pp. 351–354.

[73] See G. H. Villiers's minute, "The German Financial Crisis," *BD*, vol. 7, p. 805; and Grey's similar explanation in his memoirs, *Twenty-Five Years, 1892–1916* (New York: Frederick A. Stokes, 1925), p. 231.

[74] See Lord Stamfordham to Churchill (October 25, 1911), *BD*, vol. 7, No. 649, p. 642. Or perhaps Lloyd George was right in thinking that his speech caused the retreat. This belief is neither clearly situational nor dispositional. See Lloyd George to his wife (undated, probably late July or early August 1911), in *Lloyd George Family Letters, 1885–1936*, ed. Kenneth O. Morgan (London: Oxford University Press, 1973), p. 156. For a similar belief, see Tyrrell to Spring-Rice (August 1, 1911), in Fry, *Lloyd George*, p. 141.

Instead of thinking the German retreat demonstrated irresolution, British decision-makers thought the Germans were finally being reasonable. For example, Nicolson hopes the Germans will "moderate" their demands and "keep them within reasonable limits"; he thinks the Germans will have to become more "reasonable" in the face of British resolve; that they will have to "moderate" their demands and accept "reasonable" French concessions.[75] Cartwright thinks Aehrenthal will "moderate" German behavior.[76]

The Russians also characterized Berlin's retreats as reflecting German good sense rather than German irresolution. For example, the Russian ambassador to England, Alexander Benckendorff, thinks that "caution and moderation" prevail in Berlin after the Mansion House speech and Izvolsky views the "far-sighted" agreement between France and Germany as a tribute to German "moderation."[77]

As these examples illustrate, when a state pursues a policy we find desirable, we are likely to view it as reasonable. So when the Germans began to retreat, the British and Russians found this course reasonable, moderate, and cautious, but hardly irresolute. Although it is somewhat of a stretch, I contend that these are more situational than dispositional attributions. A situational attribution implies that anyone in the same situation would behave similarly. As a reasonable person flees a burning house, an unreasonable one stays inside. We expect people to be reasonable; when they are not, this failing reflects on their character. For example, Bertie characterized Spain's undesirable policy as "unreasonable."[78] If one rejects this argument and prefers to view "reasonable" as a dispositional attribution, the core of my argument still stands: calling a state reasonable does not imply that it is irresolute.

Although the British made situational explanations for the desirable German retreat, they made dispositional ones for the undesirable German challenge. British policy-makers believed the Germans were aggressive and bent on exploiting any weakness to advance their aim of continental hegemony. Only when faced with superior capability

---

[75] Nicolson to Goschen (July 18, 1911), Nicolson to Buchanan (August 1, 1911), and Nicolson to Cartwright (July 24, 1911), *BD*, vol. 7, Nos. 395, 493, 418, pp. 375, 465–466, 396.

[76] Cartwright to Nicolson (May 11, 1911), *BD*, vol. 7, No. 262, p. 235.

[77] Benckendorff to Neratov (August 1, 1911), Izvolsky to Neratov (October 25, 1911), in Siebert, *Entente Diplomacy*, Nos. 689, 707, pp. 596, 609. Many examples could be culled from my other two empirical chapters. For example, see Holstein's characterization of Rouvier in the first Moroccan Crisis (Chapter 3); or see the Austrians' view of Russia's Bosnian retreat (Chapter 4).

[78] Bertie to Grey (May 14, 1911), quoted in Barlow, *Agadir Crisis*, p. 203.

would the Germans back down. In short, they thought Germany was habitually cruel to those who were weaker—they thought the Germans were bullies. Grey wrote that England supported "backing up France against the attempt of Germany to bully her"; Nicolson was pleased that Churchill and Lloyd George would not "permit Germany to assume the role of bully"; and Lloyd George thought the kaiser had behaved "like a cad" while Bethmann was a "coarse bully."[79]

British policy-makers did not think Germany a proud nation resolved to force France to compensate it, just as France had compensated England, Spain, and Italy. Instead, they thought aggressive German behavior was motivated by a German bullying character. When the bully fell into retreat, this showed only that the situation had compelled a retreat rather than any change had occurred in the German character (except perhaps that the retreat showed them to be occasionally moderate and sensible). Berlin had even shown that it would risk recreating a situation in which it had earlier lost.

Nicolson thought the German retreat offered no occasion for celebration; he assumed the Germans would say "Never again!"

> That Germany will seize the first opportunity for recovering her position I have very little doubt. We are evidently entering into a period in which we shall be obliged . . . to meet all possible contingencies. Paul Cambon considers that even if negotiations succeed a conflict will by no means be improbable within the next two or three years. The bitter feeling against us will necessitate our being constantly on the watch. The future, therefore, is not very bright.[80]

Nicolson assumed that the Germans, having now lost twice in Morocco, would challenge again, if only because they had lost. Grey echoes this sentiment in his memoirs: "The militarists in Germany were bitterly disappointed over Agadir, and when the next crisis came we found them with the reins in their hands at Berlin."[81] As discussed in Chapter 1, deterrence theorists do recognize the possibility that the defeated state may say "Never again!", but they fail to note that the victor may expect this response of the vanquished.

[79] Grey to Bertie (October 14, 1911), in Lowe and Dockrill, *Documents*, pp. 438–439; Nicolson to Hardinge (August 17, 1911), quoted in Steiner, *Foreign Office*, p. 127; Murray diary (July 22, 1911), quoted in Fry, *Lloyd George*, p. 139.

[80] Nicolson to Cartwright (September 18, 1911), quoted in Harold Nicolson, *Portrait of a Diplomatist*, p. 256.

[81] Grey, *Twenty-Five Years*, p. 233.

In short, undesirable German behavior led the British to make dispositional attributions, whereas desirable German behavior led to situational ones. This pattern confirms my hypothesis. The deterrence hypothesis gets it only half right: it is true that the British will view the German challenge as demonstrating German resolve, but wrong to think that this opinion is erased by the German retreat. This example shows why adversaries rarely get reputations for lacking resolve, but can get reputations for having resolve.

British views of France. British decision-makers found French behavior both undesirable for causing trouble with Germany, and desirable for not giving up British interests or deserting the Entente. Considering the alternatives, they were pleased with the outcome of the Agadir Crisis. As a result, I would expect them to explain away French resolve by using situational attributions. In contrast, the deterrence argument expects the British to view France as a resolute ally for standing up to German aggression.

British decision-makers viewed French policy in Morocco as "stupid and dishonest," but they felt that supporting France was essential to guaranteeing British security.[82] In a note to Grey, Nicolson explains why London must support France:

> Were [France] to come to distrust us, she would probably try to make terms with Germany irrespective of us . . . In any case, France would never forgive us for having failed her, and the whole Triple Entente would be broken up. This would mean that we should have a triumphant Germany, and an unfriendly France and Russia and our policy since 1904 of preserving the equilibrium and consequently the peace in Europe would be wrecked.[83]

It is hard to tell whether the threat of French defection stems from French irresolution or capability; presumably it is some combination of both that alarms Nicolson.

As the crisis wears on and heats up, Nicolson becomes more confident in French resolve and capability. The French army, he says, "has never been in a better state of equipment, organization, and armament"; they have "never been better organized or in a fitter state to undertake a campaign"; "their whole organization, and material are in a

---

[82] Tyrrell to Hardinge (July 21, 1911), quoted in Lowe and Dockrill, *Documents*, p. 434.
[83] Minute by Nicolson (July 21, 1911), *BD*, vol. 7, No. 409, p. 386.

perfectly satisfactory state."[84] These quotes show that Nicolson used French capability to explain their desirable behavior. At the same time, and contrary to my expectations, Nicolson stressed French resolve: the French have never "been inspired by so strong a feeling of perfect confidence and unity." "I may tell you quite confidentially and for your own personal information, that the French would not flinch from accepting war with Germany. They are full of confidence."[85] Though this resolve springs from French capability, as well as from British resolve and ability to defend France, it nonetheless shows that an ally's desirable behavior can elicit a dispositional explanation.[86] In this instance, my hypothesis fails the first test—desirable behavior led to a dispositional attribution—and the deterrence hypothesis passes.

Yet the deterrence hypothesis passes the first test only by dropping its interdependence assumption and instead assuming that immediate behavior determines type of attribution. Past French behavior cannot account for both Nicolson's early belief in French irresolution and his subsequent belief in French resolve. In other words, my hypothesis passes the second test—past French behavior could not have governed Nicolson's explanations—and the deterrence hypothesis fails this test.

Recall that an attribution for resolve does not mean a reputation for resolve. If at a later time Nicolson thinks the French will be resolute, he would show that an ally can acquire a reputation for being resolved.

[84] Nicolson to Hardinge (September 14, 1911), quoted in Harold Nicolson, *Portrait of a Diplomatist*, p. 253; Nicolson to Buchanan (September 12, 1911), *BD*, vol. 7, No. 546, p. 525; Nicolson to Goschen (September 12, 1911), quoted in Cosgrove, "Note on Lloyd George," p. 701. Nicolson may have thought the French capable of fighting the Germans, but neither the Quai d'Orsay nor the French military thought so. Caillaux asked French general and chief of staff Joseph Joffre whether there was a seventy percent chance of victory in a French-German war and Joffre said no. See Williamson, *Politics of Grand Strategy*, pp. 159–160. See also Geoff Eley, *Reshaping the German Right: Radical Nationalism and Political Change after Bismarck* (Ann Arbor: University of Michigan Press, 1990), pp. 22–23.

[85] Nicolson to Hardinge (September 14, 1911), quoted in Harold Nicolson, *Portrait of a Diplomatist*, p. 253; Nicolson to Goschen (September 12, 1911), quoted in Cosgrove, "Note on Lloyd George," p. 701.

[86] Anglo-French military talks were held in late August. Nicolson repeatedly referred to this important development, e.g., "I may tell you in confidence that preparations for landing four or six divisions on the continent have been worked out to the minutest detail." "We also have been making certain preparations very quietly, and if need be, we shall be quite prepared to render very efficient aid to the French troops." Nicolson to Hardinge (September 14, 1911), quoted in Harold Nicolson, *Portrait of a Diplomatist*, p. 253; Nicolson to Goschen (September 12, 1911), quoted in Cosgrove, "A Note on Lloyd George," p. 701. For details on the Anglo-French talks, see Frank Laney, "The Military Implementation of the Franco-Russian Alliance, 1890–1914" (Ph.D. diss., University of Virginia, 1954), pp. 335–352.

This process is analogous to Nicolson's explanation of Russian behavior in the Bosnian Crisis. As discussed in Chapter 4, Nicolson thought the Russians irresolute for yielding to Berlin's ultimatum. Only if he then expects the Russians to be irresolute in the next crisis—Agadir—could we say that Russia had a reputation for being irresolute. As discussed below, dispositional attributions in this instance appear to be more independent than interdependent.

British views of Russia. The British found Russian behavior in the Agadir Crisis to be neither highly desirable nor undesirable. Perhaps as a result, London did not pay much attention to its Russian ally. Either way, they should not view the Russians as resolute. Because Nicolson expects the Russians to be resolute, my hypothesis fails (and the deterrence hypothesis passes) the first test. Although my argument fails the first test, it passes the second: past Russian behavior did not govern London's expectations of future Russian behavior—and this outcome contradicts the deterrence argument.

After noting that Britain will resolutely support France against Germany, Nicolson adds: "I am quite sure that Russia will do the same and Germany will see that the Triple Entente is not so weak a combination as she apparently imagines."[87] While it is unclear why Nicolson thought the Russians could be counted on to support France, he nonetheless implies that the Russians are resolved. Contrary to my expectations, Nicolson uses a dispositional explanation to describe desirable behavior: the Russians will be resolute.

My hypothesis fails the first test, but not the second. Nicolson's view of Russia after the Bosnian Crisis was a mix of situation and disposition, captured best when he said: "Russia is temporarily weak, with a timorous Foreign Minister"; he also said at the time that he wished "that Izvolsky and his colleagues had stiffened their backs."[88] Izvolsky's personal failings, and those of his colleagues, were compounded by the situation. Nevertheless, Nicolson expects the Russians to be resolute in the Agadir Crisis. Contrary to the deterrence hypothesis, Russia's irresolution in 1909 did not govern Nicolson's expectations of Russian behavior in 1911—indeed, he fails to even mention the Bosnian Crisis. Nicolson did not give the Russians a reputation for lacking resolve after their Bosnian defeat.

[87] Nicolson to Buchanan (August 1, 1911), *BD*, vol. 7, No. 493, pp. 465–466.
[88] Nicolson to Grey (March 24, 1909) *BD*, vol. 5: *The Near East: The Macedonian Problem and the Annexation of Bosnia, 1903–1909*, No. 764, p. 736.

My hypothesis also fails to predict Lloyd George's explanation of Russian behavior during the Agadir Crisis. In this case, I determine desirability of behavior by looking at the decision-maker's attribution. It is evident that Lloyd George found Russian behavior undesirable; it is also evident that he explains this behavior in situational terms:

> I have been quite unhappy about the position of Russia from the start. . . .
> I have had serious doubts as to whether they would come in, if they possibly could avoid it. We have substantial interests in Morocco; they have none. Besides, they have just had as much war as they can stand, for some years at least. Their internal situation is not very satisfactory. But, even if they stand out altogether, their abstention would not be necessarily fatal to success.[89]

Lloyd George's attribution illustrates two points. First and most important, it shows that even undesirable behavior may be explained away, and this possibility confounds both hypotheses: both expect dispositional attributions. It may be harder than I expected for an ally to get a reputation for lacking resolve. Second, it illustrates a nice methodological point discussed in Chapter 2. Lloyd George's explanation shows that I can base the independent variable—desirability of behavior—on a particular attribution and still disconfirm my hypothesis. This demonstrates that my method is not circular even when desirability cannot be deduced directly from the situation.

I discuss these and other bits of disconfirming evidence in the conclusion. For now, note that while the desires hypothesis fails the first test, the deterrence hypothesis does no better. Since British decision-makers described the Russians as irresolute after their Bosnian adventure, the deterrence hypothesis predicts the British will expect them to be irresolute in Agadir. But as shown this is not the case. Nicolson thought St. Petersburg resolved and Lloyd George explained away Russia's undesirable behavior rather than attribute it to Russian irresolution.

British views of Austria-Hungary. Austria gave Germany very little support in the Agadir Crisis, which pleased the British. Therefore, I expect London to explain away Austrian behavior. The deterrence hypothesis expects them to view the Austrians as either resolute or irresolute: resolute because Austria had stood firm in the previous cri-

---

[89] Lloyd George to Churchill (September 3, 1911), quoted in Fry, *Lloyd George*, p. 146.

sis, or irresolute for failing to support Germany in the Agadir Crisis. Either way, the evidence supports the desires hypothesis and contradicts the deterrence hypothesis.

Nicolson noted that "Austria—though, of course, she will have to fulfill her part of her Treaty—will not do so with any enthusiasm."[90] Cartwright even doubted that Austria would fulfill its treaty obligations to Germany. He thought it possible that Aehrenthal would sign a secret agreement promising France Austrian neutrality in a Franco-German war. Even without this secret pledge to France, Austria could be expected to give the Germans very little support. "One thing I am pretty certain of," wrote Cartwright, "and that is that if convenient to him Aehrenthal will merely stick to the very letter of the Treaty and to nothing more."[91] British decision-makers viewed Austria's behavior as desirable.

Cartwright explained Austria's behavior as resulting from two things: Austria's effort for greater independence from Berlin; and related to this, Aehrenthal's efforts to secure a loan from the French.[92] During the crisis, Cartwright depicted Austria as a "sort of regulator" maintaining the equilibrium between the two alliances: "When the Triple Entente weakens he swings away from Berlin; when it is stronger he tightens the links uniting the Triple Alliance."[93] By not supporting the Germans, the Austrians were simply maintaining an equilibrium.

What little evidence I found shows the British explaining desirable Austrian behavior in situational terms. The thought that Vienna might be irresolute probably never crossed their minds. London's failure to view the Austrians as either resolute or irresolute contradicts the deterrence hypothesis.

Summary of British views. The most important point in the above section concerns the independence or interdependence of dispositional attributions. Past German behavior strongly influenced the British. After the German defeat at Algeciras in 1906, they feared the Germans would seek revenge, and they used this motive to explain German behavior in the Bosnian Crisis. Entering the Agadir Crisis, they depicted the Germans as bullying extortionists out to gut the Triple Entente. In a private letter to President Theodore Roosevelt, Grey remarked: "The Germans,

---

[90] Nicolson to Buchanan (September 12, 1911), *BD*, vol. 7, No. 546, p. 525.
[91] Cartwright to Nicolson (November 23, 1911), *BD*, vol. 7, No. 708, pp. 714–715.
[92] Ibid.
[93] Cartwright to Nicolson (July 21, 1911), quoted in Wilson, *Empire and Continent*, p. 82.

or rather the Prussians—for the south Germans are of different ideals and temperament—are very difficult people. Their way of beginning a conversation is to stamp upon your foot to attract your attention when you aren't looking, and then they are surprised and very annoyed when the conversation doesn't go smoothly afterwards."[94] Because London explained away the German defeat at Agadir, this defeat did not affect London's image of the unreasonable German bully. Although the Germans were ultimately compelled to be reasonable and moderate in Agadir, London believed they seethed with anger and would continue their aggression. But dispositional attributions are not always interdependent. Whereas Nicolson thought the Russians had been irresolute in 1909, he thought they would be resolute in 1911.

As expected, during the Agadir Crisis policy-makers did not refer to a state's past behavior when they had explained that behavior in situational terms. The British made no mention of French resolve in 1906 because they explained that behavior in situational terms. Nor did they refer to French behavior in the Bosnian Crisis, which they also explained primarily in situational terms.

Overall, the evidence in this section supports my four propositions. Adversaries can get reputations for being resolute, but rarely for being irresolute. London thought the Germans resolute, but did not think the Austrians irresolute. My propositions do less well in explaining impressions of allies. I argue that allies can get reputations for being irresolute, but rarely for being resolute. Because London viewed St. Petersburg as first irresolute (1909) then resolute (1911), a reputation for resolve has not formed. By viewing Russia as resolute in 1911, the British make it possible for a reputation for resolve to form. The same is true with their view of France. Although British decision-makers had doubted French resolve, Nicolson now viewed the French as resolute. If he uses this attribution to predict future French resolve, then he has given the French a reputation for having resolve.

The deterrence hypothesis was partially right. British decision-makers expected the Germans to be resolute. However, this hypothesis wrongly expected the British to view the German defeat as a sign of Berlin's irresolution. Past Austrian, French, and Russian behavior appears to have had no influence on British explanations.

---

[94] Grey in a private letter to Roosevelt (no date provided, but evidently after the Agadir Crisis), quoted in George Macaulay Trevelyan, *Grey of Fallodon: The Life and Letters of Sir Edward Grey* (Boston: Houghton Mifflin, 1937), p. 184.

French Explanations

The deterrence hypothesis expects the French to view the Germans as irresolute for backing down, the Austrians as irresolute for not supporting their ally, and the British and probably the Russians as resolute and loyal allies. In contrast, the desires hypothesis expects the French to view the Germans as resolute, and to explain away British, Russian, and Austrian behavior.

French views of England. Based on past behavior, the French should have been confident that England would support them. Because the deterrence hypothesis expected the French to credit Britain for its loyal support of both France in 1906 and Russia in 1909, Paris should give the British a reputation for being a resolute and loyal ally after the Agadir Crisis. In contrast, I argue that because British behavior was desirable, the French will explain this behavior in situational terms. Since Paris explained away past instances of British support, there is no reservoir of goodwill from which to draw in 1911.

Delivered on the heels of Anglo-French military talks, the Mansion House speech pleased most French policy-makers.[95] For example, Paul Cambon wrote that he was "not badly impressed" with the speech. He thought the speech would influence Kiderlen, since "he must have believed that Lloyd George and the radicals would never trumpet the patriotic news and that [Britain] would let us take care of ourselves by ourselves."[96]

While the British were talking tough to Berlin, they were also talking tough to the French, urging them to settle and advising them of the impossibility of going to war over Morocco. French policy-makers found alarming the British talk of calling a conference if negotiations failed. London had no objections to a conference, said Jules Cambon, because England "has nothing to sacrifice and everything to gain." England having been removed from Morocco in 1904, there was now a danger, he continued, that London might return: "In a word, we must not hand over our interests, foot and fist bound between the hands of England. However loyal she is, her own interests will always be more important than ours."[97]

---

[95] See Williamson, *Politics of Grand Strategy,* p. 158.

[96] Paul Cambon to his son (July 25, 1911), *Correspondance,* p. 333.

[97] Jules Cambon to Selves (July 24, 1911), *DDF,* No. 98, p. 105. Also see Barlow, *Agadir Crisis,* p. 328.

Selves agreed with Cambon's view that British interests dictate British behavior and that those interests may diverge from French interests. Selves wanted to keep negotiations with Germany on a bilateral basis and avoid a conference. As for specific military promises from the British, Selves doubted that any military collaboration would be resolved to French advantage.[98] For both Jules Cambon and Selves, British support demonstrated that London thought British interests were at stake, not that the British were resolute.

Caillaux thought the Mansion House speech was of some value, but he deplored the absence of a firm British military commitment. He became so alarmed at the direction of events that he began secret negotiations with the Germans behind the back of his foreign minister. He did not trust the British and feared France would be left to fight Germany alone.[99] Throughout the crisis the French pressed London for a firmer commitment, but they always received the same advice: give away a Moroccan Atlantic port if necessary, yield in the Congo, a conference if talks fail, and British support for France in a war would depend upon the situation.[100]

For example, Caillaux asked for the British position if the Germans should occupy Agadir: would Britain send a ship to Mogador? Grey responded that any such action would require cabinet consultation. In his memoirs, Caillaux notes: "Evasive reply! and somewhat disquieting."[101] "The assurances of the incontestable goodwill of the British without specific engagement," recalled Caillaux, were not sufficient.[102] Caillaux wanted specific commitments; he was not reassured by promises of goodwill or a British record of supporting its allies.

Far from being grateful for British support, Caillaux complained to Bertie that "France might long ago have come to terms with Germany" had it not been for British interference.[103] Later, as Bertie reports, Caillaux softened his line a bit, saying he meant only that "he thought that

[98] Selves to Jules Cambon (July 26, 1911), *DDF*, No. 108, p. 123.
[99] For this interpretation, see Barlow, *Agadir Crisis*, pp. 315, 328, and on the secret talks, pp. 328–334; also Albertini, *Origins of the War*, pp. 331–332; Barraclough, *From Agadir*, pp. 132–135.
[100] For more French requests and British responses, see Williamson, *Politics of Grand Strategy*, pp. 158–163.
[101] Quoted in Dickinson, *International Anarchy*, p. 204.
[102] Joseph Caillaux, *Agadir: Ma politique extérieure* (Paris, publisher n.a., 1919), p. 141. Caillaux also doubted the usefulness of Britain's support, complaining that its army was too small. See Williamson, *Politics of Grand Strategy*, p. 160.
[103] Bertie to Grey (November 4, 1911), quoted in K. A. Hamilton, "Great Britain and France, 1905–1911," in *British Foreign Policy under Sir Edward Grey*, ed. F. H. Hinsley (Cambridge: Cambridge University Press, 1977), p. 325.

[the Entente] was being made to work to the disadvantage of French interests."[104] It is possible that Caillaux's comments were intended to shake up the British, who were pressing him to settle with Spain over Morocco. Caillaux's attitude did concern the British, who continued to question French reliability.[105]

Contrary to the expectations of the deterrence hypothesis, France did not mention, let alone credit, England for its support of France in 1906 or its support of Russia in 1909. Nor were the British credited for their resolute support of France in the Agadir Crisis. Instead, France explained this support in situational terms: Britain was defending its own interests which this time coincided with French interests. Rather than being grateful, French decision-makers were annoyed that London did not offer them more support. This example illustrates why it is hard for an ally to get a reputation for being a resolute or loyal ally: Paris explained British support in situational terms.

These explanations also usually correspond with decision-makers' tendencies to make worst-case assumptions. For example, during the crisis Paul Cambon became convinced that London would probably offer France military support if necessary, but this resolve in itself was not enough: "Militarily, England is ready: we know that the English Government wants to support us; but to move from desires to action, it must be pushed by a great national spirit."[106] Even if Grey and his cohorts were resolved to defend Paris, Caillaux worried about the influence of the pro-German radicals in the British cabinet.[107] Even if key British decision-makers were resolved to assist France, situational factors could still prevent them.

While Cambon and Caillaux wondered if London could be resolved even if it so wanted, Jules Cambon wondered if the Germans could compromise even if Kiderlen wanted to. Jules Cambon stressed all the factors that might force the Germans to stand firm, including German public opinion, Bethmann's supposed opposition, the Reichstag's opposition, the approaching elections, the kaiser's prestige, and more.[108]

---

[104] "Extract from Annual Report for France for the Year 1911," quoted in Williamson, *Politics of Grand Strategy*, p. 164. See also Barraclough, *From Agadir*, p. 117.

[105] See for example Crowe's minute, Bertie to Grey (November 6, 1911), No. 627, p. 619.

[106] Paul Cambon to Selves (September 6, 1911), *DDF*, No. 272, p. 358.

[107] See Williamson, *Politics of Grand Strategy*, p. 158.

[108] See Jules Cambon's reports to Selves through October, *DDF*, Nos. 463, 466, 472, 479; Tabouis, *Life of Jules Cambon*, pp. 215–216; and *The Cambridge History of British Foreign Policy, 1783–1919*, ed. Sir A. W. Ward and G. P. Gooch, vol. 3: *1866–1919* (New York: Macmillan, 1923), pp. 450–451.

Even if the Wilhelmstrasse was irresolute, Germany was not necessarily irresolute: "It is false that in Germany the nation is peaceful and the government bellicose—the exact opposite is true."[109] One could not count on the Germans being irresolute, for situational factors could force them to be resolute.

The same worst-case thinking is common among British policy-makers.[110] For example, Lloyd George thought the Germans had probably decided not to fight over Morocco, however: "Nations drift into war without any clear conscious intention, by gradually floating into positions from which they cannot withdraw."[111] Earlier, Hardinge and Grey dismissed French prime minister Georges Clemenceau's belief that Germany would not support Austria in the Bosnian Crisis due to the kaiser's irresolution; they note that even if the kaiser were irresolute, the situation would compel him to war. Whether or not the German leadership is resolute, Berlin may find itself in a situation where it has no choice but to be resolute.

French views of Germany. The deterrence hypothesis expects the French to view Germany's Agadir retreat as a sign of Berlin's irresolution. In contrast, I argue that because past German challenges were undesirable, the French would continue to view the Germans as resolute. They will be able to maintain this view after the German retreat since they should explain this retreat in situational terms.

The German financial crisis was as important an explanation for the French as it was for the British. Jules Cambon's dispatches from Berlin stressed the severity of German financial problems.[112] In mid-September, Cambon reported: "I should give you the impression created here by the financial debacle of last week. I believe that it has been very important in changing the German government's attitude. Mr. Kiderlen realized that when he speaks of war, he unleashes something he did not expect. I admit that we have a certain interest in seeing this crisis continue."[113]

Apparently Caillaux also thought the financial crisis was instrumental in causing the German retreat. In his memoirs, Caillaux takes credit

---

[109] Quoted in Konrad H. Jarausch, *The Enigmatic Chancellor: Bethmann-Hollweg and the Hubris of Imperial Germany* (New Haven: Yale University Press, 1973), p. 124.

[110] For a Russian example, see Benckendorff to Neratov (February 8, 1911), quoted in Siebert, *Entente Diplomacy*, pp. 618–619.

[111] Lloyd George to Churchill (September 3, 1911), quoted in Fry, *Lloyd George*, p. 146.

[112] See for example Cambon's reports to Selves or Caillaux on September 5, 8, 9, 16, *DDF*, Nos. 264, 288, 296, 326, pp. 349–439.

[113] Jules Cambon to Caillaux (September 16, 1911), *DDF*, No. 326, p. 439.

for setting off the stock market panic by making "a few phone calls."[114] While this claim is not true, it does show that he thought the crisis significant enough to try to take credit for it.[115]

I found no evidence that the French thought the Germans irresolute. Even when Jules Cambon was reporting to his superiors his great victory at the bargaining table, he made no mention of German irresolution (or British resolution).[116]

Far from thinking them irresolute, French decision-makers assumed the Germans were bent on further aggression. Delcassé was pessimistic for the future:

> I think that this time an agreement will be reached, but it will not settle anything, because war is inevitable. No durable arrangement can be concluded with Germany. Her mentality is such that one can no longer dream of living in lasting peace with her. . . . Paris, London, and St. Petersburg should be convinced now that war is, alas! inescapable and that it is necessary to prepare for it without losing a minute.[117]

Delcassé evidently did not think the German "mentality" irresolute, nor did Stephen Pichon (the former French minister for foreign affairs), as shown by this warning delivered to French prime minister Raymond Poincaré: "Be prepared. The event can occur much quicker than one imagines. Advise Mr. Poincaré to summon the Ministers of War and Marine with the chiefs of the General Staff and yourself. Let him remember his responsibilities. Let him not be taken unawares."[118] Poincaré did not need to be warned. He, too, was convinced of the German menace and immediately began working to strengthen French capability and to tighten its alliances.[119]

---

[114] Quoted in Rudolph Binion, *Defeated Leaders: The Political Fate of Caillaux, Jouvenel, and Tardieu* (Westport, Conn.: Greenwood Press, 1975), p. 50.

[115] On the British side, Harold Nicolson credits the British for causing the financial crisis (*Portrait of a Diplomatist*, p. 253).

[116] See for example, DDF, Nos. 342, 369, 519, 520, pp. 483, 529, 746, 747.

[117] From a written memoir of the conversation made immediately afterwards by André Mévil (September 13, 1911), quoted in Charles Porter, *The Career of Théophile Delcassé* (Pennsylvania: University of Pennsylvania Press, 1936), p. 289.

[118] Pichon to Poincaré via Paléologue (probably late 1911 or early 1912), quoted in G. P. Gooch, *Before the War*, vol. 2: *The Coming of the Storm* (New York: Longmans, Green, 1938), p. 140.

[119] See Geoffrey Chapman, "Decision for War: The Domestic Political Context of French Diplomacy, 1911–1914" (Ph.D. diss., Princeton University, 1971), p. 155; Eley, *Reshaping the German Right*, p. 28.

Here the evidence again supports my argument but not deterrence's argument. The French did not think the Germans irresolute for backing down in the crisis or the British resolute for standing firm. Instead, they credit themselves and the financial crisis. Early in the crisis, the German challenge elicited both dispositional and ambiguous explanations from Paris; but here, the German retreat elicited situational ones. As in London, the French view of German aggression was in no way ameliorated by the German retreat—nor could it be since they explained it in situational terms: adversaries rarely get reputations for lacking resolve.

French views of Russia. The French held an ambiguous view of Russia's support in the crisis. Because they viewed it as neither highly desirable nor undesirable, I cannot predict their attributions. Based on the Russian defeat in 1909, the deterrence hypothesis would expect Paris to view St. Petersburg as irresolute and therefore as an unreliable ally.

The French knew that British, not Russian, interests were at stake in Morocco.[120] Naturally they wanted their eastern ally's support, but they also knew it would not be decisive. As one student of the affair observed: "There is no indication that the Russian reaction to [the Agadir Crisis] had any appreciable affect on the final outcome of the crisis."[121]

From the beginning, the Russians offered France political support, and on July 31 and August 14 promised military support. As the crisis heated up the Russians worried that there might actually be a war. Neratov charged Izvolsky with advising Paris not to expect Russia's "energetic intervention at Berlin."[122] On August 29, the Russian leadership met to discuss the Agadir Crisis. These leaders concluded that Russia was not ready for war and that the public would not support a war over Morocco. They instructed Izvolsky to inform Paris of this "in the most cautious form." They decided not to inform Paris that, if war broke out over Morocco, Russia would mobilize against Germany but would not go on the offensive as promised.[123]

Izvolsky began pressing the French to yield to German demands, first offering Russian mediation, then suggesting Austrian mediation.

---

[120] See Georges Louis to Caillaux (July 7, 1911), *DDF*, No. 41, p. 38.

[121] Mathieu, "Role of Russia," p. 56.

[122] Neratov to Izvolsky (August 25, 1911), quoted in Robert Allshouse, "Aleksander Izvolskii and Russian Foreign Policy: 1910–1914" (Ph.D. diss., Case Western Reserve, 1977), p. 203.

[123] See Philip E. Mosley, "Russian Policy in 1911–1912," *The Journal of Modern History* 11 (March 1940): 85; William C. Wohlforth, "The Perception of Power: Russia in the pre-1914 Balance," *World Politics* 39 (April 1987): 365–366.

Izvolsky warned Selves that the Russian army was not yet ready, that Russian public opinion would not understand "a war for the sake of colonial territories," and that Russia needed peace for its internal development.[124]

There is little evidence bearing on French explanations for Russian behavior. French ambassador Georges Louis's explanation of Russian behavior is interesting because he refers to the Bosnian Crisis and this reference bears on the argument that past behavior governs expectations of future behavior. Louis was trying to figure out Russian policy in late August. He thought Izvolsky's urgings for compromise stemmed from his "burning memory of his personal failure in 1909."[125] Izvolsky was getting revenge for what he thought was a lack of French support in 1909.

Louis argues that the French role had nothing to with the defeat: "The truth is that the Bosnian affair had been so poorly handled by Izvolsky that it could only end up in a defeat for his policy." Izvolsky was not irresolute, but he did bungle the affair. "Besides," he continues, "we know since then that Russia, even assured of our most complete support, would not have gone to war: it was not ready. Today the situation is better. In the last two years preparations in Russia have made, in everyone's opinion, great progress. However, one would like to wait."[126] In other words, the outcome was largely determined by the situation, not by Russian irresolution. Nor does he think the Russians irresolute in the Agadir Crisis; they have made much progress, but are not yet ready to wage war against Germany.

Because the French viewed Russian behavior as neither strongly desirable nor undesirable, I cannot say how the French should explain Russian behavior. However, I can predict that because the French did not view the Russians as irresolute for yielding in 1909, they should not expect St. Petersburg to be irresolute in 1911 because of Russia's Bosnian defeat. The evidence supports my argument. The deterrence hypothesis was wrong to expect the French to view the Russians as irresolute in 1909, and therefore wrongly expected France to view Russia as irresolute in 1911.

---

[124] Quotation is Allshouse's paraphrase of an August 21 message to Neratov from Izvolsky in Allshouse, "Aleksander Izvolskii," pp. 206–207; Barlow, *Agadir Crisis*, pp. 358–361.

[125] Louis to Selves (August 22, 1911), DDF, No. 201, pp. 256–257.

[126] Ibid.

Summary of French views. French explanations of British and German behavior support my argument and count against the deterrence argument. Rather than consider the British loyal allies, as the deterrence hypothesis expected, Paris explained away British support and even blamed them for not offering more support. French decision-makers did not recall earlier examples of British resolve because they did not think the British were resolved in earlier crises. They explained past British behavior in situational terms.

Nor did they view the Germans as irresolute after their defeat at Agadir. Instead, they expected and feared future German challenges. In Paris as in London, decision-makers explained the German retreat in situational terms. French decision-makers did not draw upon earlier German retreats to predict German irresolution because they did not explain these earlier defeats as indicating an absence of resolve; rather, they explained the first German defeat at Morocco in situational terms. Indeed, Jules Cambon feared the Quai d'Orsay might view the Agadir Crisis as analogous to the 1909 Casablanca Crisis and stressed that the two situations were different.[127] I found no references to the first Moroccan Crisis.

French explanations of the Russians also support my argument and contradict the deterrence argument. The deterrence hypothesis expected French policy-makers to view the Russians as irresolute because of their Bosnian defeat. But they could not sensibly do this because they explained that defeat in situational terms. Louis's explanations support my earlier contention that Paris viewed the Russian defeat in situational terms. He also explains Russian concern over war as a function of this same lack of capability. The Russians were more prepared for war than before, but Louis thought they were still not ready to take on the Germans.

German Explanations

Both hypotheses expect the Germans to make dispositional explanations of undesirable British and French behavior. These hypotheses differ over how German policy-makers will explain Russian behavior. Because the Germans were pleased with Russia's tepid support of France, I expect them to explain away this behavior and deterrence ex-

---

[127] See Jules Cambon to Selves (August 20 and September 3, 1911), *DDF*, Nos. 198, 251, pp. 253, 331.

pects them to attribute it to a lack of Russian resolve. My hypothesis wins this test.

German views of England. All of Germany rose in indignation at the Mansion House speech. The kaiser was now ready to fight rather than allow Germany "to be overwhelmed for the second time."[128] Kiderlen was equally outraged: "We have lost our reputation abroad, we must fight."[129] It seemed that Britain everywhere stood in the way of Germany. Nonetheless, Berlin's leadership had no stomach for a Moroccan war; they began to give way sometime after the Mansion House speech.[130]

It appears that the German leadership may have been initially pleased with the Franco-German settlement over Morocco. The kaiser telegraphed to Bethmann his "best congratulations on the termination of this delicate affair."[131] One student of the affair argues that because Kiderlen aimed only for compensation to protect German prestige, he and his government were satisfied.[132] The American ambassador to Germany had a similar view of the event:

Although not as great as the German public was led to believe would be insisted upon, the deeded territory should more than satisfy them, as everything the German government obtained can practically be regarded as clear gain, for if the French had not moved so rapidly and had acted in a more politic manner, the chances are that in the course of 8 or 10 years they would in the natural course of events have acquired full possession of Morocco, without a struggle and without compensations.[133]

---

[128] Kaiser's marginalia, Kiderlen to Treutler (July 26, 1911), quoted in Ivo Nikolai Lambi, *The Navy and German Power Politics, 1862–1914* (Boston: Allen and Unwin, 1984), p. 319.

[129] Quoted in Fischer, *War of Illusions*, p. 82.

[130] When they began to retreat is debatable. Eyre Crowe thought the Germans began to retreat by August 1. Glenn Snyder and Paul Diesing also think they began to retreat on August 1 and Fritz Fischer thinks the retreat began August 17. Note that Caillaux began secret talks with Berlin on July 25. If Berlin interpreted this approach as a sign of French irresolution (as Snyder and Diesing argue), it is not evident in German behavior. See Fischer, *War of Illusions*, p. 84, and Snyder and Diesing, *Conflict among Nations: Bargaining, Decision-making, and System Structure in International Crises* (Princeton: Princeton University Press, 1977), p. 267.

[131] Quoted in Balfour, *The Kaiser*, p. 317.

[132] Joanne Mortimer, "Commercial Interests and German Diplomacy in the Agadir Crisis," *Historical Journal* 10/4 (1967): 456; Mortimer, "Moroccan Policy," p. 201.

[133] This is the view of Ambassador John G. Leishman (November 7, 1911), quoted in Jarausch, *Enigmatic Chancellor*, p. 459.

Though the German leadership may have initially viewed the November 4 treaty as acceptable, they were soon confronted by the widespread assumption at home and abroad that the Moroccan settlement was a German defeat.

Those parts of the German leadership and press who expected the Agadir Crisis to result in the acquisition of at least some of Morocco were bitterly disappointed that Bethmann, Kiderlen, and the kaiser would settle for less. For example, Chief of the General Staff Helmuth von Moltke wrote to his wife that he was "thoroughly fed up with this wretched Morocco affair." He continued: "If once again we crawl out of this affair with our tail between our legs, if we cannot pluck up the courage to take an energetic line which we are prepared to enforce with the sword then I despair of the future of the German empire."[134] The Conservative party leader, Ernst von Heyderbrand, was similarly critical of the settlement: "Our peace is assured by standing firm, not by agreements or settlements but solely by our German sword and also by the feeling . . . that we can look to a government which will not let this sword rust when it is needed." He saw in the Mansion House speech a "humiliating challenge."[135]

The nationalist press boiled with contempt over the agreement: "Have we become a generation of women? The kaiser has become the strongest supporter of the English-French policy."[136] The German right, the pan-nationalists, the heavy industrialists, the traditional conservatives, and much of the officer corps were disgusted by the agreement and desired revenge.[137] Like France, Germany had its own "spirit of Agadir" and its own nationalist revival.[138]

Confronted by a storm of protest in the press and in the Reichstag, Bethmann and the kaiser could not sustain their initial view of the compromise as acceptable. Defending his policy in a private letter, Bethmann argued that had he taken Germany to war, "we would now stand somewhere in France, our fleet would largely lie on the bottom of the North Sea, Hamburg and Bremen would be blockaded or bombarded, and the entire nation would ask me, why this?" They sent the *Panther* to

---

[134] August 19, 1911, quoted in Fischer, *War of Illusions*, p. 88.

[135] Quoted in Fischer, *War of Illusions*, p. 91.

[136] Quoted in Balfour, *The Kaiser*, p. 317.

[137] See Paul Kennedy, *The Rise of the Anglo-German Antagonism, 1860–1914* (Boston: George Allen and Unwin, 1980), pp. 447–448.

[138] See Fritz Fischer, *Germany's Aims in the First World War* (New York: W. W. Norton, 1967), pp. 25–26. For the nationalist wave in France, see Eugene Weber, *The Nationalist Revival in France, 1905–1914* (Berkeley: University of California Press, 1959).

Morocco, he continued, only to protect German economic interests and to show "the world that we were firmly resolved not to be pushed aside."[139] In Bethmann's view, Germany could not go to war for the stakes were too small and it would have lost anyway.

Bethmann later calls the outcome "a defeat by England" and blames it on German domestic politics, which he says is "dictated by the mood of the moment and by the political sophistication of a kindergarten."[140] In October 1912, Bethmann blamed the outcome on the situation: "In 1911 the situation was much worse. The complication would have begun with Britain; France would have remained passive, it would have forced us to attack and then there would have been no *casus foederis* for Austria—as Aehrenthal said to the delegations—whereas Russia was obliged to join in."[141] Bethmann did not explicitly mention the Entente's resolve, but he does seem to assume it. Adhering to worst-case thinking, he assumed Russia would support its ally while Austria would not. Bethmann still believed an agreement with London possible, if only he could "overcome Sir Edward Grey's opposition and above all that of his stooges in the Foreign Office."[142]

The kaiser did not think agreements with London were the way to a peaceful world. Like Bethmann, he blamed the German defeat on the situation, attributing it to a lack of German capability. This was grist for the mill of Alfred Tirpitz, the German naval minister, who wrote that "the Agadir enterprise, whatever its outcome, will be very useful to naval propaganda."[143] He wrote of "Germany's dwindling prestige" and suggested that a "major navy bill" would alleviate "the growing irritation at home."[144]

The kaiser agreed and said to Bethmann: "We have recognized the enemy, we have felt the effect of his almost humiliating activities and have been forced to put up with them gnashing our teeth in rage."[145]

---

[139] Bethmann to Karl Freiherr von Weizsäcker (November 16, 1911), quoted in Jarausch, *Enigmatic Chancellor*, p. 126.

[140] Bethmann to Karl von Eisendecher (December 26, 1911), quoted in Jarausch, *Enigmatic Chancellor*, p. 126.

[141] Bethmann reportedly said this to Walther Rathenau (October 1912), quoted in Fischer, *War of Illusions*, p. 85.

[142] Bethmann to Eisendecher (December 26, 1911), quoted in Fischer, *War of Illusions*, p. 122. Note that Jarausch translates "stooges" as "aides," see Jarausch, *Enigmatic Chancellor*, p. 126.

[143] Quoted in Berghahn, *Germany and the Approach*, p. 100.

[144] Quoted in Fischer, *War of Illusions*, p. 113; Berghahn, *Germany and the Approach*, pp. 100–101.

[145] The kaiser to Bethmann (early 1912?), quoted in Fischer, *War of Illusions*, p. 114.

Like his countrymen, the kaiser put nearly all the blame on England. When Paul Metternich suggested accepting British offers to help Germany attain more territory in the Congo, the kaiser responded "Jesuit!" It was all a British trick:

> What craftiness: the English would certainly be happy if we were to start tussling again with the French over the Congo as we did for Morocco! And when we are well entangled, they will stab us in the back! We do not want colonial wars, or complications of any kind: we want peace, and frank, definitive *political* rapprochement with London. A few more ships and maybe at last the English will understand![146]

The kaiser felt that because no British interests were at stake in Morocco, British intervention was an unexpected "stab in the back." The only way to deal with the crafty British was from a position of strength.

German views of France. Both hypotheses expect the Germans to continue to view the French as resolute after their victory at Agadir. This is both unsurprising and relatively uninteresting. What is surprising in this case is how little the Germans seemed to talk about France, instead venting their spleen on the unscrupulous British.

The Germans seem to harbor little ill will toward the French. They expected the French to resist, but ultimately to reach a reasonable agreement. As Kiderlen observed before sending the *Panther*: "It is necessary to thump the table. However, the only object of this is to make the French negotiate."[147] Because they knew their objectives were limited, they figured the British knew this too, and so did not anticipate the wild British reaction. Bethmann felt the German people were "immensely embittered" by news of British war preparations and military cooperation with France: "The people see themselves against a coalition, ready at any moment to fall upon us, and look on England as the Power which is making straight for war. For whilst France made no war preparations at all in September, it appears that England was ready to strike at any moment."[148] The Germans felt the French would have reached a

---

[146] Kaiser's marginalia, Metternich to Bethmann (November 28, 1911), quoted in *Britain and Germany in Africa: Imperial Rivalry and Colonial Rule*, ed. Prosser Gifford and William Roger Louis (New Haven: Yale University Press, 1967), p. 260. Metternich's warnings that a new Navy bill would make negotiations with England impossible elicited from the Kaiser: "Bosh!" "Rot!" and "Idiocy!" See Carroll, *Germany and the Great Powers*, p. 704.

[147] Quoted in Taylor, *Struggle for Mastery*, pp. 466–467.

[148] Bethmann to Metternich (November 22, 1911), GDD, p. 49.

settlement acceptable to all had it not been for British meddling. They took it for granted that England was pushing France toward war.[149]

German views of Russia. Because Russia offered France little support during the Agadir Crisis, the deterrence hypothesis expects Berlin to view St. Petersburg as irresolute. Indeed, the Germans should view the Russians as terribly irresolute, for not only did they barely support the French in Agadir, but they yielded to German demands at Potsdam (in August 1911) and caved in to German demands in Bosnia. In contrast, I expect the Germans to explain away desirable Russian behavior.

Just as the French government thanked Austria, the German government thanked Russia for its "correct attitude" in the Agadir Crisis.[150] Not for a second did the kaiser doubt Russian resolve. Upon reading a report that Russian capabilities were improving, the kaiser remarked: "Will my ministers at last believe that Russia is up to something and we must build up our armaments!!?"[151] Commenting on the soothing words coming from St. Petersburg, the kaiser noted: "Those fellows only want to calm us since they are not yet ready, *voilà toute.*"[152]

The German ambassador to Russia, Friedrich von Pourtalès, noted Russia's friendly attitude toward Berlin during the Agadir Crisis, but concluded that "only Russian need for peace prevented an outbreak of anti-German feeling."[153] Bethmann took a similar view of Russian behavior: Foreign Minister Serge Sazonov and Prime Minister Vladimir Kokovtsov "above all desire peace for Russia and *therefore*, not because they are in love with us—on the contrary they find us really unsympathetic—they want to be on a friendly footing with us, if possible."[154] In a note to Pourtalès, Bethmann again explains away desirable Russian behavior: "Russia likes us as little as any other Great Power. For that we are too strong, too parvenu, and generally too repulsive. Even Kokovtsov and Sazonov do not love us. If it were in the Russian inter-

---

[149] See Oswald Henry Wedel, *Austro-German Diplomatic Relations, 1908–1914* (Stanford: Stanford University Press, 1932), pp. 131–132; Fischer, *Germany's Aims*, pp. 25–26.

[150] Nicholas Dimitri Osten-Sacken to Neratov (August 16, 1911), quoted in Siebert, *Entente Diplomacy*, No. 690, p. 597. See also Barlow, *Agadir Crisis*, p. 357.

[151] Pourtalès to Bethmann (August 12, 1910), quoted in Lambi, *Navy and German Power*, p. 313.

[152] Pourtalès to Bethmann (August 22, 1910), ibid., pp. 313–314.

[153] This is Barlow's paraphrase of Pourtalès to Bethmann (September 1, 1911), in Barlow, *Agadir Crisis*, p. 362.

[154] Memorandum by Bethmann (July 6, 1912), quoted in Jarausch, *Enigmatic Chancellor*, pp. 117–118.

est to make war on us tomorrow, they would do so in cold blood."[155] Neither the kaiser, nor Bethmann, nor Pourtalès doubted Russian resolve.

Nor did Kiderlen think the Russians irresolute for failing to vigorously support France during the Agadir Crisis. As mentioned earlier, the deterrence argument expects the Germans to view the Russians as irresolute. For example, Kiderlen may view Russia as irresolute either because of its Bosnian capitulation, its Potsdam concessions, or its tepid support for France in 1911. The following explanation by Kiderlen undercuts these expectations:

> At the moment the [Russians] played the same role as the French had two years ago in the Bosnian-Serbian question: they indeed pledged the *nation amie et allié* their firm loyalty as an ally, but most urgently advised an understanding in Paris; the English, on the other hand, played a doubly crooked game since they wanted only to assure themselves . . . of the support of the French in case of later conflict.[156]

Kiderlen thought the Russians were loyal French allies encouraging their friends to reach a sensible agreement, just as the French had urged the Russians to do in 1909. He thought of neither France in 1909 nor Russia in 1911 as irresolute; these beliefs fit my hypothesis. Kiderlen's view of England also supports my argument. He did not portray the English as loyal French allies, but rather depicted their undesirable support in dispositional terms: the British "played a doubly crooked game."

German views of Austria. According to the deterrence hypothesis, the Germans should view Austria as irresolute for its weak support during the Agadir Crisis. I also argue that because Berlin viewed Austria's tepid support as undesirable, they should use dispositional attributions to explain this behavior.

I found little evidence revealing German views of their Austrian ally. They consistently doubted Austrian resolve in the past; there is no reason to think they would change their view after the Agadir Crisis. After the Bosnian Crisis, Bethmann noted: "Should extreme things come to pass, it would be better if the first attack were directed against Austria,

[155] Bethmann to Pourtalès (probably in July 1912), ibid., p. 118.
[156] Kiderlen to the Baden Minister (September 12, 1911), quoted in Lambi, *Navy and German Power*, p. 322.

which will then need *our* help, and not against us, so that [the outcome] does not depend upon Austria's [decision] if it wants to be loyal."[157] Kiderlen took an identical view.[158]

If past behavior governs expectations of future behavior, then the Germans should have expected their ally to be resolute because of its 1909 victory. But understandably, and as I argue, they saw no reason why Austrian behavior in the East should have any bearing on Austrian behavior in the West. Indeed, they did not even credit Vienna for being resolute in the Bosnian Crisis, so they could hardly use this event to predict similar behavior in Agadir. In short, my hypothesis was right to expect the Germans to doubt Austrian resolve after the Agadir Crisis. The deterrence hypothesis was also right (but only after dropping its interdependence assumption). Though there is little evidence that Berlin gave Vienna a reputation for being irresolute, the Germans certainly did not view the Austrians as resolute (even after their Bosnian victory). This outcome illustrates that it is possible for an ally to get a reputation for being irresolute, but hard to get a reputation for being resolute.

Summary of German views. The evidence in this section supports my argument and usually contradicts the deterrence argument. Both hypotheses correctly anticipated the German view of London: Berlin continued to view British policy-makers as resolute and aggressive. The German view of Austria and France also supports my hypothesis. It appears that undesirable behavior by the French and the Austrians led Berlin to continue to expect French resolution and Austrian irresolution. The deterrence hypothesis could make the same predictions, but only if we drop its interdependence assumption.

In the case of German views of Russia, the deterrence hypothesis cannot be saved even by dropping its interdependence assumption. Because the cautious Russian policy pleased Berlin, the Germans explained it away and continued to view the Russians as a resolute adversary. The deterrence hypothesis expected Berlin to view Russia as irresolute both because of its past and its immediate behavior. Deterrence's expectations are wrong on both counts.

The evidence in this section supports my four propositions on when reputations form. One, it is difficult for adversaries to get rep-

---

[157] Quoted in Jarausch, *Enigmatic Chancellor*, p. 131.
[158] Kiderlen to Bethmann (probably early 1910), quoted in Wedel, *Austro-German Relations*, p. 119.

utations for being irresolute. In spite of past Russian defeats, Berlin continued to view the Russians as resolute. Two, it is possible for adversaries to get reputations for being resolute. The Germans appear to view the British, French, and Russians as resolved. Three and four, it is possible for allies to get reputations for being irresolute, but difficult for allies to get reputations for being resolute. It appears that German policy-makers did not think the Austrians resolved because of their Bosnian victory, and continued to doubt the reliability of Vienna after Agadir.

Austrian Explanations

Vienna pursued at best a policy of benign neutrality toward the ally that had led it to victory in the Bosnian Crisis. The Austrians had mixed feelings about the German and French confrontation and therefore I cannot predict their views of Berlin's retreat or the Entente's victory. I can say that the Bosnian Crisis should play no role in Austrian policy-makers' explanations: they used situational attributions to explain their 1909 victory. The deterrence argument expects Vienna to view Germany as irresolute for yielding and the Entente as resolute for standing firm. The evidence supports my expectations (on the role of past behavior).

A. J. P. Taylor observes that Austria-Hungary was "ostentatious" in its non-support of its ally.[159] Aehrenthal was dying of leukemia and was replaced by Count Johann Pallavicini from March to May. Pallavicini constantly professed his "total ignorance" of all things Moroccan; he raised no objection to the French march to Fez and gave the French great leeway in interpreting its treaty obligations.[160]

Upon his return to office, Aehrenthal continued Austria's disinterested policy. When the Hungarian prime minister said the Moroccan issue lay beyond the scope of the Dual Alliance, Aehrenthal quickly defended him against loud German complaints.[161] Even after the Mansion House speech, Vienna failed to rush to Berlin's side, but merely viewed the speech as "inopportune intervention" by London.[162] Vienna contin-

---

[159] See A. J. P. Taylor, *The Habsburg Monarchy, 1809–1918: A History of the Austrian Empire and Austria-Hungary* (London: Hamish Hamilton, 1948), p. 220.

[160] See F. R. Bridge, *From Sadowa to Sarajevo: The Foreign Policy of Austria-Hungary, 1866–1914* (London: Routledge and Kegan Paul, 1972), p. 333; Bridge, *Great Britain and Austria*, p. 173.

[161] See Bridge, *Great Britain and Austria*, p. 175.

[162] Aehrenthal to Szögyény (July 31, 1911), quoted in ibid., p. 176.

ually warned Berlin that Austria could not fight over Morocco, maintained good relations with Paris throughout the crisis, and offered little more than benevolent neutrality to Germany.[163]

Aside from Austria's annoyance at Berlin's failure to consult or even to inform Vienna of its plans or objectives in Morocco, there are two complementary explanations for Austria's policy.[164] The first concerns Vienna's preoccupation with the Balkans, which illustrates how states' priorities differ and the effect this difference of attention may have on attributions; the second concerns their view of Germany as an ally, which highlights the role of past behavior.

Austria was always more concerned with the East than the West. During the Agadir Crisis, Vienna's attention was riveted first on turmoil in Albania, then on the dangers of a general Balkan war that might be sparked by Italy's war against Tripoli (then part of the Ottoman Empire). In 1910, Albanians revolted against oppressive Turkish rule and the Turks responded with violence. Although Aehrenthal worked out a negotiated solution, the Turks continued to brutalize the Albanians by attempting to squash all non-Turk expressions of nationalism. By March 1911—about the same time the French began their moves into Morocco—5,000 Albanian tribesmen were in revolt, causing a huge refugee problem that threatened to develop into a war between Turkey and Montenegro.

Although Hungarian Catholics were demanding that Vienna protect the Albanians, the Dual Monarchy was also pushed to action by its strategic interests in the lower Adriatic: if the Albanians were crushed, Serbia might pick up the pieces; if Montenegro was crushed, Hungary would lose a valuable buffer between it and the turbulent Ottoman Empire; and if they did nothing, the Albanians might appeal to Rome (which viewed Albania as the western gateway to the Balkans and important in affecting the balance in the Adriatic). To make matters worse, on June 25 Germany declared its support for Turkey in the Albanian conflict.[165] In addition, Italy's declaration of war against Tripoli at the end of September, and Russia's efforts to exploit this turmoil to capture the straits, account further for Vienna's relative disinterest in events in Morocco.

---

[163] See Wedel, *Austro-German Relations*, p. 133; Barlow, *Agadir Crisis*, pp. 356–357. Barlow notes that Vienna put some pressure on Paris to be moderate in early September.

[164] For Austria's annoyance, see Bridge, *Great Britain and Austria*, pp. 175–176.

[165] For details, see Bridge, *Sadowa to Sarajevo*, pp. 326–333; Andrew Rossos, *Russia and the Balkans: Inter-Balkan Rivalries and Russian Foreign Policy, 1908–1914* (Toronto: University of Toronto Press, 1981), pp. 34–37; Anthony di Iorio, "Italy, Austria-Hungary and the Balkans, 1904–1914: Italy's Appraisal" (Ph.D. diss., University of Illinois at Urbana-Champaign, 1980), pp. 254–259.

This background helps to explain Austrian policy in the Moroccan Crisis and may also explain why I found little evidence bearing on Austrian views of German or French behavior. Vienna was actually relieved that Germany found itself embroiled in a Moroccan conflict, for the distraction checked Berlin's unwelcome interventions in the Balkans.[166] Deterrence theory assumes that everyone pays close attention to everyone else. This is often not the case. As in 1906 when the Austrians were consumed by a constitutional crisis rather than the Moroccan Crisis, so in 1911 was Vienna's attention directed elsewhere during the Agadir Crisis. Morocco was not a priority and, consequently, it would not be surprising if Vienna spent little time thinking about who was and was not resolute in the crisis.

It appears that Austrian decision-makers felt no debt of gratitude to Germany for its support in the Bosnian Crisis. What came to mind was Berlin's present support for Turkey, not its 1909 support for Austria in Bosnia. While Aehrenthal referred to Berlin's present undesirable Balkan policy as a reason for not supporting Germany, he failed to mention the earlier support.[167] This earlier support had not faded from memory; it was never in their memory because Austrian decision-makers did not credit Berlin for Vienna's victory, but instead explained it away.

The evidence in this section suggests that Austria paid little attention to the Agadir Crisis. Rather than worry about who got what in the Congo, they were busy putting out brush fires in the Balkans. It does not appear that Austria thought the Germans irresolute or the Entente resolute. Rather than thinking Berlin resolute for its Bosnian support (as the deterrence hypothesis expected), Aehrenthal was annoyed at Berlin for failing to support his current Balkan line. This evidence supports my argument about interdependence and illustrates the more general point: allies rarely get reputations for having resolve.

Russian Explanations

Because Russian decision-makers blamed French irresolution for contributing to their 1909 defeat, the deterrence hypothesis expects the Russians to anticipate French irresolution in Agadir. After the French victory at Agadir, this hypothesis expects the Russians to view France

---

[166] See Bridge, *Sadowa to Sarajevo*, p. 333; Bridge, *Great Britain and Austria*, p. 175.
[167] See Aehrenthal's July 4, 1911 memo, quoted in Barlow, *Agadir Crisis*, p. 249.

as resolute for standing up to the Germans. In contrast, I argue that the Russians will explain away French resolve in Agadir by making situational attributions. Because they depicted the French as irresolute in 1909, and because I expect them to explain away the French victory, the Russians should not give the French a reputation for resolve. In this section, some of the evidence supports my argument, but some contradicts it and supports the deterrence argument.

Russian views of Germany and France. The initial Russian reaction to the German retreat mostly supports my argument. Russian policy-makers explained this desirable retreat in situational terms and did not think the Germans irresolute (as expected by the deterrence argument). Later, Izvolsky begins crediting the French for their resolve in the Agadir Crisis—these explanations partially confirm the deterrence argument and partially contradict my hypothesis. Nonetheless, Russian decision-makers continued to view the Germans as resolute; this response supports my argument, but not deterrence's.

Rather than think the Germans irresolute for backing down at Agadir, Russian decision-makers thought Berlin demonstrated good sense. Izvolsky called the agreement "far-sighted" and added: "The French Minister òf Foreign Affairs does justice to the moderation shown by Germany during the second stage of the negotiations."[168] It was the German retreat—what Izvolsky calls the "second stage"—that he labeled as moderate. After the Mansion House speech, Benckendorff thought he detected the beginnings of a German retreat. Rather than believe the Germans were irresolute, he thought that "caution and moderation won the upper hand."[169] As did British decision-makers, Russian decision-makers found the German concessions desirable and so felt Berlin was demonstrating caution and moderation, but not irresolution.

Benckendorff puzzled over Germany's "more conciliatory attitude towards France" and said he could find only one explanation for the change: "Germany was entirely mistaken in her estimate of the English attitude. . . . If this be true then it was all a tremendous error of judgment."[170] The British and French also attributed the German move and retreat to a misperception; they blundered, as Nicolson put it. A misperception could be either a situational or dispositional attribution, de-

---

[168] Izvolsky to Neratov (October 25, 1911), quoted in Siebert, *Entente Diplomacy*, No. 707, p. 609.
[169] Benckendorff to Neratov (August 1, 1911), ibid., No. 689, p. 596.
[170] Ibid.

pending upon why an actor blundered. Either way, it does not suggest they thought Berlin irresolute, as the deterrence argument contends.

Rather than think the Germans irresolute, the Russian ambassador to Germany thought the kaiser in this instance resolved for peace: the settlement should be ascribed "to two circumstances: First, Emperor William, at the first outbreak of the crisis, resolved not to let it come to war; and, secondly, [Cambon] here has displayed unusual cleverness and tact."[171] This attribution contradicts the deterrence argument, which expects St. Petersburg to view the Germans as irresolute and the French as resolute. But it also contradicts my argument. Because the outcome was desirable, I expected the Russian ambassador to use situational attributions to explain the outcome, rather than attribute it to Cambon's "cleverness" and the kaiser's resolve for peace.

Izvolsky's attributions provide the best evidence I have found against my argument. After the crisis, in December 1911, Izvolsky reported that Germany had "retreated only before the perspective of a clash with France, England, and with us."[172] Although this attribution is ambiguous, for we do not know if Izvolsky has capability or resolve in mind, his next reports are unambiguous.

On December 20, Izvolsky attributes his Bosnian defeat to a lack of unity in the Triple Entente; he then notes that now the Triple Entente "has not only demonstrated its inner strength, but has also shown that it is in a position to act in favor of the preservation of general peace. . . . Should it not be ascribed to the resolute attitude of the three Entente Powers, that Germany showed that compliance which finally led to the signature of the Agreement of November 4?"[173] Not only does Izvolsky stress the importance of resolve to the Entente in general, but he later explicitly credits the French with demonstrating resolve in contrast to their behavior in 1905. Izvolsky writes that France "has shown her unshakable resolve not to shrink from defending her rights and interests even at the cost, if need be, of resort to arms."[174]

Izvolsky's attributions cause my hypothesis to flunk the first test: in this case, Izvolsky explained France's desirable behavior in disposi-

[171] Osten-Sacken to Neratov (October 13, 1911), quoted in Siebert, *Entente Diplomacy*, No. 706, p. 609.

[172] Izvolsky to Neratov (December 7, 1911), quoted in Firuz Kazemzadeh, *Russia and Britain in Persia, 1864–1914: A Study in Imperialism* (New Haven: Yale University Press, 1968), pp. 637–638.

[173] Izvolsky to Neratov (December 20, 1911), quoted in Siebert, *Entente Diplomacy*, No. 710, p. 611.

[174] Izvolsky to Sazonov (February 15, 1912), quoted in Stieve, *Isvolsky*, pp. 56–57.

tional terms. His choice contradicts my argument but supports the deterrence argument. At the same time, my hypothesis passes the second
test. In spite of Izvolsky's belief that the French were bad allies and irresolute in 1909, he nonetheless thinks them resolute at Agadir. Even if
he expected the French to be irresolute—and as earlier discussed this
does not appear to be the case—the French were able to erase this image
by standing firm in the next crisis. This sequence fits the deterrence argument only if immediate behavior governs attributions.

In short, even when an observer thinks another is irresolute in one
crisis, this attribution may not be carried over into the next crisis. We
may recall Nicolson's view of the Russians in 1909 and 1911. He first
thought St. Petersburg irresolute in Bosnia, but then thought it resolute
in Agadir. Like Nicolson's newfound belief in Russian resolution, Izvolsky's view of French resolution may only be called a reputation if it is
later used to predict or explain future behavior.

My argument that it is difficult for allies to acquire reputations for resolve still stands, but it has been shaken. Both Nicolson's view of Russian and French resolution, and Izvolsky's view of French resolution in
the Agadir Crisis open the door for an ally to get a reputation for resolve in the next crisis. I hasten to add that these attributions are the ex-
ception; I can account for nearly all the attributions I have found over
the course of three major crises. Nonetheless, these attributions are disquieting.

Finally, note that while Izvolsky may have thought the Triple Entente
resolute, neither he nor his colleagues thought the Germans irresolute.
For example, after ascribing the Agadir victory to the Entente's resolve,
Izvolsky notes that the European political situation is "less secure than
ever" and that "any local collision between the Powers is bound to lead
to a general European conflict" in which Russia will have to participate.[175] And after noting French resolve, Izvolsky warns Sazonov to expect "fresh international complications" in the spring.[176]

The Russian ambassador to Germany noted during the crisis: "Whatever the result of the present negotiations may be, in the soul of the German people will long remain the sting of wounded pride, because
Germany has again yielded to England's effectual protest."[177] Echoing

---

[175] Izvolsky to Neratov (December 20, 1911), quoted in Siebert, *Entente Diplomacy*, No.
710, p. 612.
[176] Izvolsky to Sazonov (February 15, 1912), quoted in Stieve, *Isvolsky*, p. 57.
[177] Osten-Sacken to Neratov (August 18, 1911), quoted in Siebert, *Entente Diplomacy*,
No. 692, p. 599.

this "Never again!" sentiment, Benckendorff noted how upset the Germans were after Agadir and observed: "Success is calming; failure exasperates."[178] As I argue, and contrary to the deterrence argument, the Russian leadership explained away the Germans' defeat at Agadir and continued to view them as dangerous and resolved.

Russian views of Vienna and London. The deterrence hypothesis expects the Russians to view the Austrians as irresolute (for failing to back the Germans) and the British as resolute (for their staunch support of France). I expect St. Petersburg to use situational attributions to explain away the behavior of both Austria and England.

Perhaps because Austria played such a minor role in the crisis, I found no Russian explanations of its behavior. I also found little evidence bearing on their views of British behavior. As I discuss in the conclusion, Anglo-Russian relations revolved more around Persia than Morocco. As noted above, it appears that at least Izvolsky thought the British resolute in Agadir. This counts against my argument and supports the deterrence hypothesis.

Summary of Russian views. My hypothesis took a beating in this section. Though it never failed the second test (for interdependence), it frequently failed the first. For example, Izvolsky viewed the French and British as resolved at Agadir, when I expected him to explain away their behavior.

My hypothesis did better on the second test. For example, Izvolsky's assessment of French decision-makers appears not to have been influenced by their earlier behavior in the Bosnian Crisis (where he thought the French were irresolute). This response highlights the possibility that dispositional attributions may be independent. However, St. Petersburg's view of Germany illustrates that dispositional attributions are sometimes interdependent. Because they explained away the desirable German defeat, the Russian leadership stuck to their belief that the Germans were dangerous and resolved adversaries. This evidence supports my argument that it is difficult for adversaries to get reputations for lacking resolve. The Russians did not doubt their adversary's resolve; if anything, they thought the defeat would make Berlin ever more resolved.

I also argue that it is difficult for allies to get reputations for having resolve. On this score, the evidence in this section is mixed. On the one

---

[178] Benckendorff to Neratov (February 8, 1912), quoted in Siebert, *Entente Diplomacy*, No. 712, p. 617.

hand, Russian decision-makers did not use past dispositional attributions to predict future behavior. On the other hand, Izvolsky did credit the French for being resolved. Whether he has given France a reputation for resolve depends on what attributions he makes in the next crisis.

CONCLUSIONS

Most of the evidence in this chapter supports my arguments about when reputations form. As in the earlier empirical chapters, the desirability of another's behavior determines whether we view that behavior in more situational or dispositional terms. There were some exceptions. Before addressing these disconfirming attributions, this section summarizes how well the deterrence argument did against the evidence.

The Deterrence Hypothesis

If we assume that behavior in the previous crisis governs expectations of future behavior, then decision-makers will expect an adversary who retreats in one crisis to be irresolute in the next. For example, because the Germans retreated at Algeciras, London should predict that the Germans will display similar irresolution in the Bosnian Crisis. As discussed in the previous chapter, London did not doubt German resolve in 1909. Starting anew, because the Germans stood firm in Bosnia, London should expect them to be resolute in Agadir. This time the deterrence hypothesis got it right. However, because the Germans were then defeated at Agadir, the British should view the Germans as again irresolute—but they do not. The same story could be told for German views of the French and Russians. Because the British stood firm in all three crises, the deterrence hypothesis accurately predicted that the Germans would think the British were resolute.

If we narrow the scope of the deterrence hypothesis by assuming that states get reputations for resolve only in specific regions or over specific issues, it still fails. For example, after the first Moroccan Crisis, the deterrence hypothesis expects the British and the French to view the German retreat at the Algeciras Conference as revealing German irresolution. As a result, London and Paris should expect Berlin to be irresolute in Agadir where the region, the issues, and many of the key decision-makers were the same as in 1906. We should at a minimum see the Entente decision-makers referring to earlier German irresolution in the first crisis, but I found no evidence that supports this expectation. Far from expecting the Germans to be irresolute, they assumed them to be dangerously resolute adversaries who dared to challenge again in the same region over the same issue.

The deterrence hypothesis did no better with allies than it did with adversaries. For example, the British were steadfast supporters of France in Morocco and led them to victory in both Moroccan Crises. After the first crisis, the French should view the British as resolute and trusted allies. Paris should also expect British resolve based on London's strong support of Russia in the Bosnian Crisis. In the next Moroccan Crisis, they should at least make reference to the valorous British support. But they do not. French policy-makers fail to draw on either the first Moroccan or Bosnian Crisis because in both cases they explained British behavior in situational terms, just as they explain their victory in the second Moroccan Crisis in situational terms. The French believed the British were acting to advance British interests; should those interests change, so would British support.

If we assume that the most recent attribution governs expectations, then the British might expect the French to be irresolute because of France's tepid support of Russia in 1909. In fact, London did doubt French resolve, although this irresolution was usually attributed to a lack of French capability. The British never brought up French behavior in the Bosnian Crisis. If we assume past behavior in a specific region or over a specific issue governs, then the deterrence hypothesis fails completely to predict the British attributions of their French ally. Because the French had faced down the Germans in 1906, British decision-makers should have been confident the French would do so in 1911. But as just pointed out, they had their doubts.

The deterrence hypothesis did no better when an ally behaved in a desirable way. Even when this hypothesis passes the first test, it flunks the second. For example, because Nicolson thought the Russians were irresolute in 1909, he should have expected them to be irresolute in 1911. In fact, he expected them to be resolute. And although Izvolsky thought the French were irresolute in the Bosnian Crisis, he nonetheless viewed them as resolute in the Agadir Crisis.

Resolve reputations did not form the way deterrence theorists expect. This hypothesis consistently failed to pass the second test on when reputations form. Even narrowing the scope of the hypothesis did not help. It was clearly right in only one case: the Germans gave the British a reputation for resolve.

A Theoretical Amendment to the Desires Hypothesis

Rather than review how the èvidence supports my four propositions, this section discusses the proposition that seems most vulnerable; namely, that allies rarely get reputations for being resolute. Most of the evidence supports this proposition. For example, the French did not think England resolute in spite of its strong support of its allies in all three crises. Instead, French decision-makers explain away Britain's support as a function of British interests, rather than British treaty obligations, moral commitments, or character. Similarly, the British never stop worrying over a possible French defection to the Triple Alliance. Most British policy-makers stress French capability rather than resolve to explain their ally's behavior. The Germans also doubt their Austrian ally's reliability. They worried that Austria would go to war only in the East, but never in the West. The French took a similar view of Russia. The only way to ensure Russian participation in a war against Germany was for the war to start first in the Balkans.[179]

However, there may be trouble on the horizon for this proposition. As pointed out above, Nicolson's view of French and Russian resolve, Lloyd George's use of situational explanations to account for undesirable Russian behavior at Agadir, and Izvolsky's view of French resolve, cause my hypothesis to fail the first test. In failing the first test, I set myself up to fail the second. Because two of these decision-makers, Nicolson and Izvolsky, thought their allies were resolved in the Agadir Crisis, it is possible that they will use this characterization to predict or explain their future behavior.

A solution to the puzzle may be found by returning to my assumptions regarding in-group and out-group attributions. I assumed a state would view even its allies as part of the out-group. Though this simplifying assumption has worked well up to now, it may be that as the external environment becomes more threatening and alliances become tighter, states view their allies as part of the in-group. In this case, decision-makers would explain away their allies' undesirable behavior, and

---

[179] See John C. Cairns, "International Politics and the Military Mind: The Case of the French Republic, 1911–1914," *Journal of Modern History* 25 (September 1953): 276.

credit them for their desirable behavior. As a result, allies could get reputations for being resolute, but not for being irresolute.

For example, Izvolsky used his explanation in part to convince St. Petersburg of the importance of holding fast to the Triple Entente. Grey was under enormous pressure in this period to do something about Russia's Persia policy; both Benckendorff and Izvolsky feared that by continuing the present policy, Neratov could seriously damage the Entente, perhaps even cause Grey's resignation and the ascendence of the pro-German Liberals.[180] Izvolsky thought the key to Russia's security was to be found in the Triple Entente and, perhaps, came to see London and Paris as part of the in-group. As a result, he began to view Russia's allies as resolute. Germany was still an out-group, and correspondingly he did not attribute to them a lack of resolve.

There are some problems with this argument. First, Izvolsky's explanations may have more to do with politics than perceptions. He may have been trying to bolster his arguments on the centrality of the Triple Entente to Russian security by billing France as a trustworthy and resolute ally. The same explanation could be made of Nicolson's views of France and Russia during the Agadir Crisis. Second, changing my assumption leads to a methodological morass. How do we know when the external environment becomes threatening enough to switch assumptions? We cannot use attributions to account for the switch without risking some circularity. These difficulties aside, altering the in-group/out-group assumption may give us insight into how allies explain one another's behavior.

To illustrate this idea further, consider British explanations of undesirable Russian behavior at Potsdam (before the Agadir Crisis), and in Persia (during and after the Agadir Crisis). To illustrate the differences in the two in-group/out-group assumptions, I present these hypotheses in stark terms. It is possible that a more nuanced assumption, something like in-group, "in-law-group," and out-group might capture the relations between allies.

The British explained undesirable Russian behavior during its Potsdam negotiations with Germany in sharply dispositional terms. The Russians and Germans first met in November 1910 to discuss Persia and the Baghdad railway. In August 1911, they reached agreement: Germany recognized Russia's rights in northern Persia, and Russia agreed not to oppose the Baghdad railway and to connect it with a line

---

[180] See Kazemzadeh, *Russia and Britain*, pp. 632–669.

from Persia—this solution would allow for German economic penetration of that region.[181]

Because the Russian veto over the Baghdad railroad was about to expire, and in order to avoid a deterioration of relations with Germany, Sazonov sanctioned what he could not prevent.[182] Sazonov reasoned it would take ten to fifteen years before the railroad would reach Baghdad, and the line connecting it to Persia would not begin until the main line was complete. This interval gave Russia time to strengthen its position in Persia and hope that a change in the international situation would help Russia break its promise.[183]

Britain and France found these negotiations undesirable: they did not want the Russians negotiating unilaterally with the Germans and especially did not like the results, which damaged British interests in Persia. For example, Nicolson minuted: "We have new surprises daily. I feel that one must be continually at [Sazonov], as he is so deficient in backbone."[184] In another note complaining about Russian behavior at Potsdam, Nicolson writes that Sazonov seems disposed to "yield to whatever demands are made to him from Berlin."[185] The only explanation Nicolson could come up with to explain Sazonov's undesirable behavior was that he lacked resolve. Bertie shared Nicolson's disdain.[186]

Both Jules Cambon's and Goschen's alarm can be seen in the latter's report to Nicolson:

> Cambon is furious with the whole thing. He told me yesterday that officially he took the line that nothing that had occurred at Potsdam, or afterwards, could disturb the relations between France and Russia; but he added, "Would you like to know my opinion? Well, it is that the Franco-Russian Alliance is f—." I think that we may take it for granted that Kiderlen's policy is to detach Russia from France and us, and that he has already gone some way towards its realization. He has evidently been too much for Sazonoff, and I think that the latter is much mistaken if he thinks that he can wriggle out of what he has been brought to say and write.[187]

[181] For details, see Lee, *Europe's Crucial Years*, pp. 216–220; Taylor, *Struggle for Mastery*, pp. 463–466.

[182] See Allshouse, "Aleksander Izvolskii," p. 145.

[183] Kazemzadeh, *Russia and Britain*, pp. 595–596.

[184] Quoted in Gooch, *Before the War*, p. 301.

[185] Nicolson to Lowther (January 23, 1911), Lowe and Dockrill, *Documents*, p. 469.

[186] Bertie to Nicolson (May 14, 1911), Lowe and Dockrill, *Documents*, p. 433.

[187] Goschen to Nicolson (January 7, 1911), quoted in Nicolson, *Portrait of a Diplomatist*, p. 245. Also see Pichon's views in Gooch, *Before the War*, p. 301; and Buchanan's views in Sir George Buchanan, *My Mission to Russia and Other Diplomatic Memoirs* (Boston: Little, Brown, 1923), p. 93.

Neither Cambon nor Goschen had any doubt that Sazonov was an irresolute man whom the Germans now had on the run. Compare these attributions with the ones British decision-makers used to explain undesirable Russian behavior in Persia. Unlike the attributions just presented, the following attributions occurred during and after the Agadir Crisis. These attributions suggest that some British decision-makers had begun to view the Russians as part of the in-group.

In their 1907 treaty, the British and Russians agreed to split Persia in half, with the Russians controlling the north, the British controlling the south, and a neutral zone in the middle. Neither state was to turn its sector into a protectorate. Since the British were preoccupied with the Germans during the Agadir Crisis, Neratov reasoned that now was the time to push for greater control of the Russian sector in Persia.

Although British decision-makers strongly objected to the Russian move, the need for the Russian alliance led them to explain undesirable Russian behavior in more situational than dispositional terms. For example, after Agadir Nicolson felt strongly that the Russian alliance must not break down because of Persia: "It is of the highest importance that we should remain on the most friendly terms with Russia. It would be disastrous to our foreign policy were the understandings with Russia, France and ourselves to be weakened in any way."[188]

An anecdote told by Nicolson's son captures his view of the Russians after the Agadir Crisis: "It is still recounted in the Foreign Office that [Nicolson] minuted a bulky memorandum on Russian violations of the Convention [of 1907] with the words: I have not read this document. But if, as I assume, it contains criticisms of Russian procedure in Persia, it is largely based on prejudice and false assumptions."[189] Nicolson, who had been quick to spot Russian irresolution and was willing to sacrifice the Entente before Agadir, now calmly dismisses any suggestion of Russian misbehavior. In his memoirs, Buchanan also turns a blind eye to Russian treaty violations, arguing that Sazonov had no choice for he had to vindicate Russia's "outraged honor."[190]

It is also clear that Grey strongly opposed Russian behavior in Persia. In public he portrayed the Russians as loyal allies acting in perfect harmony with their treaty commitments. In private he sought to keep them from taking Persia. I was unable to find out how he characterized Rus-

---

[188] Nicolson to Barclay (October 24, 1911), Lowe and Dockrill, *Documents*, p. 471.
[189] Quoted in Harold Nicolson, *Portrait of a Diplomatist*, p. 258.
[190] See Buchanan, *My Mission*, p. 101.

sian policy in private.[191] Nonetheless, it is clear that London viewed Russian behavior in Persia as undesirable, and it appears that they refrained from using dispositional attributions to explain this behavior. After the close call at Agadir, London may have begun to view the Russians as part of the in-group.

A. J. P. Taylor suggests that the confrontations before Agadir had been crises of diplomacy; after Agadir, nations confronted each other in a prewar spirit.[192] As the bonds of the Triple Entente and Triple Alliance tightened and nations girded for war, it is possible that they began viewing their allies as part of the in-group while still viewing their adversaries as part of the out-group. This new perspective would explain why before Agadir, the British offered dispositional explanations for undesirable Russian behavior at Potsdam, but more situational attributions for undesirable Russian behavior in Persia. It would also explain Lloyd George's use of the situation to explain undesirable Russian policy at Agadir, as well as why Izvolsky and Nicolson thought their allies resolute at Agadir. The greater the felt need to identify another as part of the in-group, the more pronounced this tendency ought to be.

Most of the evidence in this chapter supports the assumption that states view all other powers, including allies, as part of the out-group. Nonetheless, we should be alert to the possibility of allies treating one another as part of the in-group as alliances become tighter or in times of war.

---

[191] See Keith Wilson, "Grey," in *British Foreign Secretaries and Foreign Policy: From Crimean War to First World War*, ed. Keith M. Wilson (London: Croom Helm, 1986), p. 189; Keith Wilson, *The Policy of the Entente: Essays on the Determinants of British Foreign Policy, 1904–1914* (Cambridge: Cambridge University Press, 1985), p. 82; Steiner, *Foreign Office*, pp. 131–132.

[192] Taylor, *Struggle for Mastery*, p. 473.

[6]

Conclusion

> When we recall how we discussed methods for demonstrating
> "our superior resolve" without ever questioning whether we
> would indeed have or deserve to have superiority in that com-
> modity, we realize how puerile was our whole approach to our art.
>
> —Bernard Brodie

Deterrence theorists spent so much time figuring out how to demonstrate resolve that they never stopped to examine what they were manipulating. Like economists who assume a ladder to escape from a deep
hole, deterrence theorists assumed a reputation to escape from the
problem of making credible threats and promises. But as the case studies in this book show, reputations for resolve do not form the way they
are usually thought to form. By treating the formation of reputation as
a problem rather than as an assumption, we can see what Bernard
Brodie meant when he called deterrence theorists' approach to resolve
"puerile."

This book's empirical chapters confound the common assumptions
about how reputations form. The examples show that different people
often explain the same behavior differently; that these different explanations are often a consequence of whether someone views an outcome
as desirable or undesirable; and that people do not consistently use past
behavior to predict similar behavior in the future. This analysis implies
that policy-makers should not think there is a direct correspondence between their behavior and their reputation. They should recognize that
they can get different reputations, or no reputation at all, based on the
same behavior. Both theory and evidence suggest that, to the extent that
other people draw general inferences about our resolution from our behavior, they do so in ways that make some reputations much less likely
than others. For example, our adversaries will rarely view us as irres-

olute and our allies will rarely view us as resolute. This chapter reviews some of this evidence, discusses additional historical cases and issues for further research, and presents some additional theoretical and policy implications.

How Reputations Formed from 1905 to 1911

European decision-makers in crises from Algeciras to Bosnia to Agadir often could not use the past to predict the future because their explanations of past behavior were specific to the situation. Yet, even when they used another's disposition to explain behavior, this analysis was rarely used to predict similar behavior in the future. When they did use the past to predict or explain the future, a reputation formed. Using the desires hypothesis to predict when policy-makers use another's disposition to explain their behavior, I arrived at four propositions on when reputations form.

Adversaries and Reputations

The first two propositions address the question of reputations for resolve between adversaries. Although adversaries can get reputations for having resolve, they rarely get reputations for lacking it. For example, British, French, and Russian decision-makers believed their German adversaries were resolute. When the Germans challenged their opponents, they appeared to the Entente to be bullies. But when the Germans retreated, the Entente did not then think the Germans were wimps. Instead, they explained away German defeats and preserved their image of the German bully. Indeed, they thought the Germans would be more resolute in the future because they suffered defeat. Britain and France made the same sort of explanations for Austrian behavior.

German explanations of the French and Russians also illustrate why adversaries cannot easily get reputations for lacking resolve. The Germans welcomed the lackluster support that its adversary France offered Russia during the Bosnian Crisis and Berlin offered corresponding situational attributions to explain desirable French behavior. Similarly, the Germans were pleased with the Russians' half-hearted support of France in the Agadir Crisis; again, they offered situational explanations. Indeed, in spite of the humiliating Russian defeat at Bosnia, the significant Russian concessions to Germany at Potsdam, and Russian non-support of its ally in the Agadir Crisis, the Germans continued to assume the Russians were a dangerous and resolute adversary who would turn on Germany when the time was right. Adversaries rarely get reputations for lacking resolve.

Allies and Reputations

The other two propositions address reputations for resolve between allies. Although allies can get reputations for lacking resolve, they rarely get reputations for having resolve. The evidence usually supports these propositions, but there are some exceptions.

After the first Moroccan Crisis, the British and French credited themselves, but not each other, for their victory. For this reason, each had little confidence in how the other would behave in the next Moroccan crisis. The French continued to doubt British support against the Germans, and the British continued to fear that the French might defect to the enemy bloc. French decision-makers explained the strong British support after the Mansion House speech as resulting from British interests. Should British interests change, so would the level of British support for France. In spite of strong British support for France in 1906, for Russia in 1909, and for France in 1911, French decision-makers continued to explain British behavior in situational terms. Allies rarely get reputations for being resolute or loyal.

In contrast, allies can get reputations for lacking resolve. In my study, allies rarely received a reputation for lacking resolve. For example, the British were very disappointed with the Russians' capitulation in the Bosnian Crisis and explained this defeat primarily in dispositional terms: the Russian leadership was irresolute. Similarly, the Russians complained that the French were worthless allies in the Bosnian Crisis and thought them irresolute. But an attribution is not the same as a reputation. Neither the British nor the Russians expected their ally to be irresolute in the next crisis; neither state gave its ally a reputation for lacking resolve.

Some Empirical Discrepancies

Although my argument consistently offers better explanations than the rival deterrence hypothesis, it is a probabilistic argument and it will sometimes be wrong. Rather than ignore the unexpected attributions or try to explain them away, I offer some alternative explanations for the more systematic exceptions.

Sometimes actors explained away undesirable allied behavior, or they viewed an ally's desirable behavior as reflecting its resolution. As I discuss in Chapter 5, these puzzling attributions make sense if allies sometimes view each other as part of the in-group. Although changing the in-group/out-group assumption raises some methodological complications, it may be that in times of crisis (such as when war appears likely), allies will view each other as part of the in-group. However, most of the evidence I gathered supports my original assumption that decision-makers view even allies as part of the out-group.

The way ambassadors explained their host country's behavior sometimes contradicted my argument. Although ambassadors generally explained behavior as I expected, there were several exceptions. For example, during the first Moroccan Crisis the British ambassador to Paris explained undesirable French behavior in situational terms, and the German ambassador to Italy used situational attributions to explain undesirable Italian behavior. I also found that the German and Austrian ambassadors to London sometimes viewed undesirable British behavior during the Bosnian Crisis in ways my hypothesis did not anticipate.

It may be, as Chaim Kaufmann argues, that the more motivated we are to defend a policy and the less salient the disconfirming evidence, the less likely we are to change our views.[1] Because information gained on a firsthand basis is more salient than information read in a report in the home capital, we might expect foreign ambassadors in, say, Berlin to be more inclined to offer complex situational explanations for German behavior. If this expectation is correct, then they are less likely to give the Germans a reputation because they are more likely to use situational attributions to explain German behavior.

CASES AND ISSUES FOR FURTHER RESEARCH

More than sixty million people were killed in both world wars. Could European policy-makers have avoided this slaughter by taking better care of their reputations? It is argued that by 1914 the Germans had

---

[1] See Chaim D. Kaufmann, "Out of the Lab and into the Archives: A Method for Testing Psychological Explanations of Political Decision Making," *International Studies Quarterly* 38 (December 1994): 574–576.

given the Russians a reputation for being irresolute. They expected the Russians to yield before Austro-German power because the Russians' retreat in the Bosnian Crisis showed them to be an irresolute state. Similarly, it is argued that in 1938 Hitler learned that the British and French were irresolute and spineless states because of their humiliating concessions during the Munich Conference. More recently, some observers think that Iraqi aggression against Kuwait was a direct result of American irresolution in Vietnam and in the Middle East. Although the conventional view of 1914 is wrong, a careful study of the case would help us better understand some issues related to how reputations form. And while the traditional view of the Munich crisis is also wrong, only a detailed study of Hitler's explanations could tell us what role reputation played in his thinking. It is too soon to tell exactly what role reputation played in Saddam Hussein's thinking, but there is good reason to doubt that reputation played an important role.

The 1914 Sarajevo Crisis

Scholars often argue that the Russian defeat in the Bosnian Crisis was responsible for the outbreak of the First World War. Because the Russians backed down in 1909, the Germans and Austrians supposedly gave the Russians a reputation for irresolution and expected them to back down in 1914. This view must be wrong if my interpretation of the 1909 crisis is right.

Because neither Austrian nor German decision-makers thought the Russians were irresolute in the Bosnian Crisis, they could not then sensibly believe the Russians would be irresolute in 1914 because they backed down in 1909. Indeed, even after the Agadir Crisis and the Potsdam concessions, the German leadership assumed the Russians would strike when the time was right. "If it were in the Russian interest to make war on us tomorrow," said Chancellor Bethmann Hollweg, "they would do so in cold blood."[2] It is possible that the Germans and Austrians thought the situation in 1914 was similar to the one in 1909—namely, that the Russians lacked the capability to fight. This, however, has no bearing on Russia's reputation for resolve. It is one thing to say the Russians lacked the capability to fight, it is another to say they lacked the will.

[2] Bethmann to Pourtalès (probably in July 1912), quoted in Konrad H. Jarausch, *The Enigmatic Chancellor: Bethmann Hollweg and the Hubris of Imperial Germany* (New Haven: Yale University Press, 1973), p. 118.

It is also possible that the Germans and Austrians could have forgotten their earlier explanation for the Russians' Bosnian defeat and come to believe Russia had been irresolute in 1909. More generally, decision-makers may reinterpret the past to serve contemporary needs.[3] This may be particularly true of states that want to expand. In other words, if the Germans thought 1914 was similar to 1909, then a lack of Russian capability explains the challenge; if the Germans reinterpreted the past to suit contemporary needs, then a motivated bias was responsible for the challenge. In either case, Russia's reputation for irresolution is not part of the explanation.

The Munich Crisis

The most often cited illustration of the dangers of acquiring a reputation for lacking resolve is British and French appeasement of Germany during the Munich Crisis. In *The Struggle for Europe*, Chester Wilmot declared that Hitler's "personal triumph at Munich had profoundly affected his judgment of British character." Hitler reportedly said to his commanders-in-chief shortly before the Polish campaign: "Our enemies are little worms; I saw them at Munich."[4] This interpretation was picked up by Fred Charles Iklé and later used by Glenn Snyder and Paul Diesing as the only example they could find of a decision-maker using past behavior to predict future irresolution.[5] The traditional view of the Munich Crisis—that Hitler viewed the Munich outcome as desirable, but made dispositional explanations ("my enemies are worms")—contradicts my argument. I argue that only undesirable behavior should elicit dispositional explanations.

In contrast to the traditional view, historians now generally recognize that Hitler viewed the outcome of the Munich Crisis as disastrous. He wanted war, not peace, and so viewed the Munich agreement as highly undesirable.[6] There are a number of reasons why Hitler, at the last mo-

---

[3] Herbert Butterfield raises this possibility in *History and Human Relations* (London: Collins, 1951), p. 177. See also Jack Snyder, *Myths of Empire: Domestic Politics and International Ambition* (Ithaca: Cornell University Press, 1991), pp. 13–14, 30–31.

[4] Chester Wilmot, *The Struggle for Europe* (New York: Carroll and Graf, 1952), p. 21.

[5] Fred Charles Iklé, *How Nations Negotiate* (New York: Harper and Row, 1964), p. 82; Glenn H. Snyder and Paul Diesing, *Conflict among Nations: Bargaining, Decision-making, and System Structure in International Crises* (Princeton: Princeton University Press, 1977), p. 187.

[6] For example, see Lothar Kettenacker, "The German View," in *1939: A Retrospect Forty Years After*, ed. Roy Douglas (London: Macmillan, 1983); Ivone Kirkpatrick, *Mussolini: Study of a Demagogue* (London: Odhams Books, 1964), pp. 362, 366; Williamson Murray,

ment, agreed to the Munich Conference. Virtually all of his top military and political leaders were opposed to launching a war against Czechoslovakia at that time; Mussolini changed his mind, told Hitler Italy could not support a war at that time, and urged him to accept a peaceful solution; the British mobilized their navy and the French mobilized their army; the German people seemed uninterested in war. Hitler yielded to these factors and accepted compromise, but he was not happy about it.

During a break in the Munich Conference, Hitler reportedly called Chamberlain in private a "haggling shop-keeper who wrangles over every village and small detail."[7] While three of the statesmen signed the Munich Agreement with some satisfaction, Hitler reportedly "scratch[ed] his signature as if he were being asked to sign away his birthright."[8] A few weeks after Munich, Hitler declared in a speech: "We Germans will no longer endure such governessy interference. Britain should mind her own business and worry about her own troubles."[9] Hitler's greatest fear was a Munich repeat. During the 1939 Polish Crisis, Hitler remarked: "I only fear that at the last moment some swine will lay a plan of negotiations before me."[10] Hitler viewed Chamberlain as an "S.O.B."[11] Reviewing the successes and failures of the war in February 1945, Hitler reportedly blamed Munich for all his troubles: "I ought to have seized the initiative in 1938." Hitler later said, "September 1938 would have been the most favorable date. . . . We ought then and there to have settled our disputes by force of arms." Hitler blamed it all on that "arch-capitalist bourgeois Chamberlain with his deceptive umbrella in his hand."[12]

Because Hitler considered the outcome of the Munich Conference undesirable, my hypothesis correctly predicted his nasty dispositional

---

The Change in the European Balance of Power, 1938–1939 (Princeton: Princeton University Press, 1984); Esmonde M. Robertson, "German Mobilization Preparations and the Treaties between Germany and the Soviet Union of August and September 1939," in *Paths to War: New Essays on the Origins of the Second World War*, ed. Robert Boyce and Esmonde M. Robertson (London: Macmillan, 1989); Donald Cameron Watt, *How War Came: The Immediate Origins of the Second World War, 1938–1939* (London: Heinemann, 1989); Gerhard Weinberg, *The Foreign Policy of Hitler's Germany: Starting World War II, 1937–1939* (Chicago: University of Chicago Press, 1983); Telford Taylor, *Munich: The Price of Peace* (Garden City, N.Y.: Doubleday, 1979).

[7] This was Sir Ivone Kirkpatrick's observation, quoted in Taylor, *Munich*, p. 35.

[8] Ibid., p. 48.

[9] Quoted in Watt, *How War Came*, p. 38. See also Kettenacker, "German View," p. 30.

[10] Quoted in Murray, *Change in the European Balance*, p. 205.

[11] Quoted in Weinberg, *Foreign Policy*, p. 463.

[12] Quoted in Gerhard Weinberg, "Germany and Munich," in *Reappraising the Munich Pact: Continental Perspectives*, ed. Maya Latynski (Washington: Woodrow Wilson Center Press, 1992), p. 19.

attributions. The Munich Crisis illustrates how peculiar a decision-maker's desires must be for him to give his adversary a reputation for lacking resolve. As Ernest May observed, "Hitler *wanted* war."[13] Hitler made sure in his Polish campaign that he would not be tricked again into compromise and would get his war.[14] In short, Hitler's characterization of his adversaries after Munich fits my argument that undesirable behavior elicits dispositional attributions.

Although Hitler's attributions in the Munich Crisis support my argument, this does not mean I can account for all of Hitler's views or those of other decision-makers. The period from the remilitarization of the Rhineland to the Phony War would be a good test of my argument. While this period could yield interesting results, there are some problems with it. Hitler was extreme so he may be beyond the reach of our theories. Additionally, Germany was a revisionist state bent on territorial expansion. If Hitler gave France a reputation for lacking resolve, it may be difficult to determine whether this view was more a cause or a consequence of his desire to expand: did France's reputation for irresolution encourage Hitler's revisionism, or did Hitler's expansionist desire encourage him to view France as irresolute?

Revisionists and Reputation

What role does reputation play for states dissatisfied with the status quo? For example, did Saddam Hussein invade Kuwait and then stand firm against U.S. compellence because he had given the United States a reputation for being irresolute? Hussein argued that he believed the United States was irresolute: "Yours is a society which cannot accept 10,000 dead in one battle."[15] According to a number of journalists and scholars, Hussein used as evidence of American irresolution the American defeat in Vietnam and the 1983 retreat from Beirut after the Marines' barracks were bombed.[16]

---

[13] Ernest May, "Capabilities and Proclivities," in *Knowing One's Enemies* (Princeton: Princeton University Press, 1984), p. 520.

[14] See Weinberg, *Foreign Policy*, pp. 671–677.

[15] "Excerpts from Iraqi Document on meeting with U.S. envoy," Excerpts from July 25 meeting between Saddam Hussein and the U.S. ambassador to Baghdad, *New York Times*, September 23, 1990, p. A19.

[16] See Janet Gross Stein, "Deterrence and Compellence in the Gulf, 1990–1991," *International Security* 17/2 (1992): 175; John Kifner, "Iraq, Thought Vulnerable, Has Strong Cards to Play," *New York Times*, August 19, 1990, p. E3. Also see Lawrence Freedman and Efraim Karsh, *The Gulf Conflict, 1990–1991: Diplomacy and War in the New World Order* (Princeton: Princeton University Press, 1993).

Hussein might not have invaded Kuwait had the United States stayed the course in Vietnam and stood firm in Beirut. One of the problems with examining contemporary cases is the lack of reliable evidence pertaining to motive and intention. For example, the evidence that Hussein thought the United States irresolute could be dismissed as Iraqi signaling. The Iraqis wanted the Americans to believe that Iraq considered America an irresolute power; if the Americans accepted this Iraqi belief as genuine, then they might be less likely to think Iraq was bluffing. Signaling makes studying contemporary cases difficult since we generally do not have access to private internal communications.

If we assume that Hussein gave the United States a reputation for being irresolute, we must then determine if this view was a cause of his aggression, or a consequence of his desire to aggress. Although we cannot answer this riddle without more information, revisionist states may view their adversaries as irresolute because they want to expand. For example, Jonathan Shimshoni has shown the intractability of Egyptian views of Israel. Egypt was humiliated and resoundingly defeated by Israel in the 1948 war. While the Egyptians did not deny an Israeli victory, Shimshoni contends that "their explanations of it denied Israeli superiority, resting instead on transitory and remediable causes."[17] After the Six Day War in 1967, many Israeli leaders assumed they had by then acquired a reputation for resolve. According to Shimshoni, Egyptians gave Israel no such reputation: "In explaining the defeat the Egyptians concentrated more on self-examination than on Israeli superiority. What they saw in the mirror was a set of specific, sometimes episodic, and always *correctable* deficiencies, be they technological, behavioral, or organizational. A defeat caused by episodic or correctable problems, once those are rectified, is clearly not generalizable."[18] Victory in war does not guarantee a reputation for resolve—especially among those who are strongly motivated to view a state as irresolute.

The United States aimed in the ground war to devastate Iraqi forces so that Iraqis would be unable to explain away their defeat. As a senior Bush administration official put it: "If they have a clear defeat, no one in Iraq can get the idea 5 or 10 or 15 years from now that they might win

---

[17] Jonathan Shimshoni, *Israel and Conventional Deterrence: Border Warfare from 1953 to 1970* (Ithaca: Cornell University Press, 1988), p. 116.

[18] Ibid., p. 205. Not all of Shimshoni's findings support my argument. He argues that Israel obtained a reputation after its 1956 Sinai campaign (though he argues that it was forgotten by 1967). Because Shimshoni tends to conflate resolve and capability, it is not clear what reputation the Egyptians gave Israel (see pp. 69–122).

the next time if only they had a better Air Force."[19] It will be interesting to see if the Iraqis, like the Egyptians in Shimshoni's study, explain away their crushing defeat.

While pundits are quick to argue that past retreats explain future challenges, they rarely consider how past victories fail to deter future challenges. Had the United States used sanctions rather than gone to war against Iraq, this sign of American "irresolution" would probably have been the favorite explanation for subsequent aggression else-where—such as Serbian aggression in Bosnia or a military coup in Haiti.

SOME THEORETICAL EXTENSIONS

What if the German kaiser had been a Japanese woman in posses-sion of nuclear weapons? Can my argument speak to contemporary concerns, such as nuclear deterrence, and to different cultures? This section addresses the likely effect nuclear weapons, culture, and gen-der have on the way policy-makers explain behavior. My argument about how reputations for resolve form is not only generalizable over time and space, but it can also be applied to different issues, such as promises. Although promises are an important aspect of credibility, and although I often referred to them, I have not yet explicitly ex-tended my argument to address promises.

Nuclear Weapons and the Cold War

Do nuclear weapons make reputations for resolve more or less im-portant? Security regimes tend to be weak because in a self-help system the costs of cooperating when others defect can be great. The higher the stakes, the greater the incentive to cheat.[20] It would be logical for repu-tation to be less important the more important the stakes.[21] As Daniel Ellsberg observed: "Whose reputation for honesty is so great that to

[19] Quoted in Michel R. Gordon, "The Seven-Day Strategy," *New York Times*, February 23, 1991, p. A1. See also Thomas L. Friedman, "The Rout Bush Wants," *New York Times*, February 27, 1991, p. A1.

[20] See Robert Keohane and Joseph Nye, *Power and Interdependence*, 2d ed. (Boston: Scott, Foresman, 1989), p. 260.

[21] It is also possible that because the stakes are so high, decision-makers will be more inclined to use whatever information they have—including reputations. See Snyder and Diesing, *Conflict among Nations*, pp. 185–186.

wager it would make it actually *rational* to carry out [a suicidal] threat?"[22] Under the immediate threat of nuclear war, one would expect the issues at hand to be determining, rather than past behavior or concern about future reputation. For example, Thucydides reported unprecedented lawlessness and a disregard for reputation during a plague: "As for what is called honor, no one showed himself willing to abide by its laws, so doubtful was it whether one would survive to enjoy the name for it."[23] Like people caught in a plague, decision-makers in a nuclear crisis know the game may not be repeated and so discount the future.

And yet, because the threat to use nuclear weapons may seem incredible, the need for reputation as a tool to make these threats credible may seem more important than ever.[24] This tension leads to the following paradox: nuclear weapons cause actors to worry more about their own reputation than before, even though it seems that policy-makers would be less likely than before to use others' reputation as a guide to behavior in a crisis.

The Cold War offers many opportunities to test both parts of the paradoxical effect of nuclear weapons. First, do nuclear weapons increase policy-makers' concern about their reputation? Second, do nuclear weapons at the same time lead decision-makers to be even less likely to use another's past behavior to predict its future behavior (than they were before possession of nuclear weapons)? For example, examining the Korean and Vietnam wars would both test my speculation on the paradoxical effect of nuclear weapons and shed light on the similarities and differences of non-Western patterns of attributions.

Culture and Gender

I suggested in Chapter 2 that all people attribute cause essentially the same way. This proposition is worth debating since the generalizability of my argument hangs on the outcome. While my hypothesis ade-

---

[22] Daniel Ellsberg, "The Theory and Practice of Blackmail," in *Bargaining: Formal Theories of Negotiation*, ed. Oran Young (Urbana: University of Illinois Press, 1975), p. 358.

[23] Thucydides, *History of the Peloponnesian War*, trans. Rex Warner (New York: Penguin, 1979), p. 155.

[24] Robert Jervis shares this view and points out that mutual kill capability greatly weakens the link between capability and behavior; this leeway, which permits a greater role for beliefs, symbols, and psychology is another explanation for the perception that reputation is important. See Robert Jervis, *The Meaning of the Nuclear Revolution: Statecraft and the Prospect of Armageddon* (Ithaca: Cornell University Press, 1989), pp. 41, 182.

quately addresses how reputations form among European men, we still need to know whether this process differs for those with different beliefs or cultures, or for women. Surprisingly, the extent to which attributional processes differ is likely to strengthen my argument.

People are capable of making causal attributions that do not fit neatly on a situational-dispositional axis. For example, the Moroccans were thrilled with the kaiser's 1905 visit to Tangier and believed he had been sent by God to deliver them from the French.[25] The kaiser himself occasionally used God to explain an outcome, such as his success in securing the Björkö treaty: "God arranged it and willed it so."[26] A similar problem arises with the Azande tribe. The Azandes have a dual theory of causation in which there are proximate (or common sense) causes which often operate along with witchcraft causes.[27] Or consider the Myanmar (Burmese) government which believes so strongly in the causal powers of numbers that they work out their battle plans with the help of a numerologist.[28] While some individuals or groups may invest God, witchcraft, or numerology with explanatory power, these types of explanations are rare. In contrast, cross-cultural psychologists appear to provide a fundamental challenge to my argument.

Cross-cultural psychologists have identified two distinct cultural types—collectivist and individualist—which systematically affect the way people attribute causality. Hazel Markus and Shinobu Kitayama argue that Westerners have a Cartesian, dualistic tradition in which the self is separated from the other. In contrast, non-Western cultures tend toward a monistic philosophical tradition where the relationship between self and other is assumed to be much closer. In non-Western cultures, "one's actions are more likely to be seen as situationally bound, and characterizations of the individual will include this context."[29] While Westerners tend to be "inveterate dispositionists" and easy prey for the fundamental attribution error, non-Westerners tend to be more

[25] Dwight E. Lee, *Europe's Crucial Years* (Hanover, N.H.: University Press of New England, 1974), p. 115; Oron J. Hale, *Germany and the Diplomatic Revolution: A Study in Diplomacy and the Press, 1904–1906* (Philadelphia: University of Pennsylvania Press, 1931), p. 103.

[26] Quoted in Norman Rich, *Friedrich von Holstein: Politics and Diplomacy in the Era of Bismarck and Wilhelm II*, vol. 2 (Cambridge: Cambridge University Press, 1965), p. 715.

[27] Miles Hewstone, *Causal Attribution: From Cognitive Processes to Collective Beliefs* (Oxford: Basil Blackwell, 1990), p. 232.

[28] "Burmese Rebels Await a Foe's Lucky Number," *New York Times*, March 22, 1992, p. A10.

[29] Hazel Rose Markus and Shinobu Kitayama, "Culture and the Self: Implications for Cognition, Emotion, and Motivation," *Psychological Review* 98/2 (1991): 225.

situationist and less likely to be caught in this bias.[30] Japanese, Chinese, Africans, and Hindus are more collectivist than Westerners and, as a result, less likely than Westerners to explain outcomes in dispositional terms.[31]

Those who study gender differences join the cross-cultural critique that attribution theories are ethnocentric. Carol Gilligan argues that women experience the world, and explain causality, differently from men.[32] While women tend to be more collectivist and connected, men tend to be more individualist and autonomous. As a result, women tend to be more empathetic than men; they are more likely to try to stand in another's shoes.[33] According to the logic of the actor-observer difference (where actors tend to make situational explanations), because women are more likely to be empathetic they are also more likely to make situational attributions.

If it is true that collectivist cultures are more prone to situational attributions, or that women are more prone to empathy (and thus situational attributions), then Western men are more likely than anyone else to give others reputations since they are most likely to make dispositional attributions. As a result (and serendipitously), I have made my argument that reputations matter little by using the subjects most likely to give others reputations. My hypothesis has passed the hardest case: Western men.

Promises and Reputation

Extending my argument to promises might help us better understand a number of issues in international politics. For example, it makes explicable the tendency of policy-makers to worry more about their

[30] Lee Ross and Richard E. Nisbett, *The Person and the Situation: Perspectives of Social Psychology* (Philadelphia: Temple University Press, 1991), p. 90.

[31] See Markus and Kitayama, "Culture and the Self"; Joan Miller, "Culture and the Development of Everyday Social Explanation," *Journal of Personality and Social Psychology* 46/5 (1984): 961–978. However, there is also evidence supporting the assumption that culture does not significantly affect attributions between groups. One pair of psychologists concluded that "the existing evidence, though scanty, supports the view that similar attribution processes are involved across cultures in producing the group-serving bias." See Garth Fletcher and Colleen Ward, "Attribution Theory and Processes: A Cross-Cultural Perspective," in *The Cross-Cultural Challenge to Social Psychology*, ed. Michael Harris Bond (London: Sage, 1988), p. 238. Also see the studies quoted in Chapter 2.

[32] Carol Gilligan, *In a Different Voice: Psychological Theory and Women's Development* (Cambridge: Harvard University Press, 1982).

[33] Robert A. Josephs, Hazel Rose Markus, and Romin W. Tafarodi, "Gender and Self-Esteem," *Journal of Personality and Social Psychology* 63/3 (1992): 391–402.

friends than their enemies. As George Kennan noted, "It is very simple to deal with an enemy, simpler than dealing with a friend."[34] Alexander George and Richard Smoke suggest that we pay more attention to our allies than our adversaries because geographical distance makes unclear our commitment to extended deterrence.[35] There may be a simpler explanation.

Allied relations are based more on promises than threats, and adversary relations are based more on threats than promises. This aspect of inter-state relations has two related consequences. First, we know that promises are less likely to be believed than threats. Promises are costly when they succeed and threats are costly when they fail.[36] As a result, we generally must spend more time convincing allies of the sincerity of our promises than persuading adversaries of the sincerity of our threats.

An additional reason we worry more about our promises than our threats bears on a central argument in this book. Namely, states cannot easily get reputations for keeping promises, but can get reputations for breaking promises. This is so because a target will use a situational attribution to explain a kept promise (which by definition is desirable), but will use dispositional explanations for broken promises. The same logic applies to threats: it is possible for an adversary to get a reputation for keeping threats, but hard to get one for bluffing. Because we are more likely to believe threats than promises, and because it is easier to get a reputation for keeping threats than for keeping promises, we should expect decision-makers to spend more time worrying about their allies than their adversaries.

It might be argued that decision-makers worry about promises more than threats because promises are interdependent while threats are independent.[37] Since interdependence is necessary for a reputation to form, it makes sense to focus on whatever is interdependent. As I argue

[34] George Kennan, quoted in John Lewis Gaddis, *Strategies of Containment: A Critical Appraisal of Postwar American National Security Policy* (New York: Oxford University Press, 1982), p. 74.

[35] Alexander George and Richard Smoke, *Deterrence in American Foreign Policy: Theory and Practice* (New York: Columbia University Press, 1974), pp. 65–66.

[36] Thomas Schelling, *The Strategy of Conflict* (Cambridge: Harvard University Press, 1960), p. 177; David Baldwin, "The Power of Positive Sanctions," *World Politics* 24 (October 1971); Robert Jervis, *The Logic of Images in International Relations* (Princeton: Princeton University Press, 1970), pp. 81–82.

[37] Robert Jervis made this speculation in "Domino Beliefs and Strategic Behavior," in *Dominoes and Bandwagons: Strategic Beliefs and Great Power Competition in the Eurasian Rimland*, ed. Robert Jervis and Jack Snyder (New York: Oxford University Press, 1991), p. 25.

throughout this book, the independence or interdependence of a commitment is found not in the type of commitment—either threat or promise—but in how an observer interprets that behavior, as either situational or dispositional.

For example, the kaiser was annoyed at the Italians for not keeping their word by fully supporting Germany at the Algeciras Conference; he spoke of the "miserable and degenerate Latin peoples."[38] Although the kaiser thought this promise should have been kept, he welcomed and even expected other states to break their promises when this tactic was desirable. For example, he was miffed that Spain refused to inform Germany of the contents of the Franco-Spanish agreement over Morocco; the Spanish king refused because he had promised France to keep it secret. In a letter to Bülow, Kaiser Wilhelm complained: "The King of Spain expects me to visit him! But refuses me any kind of political concession. I suggest that Your Highness let Madrid know quite bluntly that if His Majesty does not inform me about the agreement with France over Morocco . . . then I will not pay a visit to Madrid this year! I am so much older than that lout that he at least owes me that!"[39] The kaiser, like British decision-makers who were untroubled by broken promises that advanced their interests, assessed the sanctity of a promise according to its desirability.

In short, the relative interdependence of a promise hinges on the perceived desirability of that commitment. If this assessment is right, then states should rarely get reputations for keeping promises, because kept promises (when desirable) elicit situational attributions. However, states can get reputations for breaking promises, because broken promises (when undesirable) result in dispositional attributions.

POLICY IMPLICATIONS

Although there are many reasons why a state may choose to go to war, and many reasons why a state may choose to continue a war, the argument that we must act to enhance or preserve our reputation can-

---

[38] Quoted in G. P. Gooch, *Before the War: Studies in Diplomacy*, vol. 1: *The Grouping of the Powers* (New York: Longmans, Green, 1936), p. 263.

[39] Kaiser Wilhelm II to Bülow (February 11, 1906), *The Holstein Papers: The Memoirs, Diaries and Correspondence of Friedrich von Holstein, 1837–1909*, vol. 4: *Correspondence, 1897–1909*, ed. Norman Rich and M. H. Fisher (Cambridge: Cambridge University Press, 1963), No. 933, p. 395.

not be sustained. This conclusion is true for three reasons. First, reputation is in the eye of the beholder. A reputation is a characteristic that we attribute to others and not a universally recognized property that we own. It is therefore difficult for us to control the image others hold of us. Second, people often explain the same behavior differently. How we act in one instance can lead to as many different reputations as there are observers, or it can lead to no reputation at all. As a result, states may not have one reputation for a type of behavior, but may have competing reputations with different states based on the same behavior.

The third reason not to fight over our reputations for resolve concerns the independence of commitments. Decision-makers do not consistently use another state's past behavior (whether in the same region or a different region) to predict that state's behavior. Rather than sum another state's aggregate behavior to conclude its resolve, decision-makers select behavior for the equation in a way that biases the findings. Allies should therefore not think of resolve as a poker chip that can be stored up or spent in successive hands of international politics. Because allies tend to explain each other's desirable behavior in situational terms, they will be unable to recall this resolve, not because they forget about it, but because they attributed it to the situation rather than to disposition. As a result, states get no credit when they behave properly, but do get blame when they misbehave.

From this analysis it follows that reputations for resolve often do not form. Most of the time actors use factors other than resolve, such as interests or capability, to explain a state's behavior. Even when actors use resolve to explain a state's behavior, these attributions often are not used to predict similar behavior in the future—that is, no reputations form. Finally, when observers do use another's resolve to explain behavior, and when they then use this attribution to predict similar behavior in the future, only two kinds of reputations are likely to form. First, adversaries can get reputations for being resolute (but rarely for being irresolute). To the extent that our adversaries do draw general conclusions about our resolve, they are likely to think we are resolute. Second, allies can get reputations for lacking resolve (but rarely for having resolve). To the extent that our allies draw general conclusions about our resolve, they are likely to think we are irresolute.

Although the possibility that our adversaries will view us as resolute (but rarely irresolute) means we need not worry about reputations with adversaries, the possibility that our allies might view us as irresolute (but rarely as resolute) is not reassuring. What should be done? Nothing. First, our allies will tend to explain away our efforts to demonstrate resolve by citing the transient situation. We cannot manipulate our allies' image of us to make them think we are resolute regardless of our interests or capabilities. They will tend to assume that our interests and capabilities determine our resolve. Second, based on my case studies it appears that allies rarely give one another a reputation for lacking resolve. Even when observers used an ally's irresolution to explain its behavior, they did not then expect their ally to be similarly irresolute in the future. Indeed, sometimes (and contrary to my expectations) observers who had thought an ally was irresolute in one crisis came to believe their ally was resolute. In short, even when observers view their ally as irresolute, this belief can result in a reputation for lacking resolve, an expectation of future resolution ("Never again!"), or no reputation at all.

Deterrence theorists advise policy-makers to pay now to avoid future costs. I argue that there is no reason to pay now because there probably will not be any future costs. This position does not mean that we should shrink from defending our interests. It means we should not view our putative reputations for resolve as interests in themselves. Decision-makers would be well served to remember one simple policy maxim: fighting to create a reputation for resolution with adversaries is unnecessary, and fighting to create a reputation for resolution with allies is unwise.

Index

Cornell Studies in Security Affairs

edited by Robert J. Art, Robert Jervis, *and* Stephen M. Walt

Breinigsville, PA USA
01 September 2010
244566BV00005B/2/P